The Latino Student's
Guide to College Success

The Latino Student's Guide to College Success

Edited by Leonard A. Valverde

Greenwood Press
Westport, Connecticut • London

Library of Congress Cataloging-in-Publication Data

The Latino student's guide to college success / edited by Leonard A. Valverde.
    p. cm.
    Includes bibliographical references and index.
    ISBN 0–313–31113–7 (alk. paper).—ISBN 0–313–31960–X (pbk.: alk. paper)
    1. Hispanic Americans—Education (Higher)—Handbooks, manuals, etc.
    2. Universities and colleges—United States—Directories. I. Valverde, Leonard A.
    LC2670.6.H57   2002
    378.19'82968073—dc21   00–064062

British Library Cataloguing in Publication Data is available.

Library of Congress Catalog Card Number: 00–064062
ISBN: 0–313–31113–7
        0–313–31960–X (pbk.)

First published in 2002

Greenwood Press, 88 Post Road West, Westport, CT 06881
An imprint of Greenwood Publishing Group, Inc.
www.greenwood.com

Printed in the United States of America

The paper used in this book complies with the
Permanent Paper Standard issued by the National
Information Standards Organization (Z39.48–1984).

10 9 8 7 6 5 4 3 2

Dedicated to

My cousins, particularly, the Bravos—
Junior, Reddie, Angie, and Diane—and
my younger brother, Ron, who were neither advised
nor encouraged to go to college by school personnel,
yet were all capable in different ways.
And to the countless other Latinos who suffered
similar neglect.

Contents

Introduction

Why is this book important to Latinos and to the staff of colleges and universities? First, to succeed in the United States and in the world economy, one will have to be highly educated. In fact, now that the world economy is based on an information society, a college education is a must. Technology will advance the future rapidly and create new opportunities presently not known. College-educated persons will be better prepared to compete in such a society. Moreover, there is an advantage factor. Those persons who have a college education will earn more money over the span of their careers than those without a college education. As shown in this book, the latest reports (as of this writing, 1997) by the Census Bureau find that Latino men with a college degree earn about $11,000 more a year than do non–college educated Latinos ($31,635 versus $20,617).[1] Throughout a forty-year working lifetime, this difference is over $440,000. Similarly, Latina women with a college degree earn roughly $28,550 a year, whereas women high school graduates earn only $14,747. Again, looking at it from a working lifespan, this constitutes a difference of $550,000.

Second, it is important that an increasing number of Latinos go to college and graduate because up to this point Latinos have been badly underrepresented, not just in the student body but also in faculty and administrative positions. Since the late 1960s, when Latinos began to be admitted into college in slightly greater numbers as a result of the civil rights movement, the national average of Latino enrollments has been about 10 to 20 percent. In 1999 the Educational Testing Service (ETS) reported that only 22 percent were enrolled in college. Of this small number, between 60 and 80 percent are enrolled in two-year technical or community colleges.[2] And the statistics get worse: of the low percentage of Latinos admitted to college, only about 5 to 10 percent graduate with a four-year college degree. Again, in 1999 ETS reported that only 8.9 percent of this population group completed four years of college. Few go on to graduate education for a terminal and/or professional degree (4 to 5%), and only about 2 to 3 percent successfully finish their program of study.

America needs well-educated Latinos; it is predicted that we are going to be the largest population subgroup and work force of tomorrow. By the year 2004, the Census Bureau is estimating that Latinos in the United States will overtake African Americans in number and thus be second only to the white population.

Last, with the recent attack on affirmative action, it is becoming more difficult for Latinos to access a college education. Moreover, state financial support of public colleges and universities is diminishing. The cost of a college education is increasing. More people are applying to college because the total population is growing, and they see that a college education is critical for getting a good job. To make matters worse for Latinos and other persons of color, there is a growing change of attitude—a negative point of view, anti–affirmative action, anti–civil rights—that puts the burden on Latinos to work twice as hard to be considered good enough or equal to Anglos. This may not seem fair, but it has been our situation for many generations. Yet the current generation of Latinos believes that our youth are up to the challenge and will be successful. This book is written to help you succeed.

The information in this book is provided to assist Latinos who are thinking about going to college. It will help you prepare, apply, find financial support, study and pass the courses, and participate in extracurricular activities in order to graduate from college. The book is divided into four parts and is organized by steps. The information provided is current and highly useful. This is due primarily to the expertise and experience of all the contributing writers.

Part I: Preparing for College discusses the first three steps you need to think about and do in order to get admitted to college. Step 1 identifies ten new ways of thinking about college; these will get you psychologically ready to succeed in college. Step 1 also tells you about getting ready for the SAT or ACT exams. Step 2 provides helpful forms to fill out, tips to use, and a sample letter to write in your efforts to select a college. Step 3 gives information about how to qualify for certain types of financial aid, the application process, where you can get financial aid, and the different types of financial assistance. It also lists Web addresses and toll-free telephone numbers.

Part II: On Campus has five steps that focus on how to be a good student and successfully meet the requirements of your program of study and, thus,

graduate. Step 4 explains the usefulness of the college catalog, campus policies, and new student orientation programs, and also gives academic strategies for being a better student. Step 5 is a guide to being an active learner,
manager of time, builder of a support group, eliminator of stress, setter of
goals, listener and note taker, test taker, and writer of formal papers. Step
6 gives tips about services on and off campus, particularly via the computer
and the Internet, and choosing mentors. Step 7 provides information about
your rights as a student on campus. Specifically, it covers class attendance,
course syllabus and requirements, adding and dropping a class, requesting
an incomplete grade, early withdrawal from class, and petitions for action.
Step 8 tells about the three types of extracurricular activities: academic,
athletic, and social/cultural. There are benefits and disadvantages from extracurricular involvement, but generally there are more advantages.

Part III: "How I Did It" provides vignettes from notable Latinos rep-
resenting various backgrounds. All tell their story of how they made it
through college. You, as a reader, should be able to relate to at least one
of these persons. Their stories provide the message that everyone can make
it, if they work hard and sincerely want to be a college graduate. As the
great Latino labor organizer Cesar Chavez would say when facing enormous challenges, *"Si se puede!"*—It can be done.

Part IV: College and University Directory provides information about
the top 50 universities and top 20 community colleges in the United States
and top 5 Puerto Rican institutions that graduate the most Latinos. Also
provided are lists of the top 10 universities and top 10 community colleges
with the highest percentage of Latinos enrolled. These are the places that
other Latinos have identified as good colleges to attend. You might want
to use this list in identifying colleges to consider making application to.
Read Step 2 when viewing these lists.

Just as the progress of each generation is dependent upon the achievements of the preceding generation, so too is the advancement of families
and of individuals. That is, for many Latino families, previous family members were unskilled laborers, many of whom migrated to the United States
from Mexico, Puerto Rico, Central America, and South America. Other
Latinos, like Cubans, were forced to leave their homeland because of political conflict. In the past, each succeeding generation has been able to
move up in social/economic status from unskilled to skilled, from low income to middle class. We, as a generation of the latter half of the twentieth
century, opened the college doors for the twenty-first-century generation of
Latinos. You, the new generation of Latinos, are now at a stage when you
can join the ranks of the professionals in large numbers. But to reach this
point, Latino youth will have to not just graduate from a four-year undergraduate program, but will have to go on and earn a terminal/professional
degree. The college gates are now open. So it is your turn. Go through the
door. And in so doing, work to make sure future generations of Latinos

will get a better college education. Each Latino/a has not only a personal responsibility to him or herself and to his or her family but to society and future generations.

NOTES

1. A. P. Carnevale, *Education Equals Success: Empowering Hispanic Youth and Adults* (Princeton, NJ: Educational Testing Service, 1997), p. 9.

2. U.S. Bureau of the Census, *Current Population Reports* (Washington, DC: U.S. Government Publishing Office, 1997).

Leonard A. Valverde
Hispanic Border Leadership Institute
Arizona State University, Tempe

Preparing for College

STEP 1

Getting Ready for a College Education (Or, What You Need to Know to Qualify for College)

CARLOTA CARDENAS DE DWYER
High school teacher, San Antonio, Texas

TO MAKE THIS POSSIBLE

For many Latinos, media images and personal experience project American society as one dominated by individuals of other colors, other races, and other cultures. Invisible lines of exclusion seem to be drawn on the basis of these visible factors, as well as on the basis of language and accent. As individuals of Latino background, we sometimes feel like people on an island looking out on an ocean full of ships sailing swiftly in various directions. From our standpoint we know where we want to go, but we are not sure how we can transport ourselves—or our children—from where we are to where we would like to be. We have a strong desire to set off on the voyage, but we hesitate because we feel uncertainty about exactly where we are going and how we will get there.

Tierra incognita is a term used on early maps to identify lands unknown to European explorers of the time. Although these places were very well known to the people who actually lived there, such locations were shadowed in darkness and danger to others. Likewise, for those approaching for the first time, success in college may seem to be a distant destination not easily reached except by those with special and, possibly, "insider" knowledge. The various steps, or chapters, of this book answer basic questions of "who," "what," "when," "where," "why," and "how" linked to college success. Yet the overall presentation of these materials and this first step are directed especially to those of us involved and concerned about Latino students in particular. We all work to make the success of our children possible.

FIRST THINGS FIRST

Once students begin to think about going to college, it doesn't take long before they—and their parents—discover that there are really two major areas of concern that demand serious consideration. The first area involves admission requirements, financial obligations, and basic questions such as which college to choose, what to major in, and where to live. These issues are fairly common to all would-be college students and are best answered through standard information materials or guidance from counselors, librarians, admissions offices, or books such as this. However, the second area of concern is more important than the details relating to campuses, courses, and expenses. This second element is actually the "missing link" between exactly where many Latino students *are* as they complete high school and where they *want to be* as successful college students. This area of concern remains to many Latino students a mysterious and almost magical, hidden formula. Excluded from what seems like an inner—and closed—circle of knowledge and power, Latinos see a world of opportunity from the outside without any apparent access available to them. Even though they may focus their attention on far-off goals, such as success in college, the key to capturing such distant achievements is actually located *within* the minds and hearts of the students themselves.

When focusing on this "heart" of the matter of student success, Latinos often make two serious errors. First, because these points are mental and psychological (that is, personal and subjective rather than physical and objective), some individuals think that the points are of little or no influence. Wrong! Second, others may mistakenly think that for Latino students to achieve success in college they must follow not only a magical but also a *secret* formula, discovered by a privileged few and beyond the reach of themselves or those in their own family. Wrong again! Just as most students—and their parents—are absolutely correct in seeking the goal of a college education to begin with, they are also correct in their hope that such a goal is possible, no matter how difficult it may seem at the start. The path to such a goal need not remain "forbidden knowledge" to those who are truly interested in achieving success.

CHARTING THE VOYAGE

When we prepare to tell someone how to find our home or when we decide to drive from one city to another, clear directions and a map are helpful, if not necessary. Because we are familiar with the route to our own home, we can usually suggest useful hints to the newcomer or offer warnings about, say, a sharp curve or an unexpected stop sign. The same idea applies when we try to guide Latino high school students as they look forward to college. Although the most valuable lessons in life are often learned from personal experience, useful hints may also be passed on from one person to another, more like a family recipe than a secret formula!

In these pages we list and explain in detail a few important concepts that are commonly included in "how to" books but are almost never related specifically to Latino students. Also, although no simple step-by-step method could possibly be useful to a group of the size and diversity of today's Latino students, some guidelines or "rules of the road" are given with detailed explanation and application. These ideas are intended to assist with what—for many students in all varieties of situations—is the most difficult step: getting started.

TEN POINTERS FOR SUCCESS

1. Develop a Positive Attitude

Attitude influences and, to a great extent, is the single most important factor to all concerned. Although the word *attitude* is defined in dictionaries in terms of a mental outlook, most people know the concept in two different contexts. In a negative context, a person who thinks he or she is better than others, particularly Latinos, is said to have "a lot of attitude," if not a "red neck." In this form, attitude tends to irritate others and is crippling and self-defeating. At the opposite extreme is the popular concept of "a very positive attitude." Although most of us probably agree on the common signs of a positive attitude, too often the term is used or recommended ("Be positive!") with only a vague suggestion of exactly what makes up this most vital ingredient to success. The key idea is that at first and always, it is not so much what you do as *what you think*.

Most of us have observed an astonished sports announcer exclaim "touchdown," "goal," "home run," or "basket" and watched a winning player or team surprise everyone by overcoming odds, injuries, and even undeniable superiority in ability or strength. What's inside—*attitude*—made the difference and enabled success to replace failure. Although such turnabouts occur at athletic events in every season of the year, few people realize that similar reversals happen every semester in the quiet seclusion of classrooms across the country from elementary school through graduate school. In different forms and with different faces, the same internal struggle is waged and won by students who have mastered the first lesson of any school (or life) experience: learn to win and win to learn. Let nothing stand in your way. Benefit from *all* experiences. However, simply wanting to succeed is not enough. Despite its key role, attitude does not stand alone; it is, in fact, made up of all the following points.

2. Divide Your Goals Between Long-term and Short-term Objectives

While we focus on the ultimate goal of college graduation as a single step, we should view that goal in terms of numerous, lesser goals that lead up to graduating from college. The secret to achieving the last goal is to meet successfully all the challenges between where you start and where you want to be. Individual actions bring individual results, so setting goals and achieving goals is really a step-by-step process with one set of goals forming a platform or staging area for the next set. Four years of classes and a grand total of 120 credits (more or less) is enough to make anyone hesitate. Breaking down such a target, especially at the beginning, is one way to place aside doubt and insecurity and simply move ahead one semester at a time.

Allowing for differences in abilities and preferences, a first-year student should tackle a reasonable number of courses and plan on finishing the first semester with a personal goal of making a particular grade point average. Some students may be able to set higher goals in the second semester, once they learn their own patterns of strength and weakness. Some students may discover that high grades are manageable in certain areas—science or history, for example—whereas simply earning a passing grade is the best to be expected in another area.

Not all courses of study are a matter of choice, one class may require more hours of effort than another. *This imbalance of tasks is a standard part of the complexity of achieving high goals.* Because roadblocks lie all along the path, an important and early decision is *not* to be stopped by such an obstacle. Often, surmounting these roadblocks demands more mental energy than physical effort. At this point, a positive attitude and deep determination are required to form a firm conviction that even though not all tasks will be equal, all will be achieved. It could be that a deceptively minor obstruction will require the greatest dedication. Getting up early, staying up late, enduring a forced companionship with an unlikeable roommate or instructor, even a visceral dislike of a required subject—all these should be expected at some point and overcome. Each encounter needs to be met with the all-important question to self: Am I going to allow this to stand in my way? Such barriers will halt your progress only if you give up and allow them to do so.

3. Identify and Accept Your Priorities

The prospect of having one's name included on a Latino magazine's list of the twenty most influential people in the nation or the country probably appeals to many of us. Equally appealing would be the opportunity to be given the local community award for outstanding service and having your photo in the newspaper. The difference between those successful few and the rest of us is not so much wanting these achievements as it is being willing to do everything that is necessary to actually reach those final goals.

Phrases such as "no pain, no gain" and "no guts, no glory" are used widely, but they carry little useful meaning to those at the beginning of their ventures who genuinely need solid guidance. An important part of setting priorities to meet goals is to understand that it is a two-stage process. The most well known stage involves a focus on what a person should do. It is an active and positive process of "do this now" and "do that next." Most people accept the necessity of taking these actions. Yet this is not enough. People do not always understand the sheer multitude of sacrifices they will have to make. When we decide to do this and do that, we must, at some point, *not* do other things.

Difficult choices will have to be made; old habits and customs may have to be changed or put on hold. For example, being prepared to accept the temporary loss of Friday night, Saturday or Sunday afternoon family get-togethers in place of staying in with books or working on a project is a requirement. Over time, recognition that long-term rewards and goals will outweigh short-term losses will provide reassurance to all involved. In college, *academic priorities* must come before recreational or social ones. Only beginning college students themselves can make these difficult choices that demand more than just a willing spirit. Yet the choices are not easy—you should not begin college with the simple notion that a successful student studies all the time. Indeed, a wise decision reflects more than just the final goal. "Know thyself" expresses the entire collection of vital ingredients that turn the dream of success into reality. Self-knowledge is, indeed, a complex idea that deserves further clarification.

4. Know—and Accept—Yourself

While you look purposefully in the distance toward your goals, you should not lose sight completely of where you are in the here and now. Important considerations about the "what" and "when" of your actions should not overlook your own individual needs and requirements. It is not merely an issue of *how* you can get something done. The key question is how you can get something done *best*.

Students should be prepared to recognize false priorities or sacrifices. At the beginning of serious effort in school, a student should establish a progress chart to record the results of various patterns of study. For example, staying up all night to cram before a test may not really contribute to improved performance if pure exhaustion destroys concentration and skill. How important is physical rest, relaxation, proper diet, or even some form of exercise or play? Look for your own personal telltale signs of wrong choices.

Most important, discover what works *for you*. Whereas some individuals work well under the pressure of last-minute deadlines, others find that such tension has a paralyzing effect on their thought processes. Did simple fatigue and weariness cause a serious mistake that would not have been made if you were sufficiently rested? Another option that may work well with some but not all students is joining a group rather than studying in isolation. Some students benefit from the lively interaction of words and ideas in a group, whereas others find that much time is wasted and they cannot concentrate with such distractions. Trying to work with two or three others may actually take more energy (and time) than simply doing it by yourself. In some situations, such as an emergency or an assigned group project, you may not be free to make the best choice that works for you; but when options are available, wise choices should be made.

Situations such as these occur all throughout a career. Regardless of the issue, close attention should be paid to what actually improves performance. Combining priorities with personal requirements results in achieving goals.

5. Learn to Understand and Develop True Discipline and Patience

Balancing goals, priorities, and individual or family requirements demands two qualities. The first is *discipline*, and the second is *patience*. Both words carry rather general and even, possibly, negative associations. Therefore, a brief elaboration is offered here to clarify how these two qualities relate to achieving success in college.

Discipline may be linked to a correction or punishment that a parent or teacher might impose on someone, usually a child, who has committed some wrong. One of the most dramatic changes occurring in Latinos' transition to college is the fact that they are leaving the traditional grip of both parents and teachers, as well as other authority figures. For most students, this release triggers an explosion of excessive behavior, particularly on some college campuses where temptations exist in many forms. However, for Latinos, there may be a greater release since most traditional Latino families have strong disciplinarian fathers and mothers with strong religious faith. All these students share one general error in their thinking: that liberty from the restrictions of others implies freedom from the necessity of self-control.

Simply put, for the first time in their lives Latinos entering college must understand that they themselves—not their parents or teachers—must make and enforce decisions about what they do on a daily basis. Many judgments about where and when to come and go, for example, become the most influential choices of their overall college experience during the first (and following) semesters. Go to the library and study, or go out with roommates for fun? This situation is a clear illustration of the ever-present conflict between short-term and long-term goals. For students beginning college, the voice and the power must become internalized.

With students' physical transition to college, a comparable mental and emotional transition must occur. A shift from passively accepting the power of others must take place, as beginning college students take control of their own lives. Development of this inner power comes from understanding the interaction among personal goals and priorities. Students must be aware that their individual sense of discipline is strongly dependent on their own capacity for patience.

The kind of patience now required must energize and support the determination *to do or not to do now because of a goal to be realized later.* This element of patience also contains qualities of sheer endurance and willingness to suffer discomfort in the present for the hope and expectation of enjoyment and reward in the future.

6. Learn How to Accept Errors and Failure

Errors or mistakes in judgment will occur. Do not view them totally negatively, as outcomes to be avoided at all costs and without any possible benefit. Whenever you are disappointed or upset—that is, surprised—by an unexpected outcome, do not give in to apologies, excuses, or emotional outbursts. Move beyond feelings and ask, "What lesson have I learned?" Perhaps the answer is that machines (computers, copiers, faxes) sometimes break down when you need them, that other people cannot always be depended on, or that a task sometimes can take twice as long as originally planned. Ask yourself, "What should I do differently next time?" Begin with the awareness that mistakes or problems of some form not only can but are likely to happen.

Similarly, be prepared to expect and accept an occasional failure. Since it is highly likely you will be the first in your family to attend college, you will encounter new situations where you will not know how to behave or what to say. Dealing with an occasional disappointment in school should encourage the growth of determination and creativity in forming new ways to achieve objectives not won at first. Progressing beyond temporary failure is much more important than becoming immobilized by feelings of embarrassment and regret. Although you cannot always control what happens, you can control how you think about it. Rather than acceptance of disappointment, attainment of goals may simply require a different approach revised on the basis of added experience.

7. Distinguish Between Network and Team

For many Latinos, starting college will become much more than just continuing into their thirteenth year of formal education. As they step through the doorway into those first college classes, they begin not only to take new courses but also to make acquaintances and establish relationships in a new world that will form a very influential part of how they function in the future. Most students maintain fairly active social lives in high school with a wide range of connections, including family members, neighbors, and peers. But when you enter college, the number and type of contacts you have with others begin to show important differences. Understanding what these different relationships are and how they affect opportunities for growth and achieving success is important. The most significant distinction is between two slightly similar but critically contrasting types of personal associations. Although each type of relationship has unique characteristics, both can make a positive contribution. Recognizing the differences between the two and not confusing one for the other is a key survival skill.

A *network* of associations can play a very useful role in a Latino's career. A true network consists of people whose knowledge and contacts reach beyond your own; these individuals should be called on to offer recommendations on how and where others might be reached who could help you. Even though you may not be aware of people who know or do something you need, someone in your network might. Obviously, once you have made such a contact, your own network (and theirs) expands. You will learn that keeping track of such contacts and cooperating with others to do so becomes increasingly important as you move forward. Many high achievers in all varieties of professions consider networking a necessity, not merely a form of social entertainment. However, although networks offer a useful aid to many of us, our needs frequently demand assistance that goes beyond the limits of a casual contact. Initially, identifying a Latino mentor should be considered a first step to professional development. Later, serving as a mentor to a developing Latino continues a positive tradition.

Unlike a network, a *team* is made up of people we actually join with in a mutually dependent and cooperative effort to achieve a common objective. The critical difference between network and team is that someone contacted through a network feels no obligation to participate on your behalf. Team members, on the other hand, are expected to contribute much more than informal information. However, team members do not always live up to this. Sometimes team members let us down because they do not have the same degree of determination and commitment.

Working in a team is much more complicated than simply being part of a network. When possible, choose individuals for your team who have a track record of achieving high goals; that is, they should be skilled, responsible, and dependable—self-motivated. These are people who will work on their own without being pushed or pulled by someone else (you!). Look for those who share many of your basic goals and values but who also represent talents and styles that are different from your own. Skills in organization, logistics, creativity, analytical thinking, technical expertise, and communication should be a part of the total resources of a successful team. Members of a network provide needed information, but members of a team actually pitch in with one another to get the job done *together*.

8. Choose Your Battles

One of the themes stressed repeatedly in this discussion is the importance of being thoroughly dedicated to a goal and not allowing others to close the doors of opportunity in your face. Although this attitude of "never say quit" is fundamental to achieving success, how you apply it in the everyday interactions of human activities often demands careful and thoughtful attention. Indeed, developing a practical sense of how and when to fight the battles that will invariably arise is one of the most necessary and complex life skills. Every time you face one of those clashes, you become part of a very uneven match of wills and power. The opponent is saying "no" or "you can't," and you are called on to perform some of type of skilled maneuver to move forward.

Unfortunately, workable solution or compromise may lie within your reach only if you control your emotions. The key to success in such conflicts is remembering that the only victory that counts is when *you* get what you want—certainly not in any kind of passing moment of verbal exchange or the like. Do not confuse a temporary skirmish with the real campaign of your success in life. Beware of trying to win a battle only to lose the war. In other words, learn to "bite your tongue" occasionally and resist the temptation to have the last word, particularly when engaged in a verbal duel with someone in authority, such as a professor. Be willing to swallow your ego today so you can be the big winner tomorrow!

However, this assurance simply to keep trying is not enough to carry you through all the conflicts associated with a long and full career of achieving high goals. Part of learning from your failures is that sometimes you do have to re-think your entire strategy. Calling on others for guidance, such as members of your network, team, or family, can help you work your way through an improved plan of action.

9. Be Prepared to Be Surprised

When you prepare yourself to do everything just right to make that final and long-awaited moment of success a reality, you can fall into a fairly common but dangerous trap of faulty thinking. Although standard wisdom is to judge future events on the basis of what has been learned from past experience, a one-to-one connection between past experiences of fewer than twenty years or so may not be adequate for life beyond high school. Much more similarity exists between college and professional work experience than between high school and college. To a great extent a new and different set of rules, practices, and values will slowly appear. In college and beyond, certain unwritten rules will have increasing impact.

Among the many new behavior patterns, only a handful are critically influential. Among the most significant is the concept of self-selection. Sometimes one only learns about this idea after it is too late. In its negative application, self-selection is a process by which people decide on their own to count themselves out without waiting for the judgment of others. In other words, these individuals give up early on, thinking "I'll never make it" or "I just can't compete with those others." Too many Latino students have this self-doubt because throughout their K–12 school experience they have so often encountered rejection rather than acceptance that they come to believe strongly that this is the end result. Sometimes it is only the fear of failure or rejection (see Rule 6) that becomes overwhelming, but more often than not the error lies in a subconscious and faulty mental calculation: that you as a beginner—or outsider seeking entry to this world—have a complete and accurate understanding of how the final judgments will be made regarding who to admit. You count yourself out without realizing that what the judge or judges (e.g., admissions committee, scholarship review board, selection group) might be looking for was someone with your particular combination of strengths and weaknesses. Remember, you are moving toward unknown territory. Your own past knowledge may serve merely as a partial guide.

Do not allow the fear of failure or rejection to rule your life. Dignity and self-respect remain undamaged when you do your best. What and how others decide is on their record, not yours. Do not fall victim to the trap of self-elimination.

Another change that you will gradually encounter should be even more reassuring: you become increasingly competitive every day you participate in the life process of working toward achieving high goals. You do change and improve daily, although you may not always be aware of it. Indeed, sometimes when we look ahead to those who have reached certain high levels of expertise, we feel overwhelmed. When we do gain entry into higher levels of performance, we become discouraged and think, "I'll never be able to do what those others are doing." It is important to remember that no one is born into these high realms of achievement. Even now, those several years behind you may be gazing in your direction and wondering if such a degree of skill lies within their own levels of possibility! So, while looking ahead to distant horizons of success, maintain confidence, faith, and trust in yourself and in the future. Learn to draw from your own reserve of emotional resources when you feel unsteady. Remember that your own circle of family can play a special role in this process.

10. Family Is the Beginning and the End

For Latinos, *la familia* is not just a concept; it is a way of life. Families do make the success of individuals possible and worthwhile. Yet family is a concept that in most circumstances requires no definition or explanation. However, just as recognizing the difference between network and team is a necessary ingredient in a successful career, it is important to clearly understand your family's very special and powerful function in your life. As you travel into the world of advanced schooling and work, people on a campus or in the workplace will look at you in a completely different way from that of your family. For the most part, they will judge you in terms of what you do. They are particularly interested in what you can do and especially in what you will do to help them achieve their own goals. Your family treasures you because of who you *are*. For others, "being" is not the issue; "doing" is. Worldly fame and fortunes are tied to actions and results, whereas genuine family feelings are little swayed by accomplishments. Your family embraces you during your moments of failure as well as those of triumph. What is important to them is who you are—not what you do.

Just as you should always be able to rely on the acceptance and affection of your family and closest associates despite temporary disappointments or losses, they should expect the same in return. In other words, you should maintain your respect and high regard for your family and friends even though some differences may increase, as you progress through school and your career. In most cases it is your family that has provided you the capacities and talents, as well as the opportunities, to succeed in the first place. Improvement of the status of daughters or sons beyond that of their parents is truly a fulfillment of the promise and the legacy extended from one generation to the next. Even though possibilities for conflict might arise, reliance on fundamental bonds and values should strengthen positive feelings. Change is inescapable in the course of human experience, but among the many challenges of achieving success is that of accepting variations in even the most basic relationships.

In the conclusion of his novel *Bless Me, Ultima* (1972), author Rudolfo Anaya presents a scene between a parent and his young child. The father, Gabriel Marez, attempts to advise his young son, who senses painful tensions between conserving precious memories of his family's heritage and undergoing a whirlwind of new experiences and changes. The father tells the boy, "Ay, every generation, every man is a part of his past. He cannot escape it, but he may reform the old materials, make something new" (236). The son is shown the path of reconciliation that is available to all of us. Valuing our origins enables us to view ourselves as part of a growing tradition in which what our parents have made possible for us is returned to them with respect, just as the author of *Bless Me, Ultima* did in dedicating his novel to his own family—"*Con Honor, Para Mis Padres.*" Progress and growth in the present draw strength from the past while creating a bridge to the future.

CROSSING THE BRIDGE TO THE FUTURE

At times, hopeful high school students and their parents feel as if the bridge to the college of their dreams is barricaded by the seemingly endless list of tasks and forms they must complete, just to be *considered* for admission. Latino parents may find this process highly frustrating, especially due to the language barrier and lack of experience. This list usually includes an official transcript of high school courses, customarily obtained from the school's registrar; recommendations from a counselor and/or a teacher; the application form itself; and, often, at least one essay. In addition many colleges require, or simply request, a set of standardized test scores. Standardized tests may represent the most formidable hurdle for Latino students. The language of these tests, as well as their format and the culture they represent, are largely Anglocentric. To enhance a Latino student's opportunities for success, the best preparation is a systematic approach.

The two most well known college admission tests are the Scholastic Aptitude Test (SAT) and the American College Test (ACT). Although the SAT is the most well known nationwide, the ACT is used extensively in many parts of the country, such as the Midwest. Although both tests roughly share a common purpose, they are quite different in form. Because of their differences, a student might actually find one test easier than the other and, therefore, do better on that one rather than the other. The first and most practical approach for students would be to examine the bulletin or informational materials from their chosen college(s) to learn which (if any) of the tests are required.

A careful plan of attack should then be devised, involving a few fundamental steps. The most important questions should be identified and considered first:

1. What are the SATs and the ACT, and how do I arrange to take them?
2. What can I do to obtain the highest possible scores?
3. When should I take these tests?
4. What do my scores actually mean, and how will they influence my dream of going to college?

Although the idea of taking college admissions tests can be nearly overwhelming, once these questions are considered and, most important, a plan is made, much anxiety and stress can be alleviated.

1. What Are the SAT and the ACT, and How Do I Arrange to Take Them?

Tests, such as the SAT and the ACT, are frequently called different things by different people—including the corporate producers of the tests themselves. These differences in titles and labels highlight the crucial differences between their format and purpose. Although the SAT is known universally as simply "the SAT," the test was originally identified by its creators as the Scholastic Aptitude Test, with an emphasis on aptitude, or innate ability, rather than mastery or memory of individual items of knowledge. A corporate collective known as the College Board has been the source of policy regarding the nature of the test, and the Educational Testing Service (ETS) in Princeton, New Jersey, is the actual test maker. Similarly, the ACT is a firm of test makers and designers located in Iowa City, Iowa, that, like ETS, produces numerous assessment measures in addition to college admissions tests.

Although it is a multiple-choice test, the SAT is labeled by its producers as a "reasoning test." It attempts to measure two types of reasoning—verbal and mathematical. On the other hand, the ACT's stated purpose is to measure the knowledge, understanding, and skills acquired throughout a student's high school education. The ACT focuses on four categories: English, mathematics, reading, and science reasoning.

Both tests, composed of their various sub-parts, involve an intense—and often exhausting—three-hour test session requiring prior registration and preparation. Because of the limited number of test sessions scheduled and the relatively formal process of registration itself, plan to start the registration process a year in advance. Registration should be initiated by students themselves at their own high school.

Registering for the SAT

Test producers provide high schools with brochures and booklets that are available freely to all interested students. These materials may be found in the counselors' office or a career and study center located right in the school building. The College Board offers two basic and important student publications. The first one is "Taking the SAT I: Reasoning Test." This free booklet describes the basic SAT, suggests preparation strategies, and includes a sample test. On the last page, a schedule of SAT tests offered throughout the entire year identifies test dates and registration deadlines (usually a month before the actual test dates). Test fees are also given—the basic fee is about $15.

The second booklet offered by the College Board is the actual "Registration Bulletin," containing the necessary names, numbers, and forms and the envelope needed to register for the test. It is also possible to register for the SAT electronically by contacting the College Board Online—

www.collegeboard.org. Students will receive immediate confirmation as well as a registration number to be used for admission to the test site. (But be aware that you will need a credit card number if you want to register online.)

Registering for the ACT

The ACT offers a large envelope labeled "Student Registration Packet" for prospective test takers. All materials necessary for registration are in this packet, and they are to be mailed back to the ACT in the envelope itself. Like the SAT, the ACT is offered throughout the year, usually once in alternating months such as October, December, February, April, and June. Once a student selects a specific test date and begins the registration process, he or she is ready for the most important step: preparation for taking the test.

2. What Can I Do to Obtain the Highest Possible Scores?

If you knew you could win $1,000 or more by running a five-minute mile twelve months from today, what would you do almost every day between now and then? Of course, you would run, run, run! Or, practice, practice, practice. After all, we do well that which we do often and with confidence. Just as you would get a coach to help you prepare for a mile run, so you should talk with Latinos who have taken the test the year before.

In the same way, effective preparation for either the ACT or the SAT begins with studying all the test preparation and practice materials available. Overall preparation for both tests should involve sustained study sessions of increased length until mental and physical stamina are strengthened for that all-important three-hour test session. A normal day of preparation should include challenging and concentrated reading followed by intense analysis of both style and content. In addition, it is useful to identify and isolate exactly what you will be asked to do in each item. In English or a verbal section, for example, it would be a major mistake to assume that you will simply recognize the correct answer because it will sound right. In fact, the SAT frequently requires the mental manipulation of many "big ideas," involving distinctions of comparison versus contrast, main idea versus supporting detail, and so on. Similarly, the ACT English test requires students to distinguish between words that serve as a transition and those that serve as supporting details. Both tests demand fine and specific judgments regarding the interpretation of words and ideas, as well as a sound knowledge of English grammar.

3. When Should I Take These Tests?

Because test scores are needed for the fall admissions process, high school students should consider taking the tests in the spring of their junior year. The PSAT, or Preliminary Scholastic Aptitude Test, is offered to sophomores and juniors in October and is considered a helpful preview for the SAT. It is also possible for students to take the test in the fall of their senior year. Whether students take the tests more than once is a decision best discussed with a guidance counselor.

4. What Do My Scores Actually Mean, and How Will They Influence My Dream of Going to College?

Increasingly college admissions officers are declaring their unwillingness to allow any one element, such as a test score, in a student's application file to determine a final decision. If low scores indicate the student might have difficulty in achieving academic success, then the admissions officers are likely to search for indications of good study skills or the ability to organize resources, assume individual responsibility, or solve problems. The admissions officers's job is to identify students who will likely graduate in four years—they are searching for applicants who show a balance of the abilities, skills, and goals appropriate for success in their particular institution. If low test scores seem to indicate potential problems in achieving success in a particular college or university, then the student should consider other colleges and options. Again, this is best discussed with a guidance counselor.

COMMUNITY COLLEGE VERSUS FOUR-YEAR COLLEGE OR UNIVERSITY

The option of attending a community college offers many advantages to Latinos who might otherwise feel somewhat "in over their head" in a high-powered academic institution. What should be remembered and maintained in all planning and preparation for college is that the question of education beyond high school is not necessarily a matter of a simple yes or no. If low scores or insufficient finances mean that you have to eliminate one choice, be aware that many others are available. You could consider a two-year community college either as a "fallback" option or as a purposefully chosen preliminary step in an extended series of moves toward the ultimate goal of success in college.

How to Choose a College (A Journey with *Familia*)

GUADALUPE ANAYA

Professor, College of Education, Indiana State University

Since the mid-1980s the Latina/o college-age population (18 to 24-year-olds) has been increasing dramatically. Each year more Latina/o youth have been making the decision to go to college, and college enrollments for Latinas/os have steadily increased across the country.

Making the decision to go on to college and selecting a college to attend is a journey you should take with your family. It is never too early nor is it ever too late to go to college. The questions you need to think about in selecting a college will include questions about yourself, your family, and the colleges you might attend. This can be a journey full of wonder and delight, as well as challenges and some frustrations. Having family, *tias, tios, primas*, and *primos*, and close *amigos* to share the uncertainties and achievements will transform the journey into an adventure. *La aventura*—the adventure—can begin with the college selection process, the task of choosing a college.

Your family and college representatives may be able to answer your questions, so you should discuss the college selection process with them. The role they play can be small or big, and your role is that of the primary actor. *La familia Latina* reflects cooperative structures, dynamics, and values found in many Latina/o cultures. The structure of many Latina/o families often includes an extended family of grandparents, aunts and uncles, cousins, *madrinas* and *padrinos*, and close family friends. Cultural values of cooperation and closeness are seen in the support provided by the family to the individual and in the obligation that each son/daughter or sister/brother has toward the family. It is common for Latina/o youth to feel a strong sense of reward in meeting family obligations, as well as a strong sense of obligation to the family. In Latina/o communities it is common to see family members of all ages fulfilling family obligations and reaping the rewards of a cooperative family unit. Sharing information about college choices with family is one more aspect of the Latina/o family dynamic. You should become familiar with the questions in this chapter. And you should think about those questions you might ask in preparation for discussions about college. Also, as you practice asking questions you will find that it becomes easier to talk about college selection. *Ya veras*: Soon you will find yourself adding your own questions to those included in this Step.

The opening sections of this Step present some questions to ask about yourself and your family and some questions to ask about colleges and universities. The next sections of this Step discuss campus visits and offer tips on selecting colleges to apply to. The last section includes checklists that will help you keep track of important information and a sample letter to write to college representatives.

Here are a few words about the best time to think about choosing a college. Middle school is an excellent time to begin to have serious discussions about college. You can discuss your interests in school subjects you might continue to study in college; you can also talk about where you might go to college and what types of jobs you think you might like to have someday. You should tell your counselor about your desire to attend college when you begin to plan for your high school classes. In order to begin college right after high school graduation, you should start reading this chapter, exploring the questions, and having discussions with your family during your junior year in high school.

COLLECTING INFORMATION ON EACH COLLEGE THAT INTERESTS YOU

You should contact the colleges you are interested in as soon as possible. Call the college admissions office. Many universities have toll-free 800 numbers or can be contacted by e-mail. Most public libraries (and some high schools) will provide you access to a computer and the Internet. You should begin collecting information before you begin your senior year. This is especially important in case you want to apply to colleges with application deadlines in October and November of your senior year. Ask for:

packages prepared by the college for new students
- admission requirements and guidelines,
- application materials, and
- financial aid and scholarship materials; as well as

information on programs
- in the areas of study you are interested in (you can ask for as many as you like),
- for first-generation college students, and
- for students from low-income families, if this is your family status.

For each college that you do research on, you should use a folder or large envelope to collect and save the information. Write the name of the college on the outside of the envelope, include all the materials you receive, and use index cards for notes. On the index cards you can make brief comments about your first impression of the college, your experiences with college representatives and staff, and your impressions during campus visits.

It is never too early nor is it ever too late to think, read, and do something about selecting a college. That's why it is good for you to share this adventure with all the members of your family: children in elementary and middle school as well as your parents, aunts, uncles, and grandparents. Any one of them is likely to be inspired by your interest in college and decide to go on to college themselves!

QUESTIONS TO ASK ABOUT YOURSELF AND YOUR FAMILY

There are many things to consider while you are trying to choose a college. You can make it an easier process if you remember that the most important questions you should ask are about yourself, your family, and the college you want to attend. This section focuses your attention on yourself and your family. For each category there is a brief discussion to help you organize your thoughts and some sample questions. Remember that this is a guide meant to call your attention to important matters. Your family, teachers, and friends may suggest other questions.

You can begin by (1) exploring your expectations and your family's expectations, or (2) making an academic self-assessment. In any case it will be good for you to return to each of these sections several times over the next few months.

Your Expectations and Your Family's Expectations

Going to college involves clarifying your expectations as well as those of your family. There are many things to consider. Among the most important are:

personal priorities
- how far from home? leave home or commute daily from home?
- financial considerations

educational goals
- A.A. or B.A. degree?
- graduate school, sooner or later?

vocational (career) goals

Personal Priorities

Families have much in common in our society, but there are also many differences in the values and traditions practiced. Providing love and support are basic expectations within most families. However, love and support can be expressed in various ways: material and spiritual. All these things can influence personal and family priorities. At the beginning of the chapter you read that *la familia Latina* often reflects cooperative cultural values and traditions. This means that the personal priorities you develop may take into account the needs and priorities of your family. As such, you will experience a strong sense of reward for keeping your family in mind. In this context you can see why it is important to ask yourself what things are important to you *and* to your family. These are your personal priorities. Priorities are the choices, options, and preferences to which you devote your attention, emotion, time, energy, and money. Figure 1 is meant to get you started. You should add other priorities of your own and keep in mind that the list may change as a result of your experiences.

A large number of individuals leave their homes to attend college. However, it is more common for Latinas/os to stay at home and commute to college due to traditional parental preferences. Often due to economic need, Latinos will stay home and work to help increase the family income. Do you want to leave home to attend college, or stay at home and commute? The decision to go away to college or to commute is often based on (1) the importance placed on remaining a part of the family on a daily basis, and (2) financial considerations. Going away to college does not mean that less importance is placed on being with family. Most often it means that a family has the money to pay for extra car, bus, or airplane trips during the school year. And sometimes it means that family members are willing to make the sacrifice not to be together as often as they are accustomed to.

If you expect to leave home to attend college, it is important to consider how far away you can go. Discuss the following questions with your parents, grandparents, aunts and uncles, and whoever is living with you now:

- How often will you travel home from college?
- How much travel time is reasonable for each trip?
- Will you be traveling by car, bus, or airplane?
- How much will your trips home cost?

Figure 1
Exploring Your Personal and Family Priorities

How important are the following? 1 = always expected (required)
                                   2 = very important
                                   3 = somewhat important or negotiable

	To you	To your family	To _____
How important is it to be with your family			
for holidays	—	—	—
(which ones?)	—	—	—
for family birthdays, anniversaries, etc.	—	—	—
(which ones?)	—	—	—
for other family events	—	—	—
(which ones?)	—	—	—
to help at home	—	—	—
(help with what?)	—	—	—
(how often?)	—	—	—

If you expect to stay at home and commute to college, it is also important to consider how far away you can go. Discuss with your parents or family questions such as these:

• Will you be traveling by car or bus?
• How much travel time is reasonable?
• How much will bus fare be?
• If you will drive daily, how much would you spend on gasoline and insurance?

Attending college will cost you some money, but not necessarily a lot. Financial issues require early consideration and have been introduced in the previous discussion. However, taking college expenses into account requires information about what everything will cost and where the money will come from. These are very important personal considerations, and a full chapter is dedicated to this topic (see Step 3).

Educational and Vocational Goals

Why are you going to college? What are your educational and vocational goals? There are many reasons given by students when they are asked this question. Some of the most common answers are:

- to learn more about my favorite subject,
- to be able to help my family financially in the future,
- to contribute to my community, and/or
- to prepare for a career.

However, there is seldom one single most important reason for any student. In most cases there are several reasons for going to college. Your reasons reflect your own educational and vocational goals and the expectations of your family.

No matter what subject, issue, or problem you are most interested in, learning more about a favorite subject is a powerful educational goal. This goal will motivate you to discover the colleges that have the most interesting and appropriate programs, courses, and opportunities for you. Fulfilling this goal through your college education will prepare you to discover career options. What does this mean? Today, or the day you start college, you may not know what career you will have after you finish college. But as you explore your favorite subject(s) in college, you will come across many opportunities to learn more about careers. It is important to explore

- what it is that you like about a subject(s),
- what you find most interesting, and
- what you find boring about it.

The desire to help your family and contribute to your community is a commendable goal that will strengthen your motivation to get a college education. The desire to contribute to the well-being of others will help you focus on their needs and the ways in which you can and want to help out. You should ask yourself three questions. Asking and answering the first two questions will point you toward colleges that can help you meet your goals. Thinking about the third question will provide you with the drive and motivation to find the best educational and career opportunities for you.

- Which group(s) of people or which community are you most interested in helping?
- What kinds of things would you like to do (or hate to do)?
- Why do you want to help your family or community?

If you are interested in going to college in order to prepare for a specific career, you have a very useful guide. For you, educational and vocational goals are tied to each other. Although once you select a major it may seem that the college puts many rigid rules on you, you will actually have a lot of flexibility. Many careers and jobs today require a specialized college education. The most important requirements in most careers are the commitment to work hard and the willingness to learn.

Another possible reason for going to college is just to have the educational and life experiences that attending college can provide. Colleges can offer many experiences and challenges for your heart, mind, body, and spirit. To take advantage of these experiences, you should think about the things you:

love	=	your heart,
are interested in	=	your mind,
like to do	=	your body, and
believe in and hope for	=	your spirit.

Practice making lists for each of the four areas; place check marks by the most important and most interesting things on each list. Which list is the longest? Which one has the most check marks? This exercise will provide you with insight about who you are and will help you understand yourself a bit better. Don't forget to talk with your parents and older brothers or sisters. They know you better than you think. They can help you prioritize some of the information.

A.A. or B.A. Degree? Graduate School, Sooner or Later?

As you begin to research educational and career opportunities, you will also think about the college degree you will earn. Will you obtain an Associate's or Bachelor's degree? Will you continue on to graduate school? This is another aspect of selecting a college that requires very careful thought.

The Associate's and the Bachelor's degrees are awarded to undergraduate students by two-year and four-year colleges, respectively. Graduate schools offer additional specialization for individuals who have earned a Bachelor's degree. There are many different degrees. The most common are listed below.

Academic undergraduate degrees
- A.A. and A.S. = Associate in Arts and Associate in Science
- B.A. and B.S. = Bachelor of Arts and Bachelor of Science

Professional undergraduate degrees
- A.S.N. = Associate of Science in Nursing
- B.S.N. = Bachelor of Science in Nursing

- O.D. = Doctor of Optometry
- Pharm. D. = Doctor of Pharmacy

Graduate degrees

- M.A. and M.S. = Master of Arts and Master of Science
- Ph.D., Ed.D., J.D., and M.D. = Doctorate and professional terminal degrees

Colleges and universities do not offer every college degree. Most colleges and universities specialize in undergraduate degrees such as two-year (Associate's) or four-year (Bachelor's) degrees, and others offer many different undergraduate and graduate degrees. The college you attend determines the exact requirements for each degree, but there are some common characteristics. Following is a description of the most common degrees and the time required to complete the requirements (for a full-time student).

An Associate in Arts degree (A.A.) and an Associate of Science (A.S.) are available in some technical, business, and health and social service fields. It is generally awarded after two years of college education at a community, technical, or junior college.

The Bachelor of Arts (B.A.) and the Bachelor of Science (B.S.) degrees are available in a tremendous number of subjects; these are generally grouped into categories by colleges (e.g., education, science, humanities). Even though most B.A. and B.S. degrees are supposed to take four years to complete, the average time to complete all classes required for a Bachelor's degree is *five* years. (Due primarily because many students work while attending college.) At some colleges you can start out in an A.A. program and stay on to complete the B.A. (Often a student begins an A.A. program at a two-year college and then transfers to a four-year college to get a B.A. or B.S.)

To earn a graduate degree you must apply and be admitted to graduate school, but you must first earn a Bachelor's degree. You may want to continue on to graduate school immediately after completing your Bachelor's degree. However, you can return to graduate school several years later. There are many types of degrees that you can earn in graduate school. The most common ones are: M.A. or M.S. degrees = Master of Arts or Science; M.Ed. = Master of Education; J.D. = Doctor of Jurisprudence (lawyers); M.D. = Doctor of Medicine (most physicians); and Ph.D. = Doctor of Philosophy (college professors, researchers, and scientists). Graduate programs range from one to six years and are not offered at all colleges.

Self-Assessment

Exploring college possibilities requires that you have a clear and accurate understanding of your own characteristics and accomplishments. A self-assessment is essentially a listing of your achievements and qualities. As you consider this activity, remember that one culturally related value commonly held by many Latina/o families is that of humility. Modesty regarding individual accomplishments is expected, thus Latina/o youth may have limited experience "selling themselves" to college recruiters. But a self-assessment is important for another reason: it is a very useful tool for selecting a college that is right for you.

Once you have begun the process, you may begin to see how this information can help you select a college and can also be useful in helping you secure admission to the college of your choice. Colleges typically seek information about your achievements and unique qualities. Achievements can include educational accomplishments such as your grade point average, honors and awards you have received, contributions to school organizations and offices you held, and participation in athletics and clubs. Colleges are also interested in non-school achievements: your experiences and accomplishments in your church, in the community, at work, and within your family. You can tailor the list according to your special interests, unique talents, and most meaningful expectations.

Perhaps the easiest place to start your self-assessment is with your educational profile (see Figure 2). Although your high school grade point average is useful in communicating your level of academic achievement, a closer examination of your high school course work is often much more helpful.

The knowledge and skills required for success in college are, for the most part, obtained in school. However, there is much that a young person can learn and achieve outside the classroom that will be useful for success in college and in life. Non-academic achievements are an important part of your self-assessment (see Figure 3). Colleges look carefully at all your other achievements, your experiences and accomplishments in your church, in the community, at work, and within your family. For example, did you participate in a community youth group, folklorico, mariachi, percussion ensemble, trio, or teatro; or were you active in a Latina/o cultural organization or Union Benefica?

The unique qualities you possess may be the most difficult to determine in your self-assessment. These can include a characteristic or skill that makes you different from others. A quality may not be very unusual in some social circles, in some groups, or in some communities; however, in others it may be very rare—for example, traveling to Mexico or Puerto Rico often, thus knowing a lot about another country. Think about students who may be going on to college while you try to decide if a quality you have is unique. The unique qualities you have are by definition those that are not very common among college-bound students. For example, the cooperative nature of Latina/o culture means that the desire and ability to get along well, to have harmonious interactions with others, is highly valued. Providing mutual support and a sense of mutual obligation is also

Figure 2
Educational Profile

Educational Accomplishments & Experiences	Number of Years	Grades & Awards	Unique Experiences or Activities & Special Projects
English			
History & social science			
Laboratory sciences (biology, chemistry, physics)			
Language other than English			
Mathematics			
Art, dance, music, theatre, other visual & performing arts			
Computer or technical subjects			
Advanced placement courses			
Special academic programs (such as Upward Bound)			
Other			

Figure 3
Non-Academic Achievements

Non-classroom Activities, Honors & Awards	Date or Number of Years	Name of Organization or Group	Unique Experiences or Activities & Special Projects
Academic or intellectual (local, state)			
Church or religious service, or volunteer work			
Community service or volunteer work			
Cultural activities			
Work			
Family or neighborhood			
Other			

highly valued. The skills necessary to maintain cooperative relationships with peers, family, and community include being considerate of another's point of view or position, as well as empathizing with others. You can include instances in which you've shown these qualities. In addition, Figure 4 lists a few examples of life circumstances and experiences that may shape unique qualities in individuals. These personal qualities are very important in completing your self-assessment (they are not reflected in your educational profile).

QUESTIONS TO ASK ABOUT THE COLLEGES YOU ARE INTERESTED IN

This section provides information about colleges and universities in the United States. It will provide you with a basis for posing important ques-

Figure 4
Unique Circumstances, Qualities, and Experiences

Characteristic, Quality, or Skill	Description or Explanation
Low-income family	
First-generation college bound (parents don't have college degrees)	
Multi-lingual proficiency: speaking, reading, writing	
Community cultural activities and cultural hobbies	
Personal qualities or characteristics: e.g., bi-cultural, cooperative	
Travel experiences outside of your home region, state, or country	
Other abilities, skills, or talents	

tions about the colleges you are interested in. You can also get information from libraries and colleges, as well as on the World Wide Web. It is also very important that you seek the guidance of your family, teachers, and guidance counselors.

Things to Know About Colleges and Universities

There are many kinds of colleges and universities to pick from. There are over 3,000 colleges and universities in the United States and several ways to group them: for example, by types of degrees offered and by type of student body. Other important characteristics can help you determine if the college is right for you: for example, campus life, college reputation, and facilities. Getting a college degree is a serious business; therefore you should make sure to select a college that is accredited by the regional accrediting association. (Part IV gives additional information on colleges and universities.) The discussion that follows includes information you may want to look for. However, keep in mind that there are many other features of colleges and universities that you might think of to add to your list of things to ask about a prospective college or university.

Types of Colleges

Colleges and universities can be grouped into three categories: (a) two-year community (junior) colleges, (b) four-year, or comprehensive, colleges, and (c) doctoral degree–granting or research universities. Most community colleges offer professional training classes, one- to two-year degree programs (A.A. = Associate in Arts degree), and general/introductory courses that are required for and count toward a B.A. degree (Bachelor of Arts degree). The comprehensive colleges offer a large variety of B.A. and B.S. programs, which require four to five years to complete. Many comprehensive colleges also offer graduate courses leading to master's degrees (M.A. or M.S. degrees). Some comprehensive colleges offer a small number of A.A. programs. Doctoral degree–granting and research universities provide a wide variety of programs granting bachelor's, master's, and doctoral degrees. Some doctoral and research universities also have law and medical programs.

In addition to the types of degrees offered, it is important to look at the academic programs offered by the college: majors, ethnic studies, and special academic programs. The greatest variety of majors is generally found at large colleges and universities (18,000–45,000 students). Students who are undecided about an academic major will have a chance to shop around for subjects they might like at a large university. You generally have until your sophomore year to declare a major. Or, if you change your mind about what you want to study, it is easier to shop around for a major at a large college. Additionally, some colleges and universities have impressive ethnic studies programs: Chicana/o and Boriqua Studies, American Indian and African American Studies, or Asian American and Caribbean Studies. If the college you are researching does not have an ethnic studies program, you should ask if the classes offered reflect the experiences of U.S. Latinas/os (Chicanos, Puerto Ricans, etc.). Many colleges have special academic programs and co-curricular programs that are very appealing to prospective students. These can include honors study, volunteer or community service learning, internships, early research experience, and international programs. Ask the college staff for information on special programs.

Some characteristics make educational institutions very extraordinary. Hispanic-serving colleges are among the newest on the American college scene. They are sometimes referred to as Hispanic-serving institutions, or

HSIs. (To find out which colleges are HSIs, look up *www.hacu.net.*) Mexican American, Puerto Rican, and other Latina/o students make up approximately 25 percent of the student body at a Hispanic-serving college or university. Historically black colleges and universities (HBCUs) have a commitment to meet the needs of African American students. Many HBCUs have large numbers of Latina/o and non-black students. There are also tribal colleges throughout the country serving the needs of American Indian students and their communities. These extraordinary colleges and universities are dedicated to providing quality educational opportunities to Latina/o, African American, and American Indian students and their communities. HSI, HBCU, and tribal colleges offer the same curricula and undergraduate degrees as the regular higher-education institutions. However, most HSI, HBCU, and tribal colleges do not offer the terminal degree.

Campus Life and Reputation

The characteristics already discussed, and the quality and variety of programs offered by a college, contribute to the experiences that a student can expect to have there. For example, most colleges are known as predominantly white institutions (PWIs) because most of the students who attend are white. The percentage of Latina/o, American Indian, African American, and Asian American students at PWIs can be as low as 1 percent or as high as 12 percent. However, there are many other features that shape the campus life of American colleges and universities.

An educational institution of any kind or size can be a residential campus. Many colleges and universities are located in small towns (campus towns); some colleges are located in large cities. A college that provides dormitories for its students is said to have a residential campus. Although some colleges do not have enough dorm space for all students, they often guarantee campus housing for all freshmen or all freshmen and sophomores. Early applications for housing assignments will ensure that you get the type of building (or floor) assignment that you prefer. The types of housing units vary from campus to campus. They generally include co-ed and single-sex (buildings or floors); special academic or theme units; and single, double, or triple rooms or suites.

There are also commuter and "suitcase" campuses. Students at commuter schools generally live at home (family home) and drive or take the bus to campus daily. Residential campuses whose students pack up their suitcases often and drive home for the weekends are sometimes referred to as suitcase campuses.

The time you spend in college is a very important part of your life. Some campuses have very strong educational or academic reputations, yet others have a reputation that is non-academic. It is true that some of what you learn during your college years will come from your experiences outside of the classroom. For this reason, colleges and universities spend a lot of time and money on extracurricular activities and on recreational and cultural programming. Student clubs that are typically found in many high schools are also found on college campuses. Additionally, the town or city may offer many diversions: local festivals, museums, and entertainment. Although this atmosphere is stimulating, students must remember that it is possible to spend too much time on diversions and lose sight of academic and educational goals.

Another important aspect of campus life is the racial climate. Does the college have a welcoming and inclusive atmosphere for all students? The presence of Latina/o and other minority students, staff, and faculty on campus, as well as of Latina/o oriented student organizations, typically contributes to a more hospitable campus climate for Latina/o students. If this is very important to you, you should consider an HSI college. This is especially true at PWIs. At predominantly white institutions the Latina/o oriented student organizations sponsor cultural, educational, service, and recreational programs. In doing so they create a sense of "home away from home" for Latina/o students, and they provide a valuable educational service for the campus. Unfortunately, Latina/o students may experience a chilly racial campus climate when they feel out of place or not welcomed because of their race. At the extreme, students may experience racial harassment. Some colleges have offices and programs to handle these incidents (affirmative action office, dean of students, multicultural affairs office).

An important distinction between some colleges is the retention and graduation rates for different groups of students. On a national level, the college graduation rate is approximately 65 percent. This means that one college may have an 85 percent graduation rate and another might have a 45 percent graduation rate. The national graduation rates for Mexican American, Puerto Rican, American Indian, and African American students are approximately 35 percent. This is true across the country. For any school that you are interested in, it would be a good idea to locate the graduation rates for Latina/o college students (or African Americans). Are the graduation rates above or below the national average of 35 percent? Obtaining graduation rates for different racial groups, and for women and men, for the schools that you are considering can help you in the college selection process. (Some of this information is found in the lists provided in Part IV of this book.)

Facilities: Classrooms, Library, Cafeterias, Snack Bars, Handicap-Accessible Features

In addition to looking into the types of programs, student body, campus reputation, and campus climate, it is very important to know about the facilities available on campus. Some facilities will be more important to you than others. You should try to get information on the quality of the classroom buildings, the college library, the number of computers available to students, and the quality and safety of the residence halls. You may also want to determine the quality and range of sports and recreational facilities, and the degree to which the campus is handicap accessible.

Most colleges and universities have fairly good cafeterias and snack bars. For some students, the food is different from what they are used to having. For many Latina/o students, the traditional or typical foods available at home are seldom served at most college campuses (with the possible exception of Hispanic-serving institutions). Thus, if you have to pay for a meal plan you should ask about the refund policy for meals you don't eat. You don't want to be surprised after you've paid for eighteen meals per week but only eaten twelve meals per week and in the end the college keeps the balance of your money. That's a lot of money out of your (or your parents') pocket!

CAMPUS VISITS

If at all possible, you should visit college campuses that you are interested in. Campus visits can be an important part of the college selection process. You will see the types and quality of facilities and can meet with students, faculty, or staff. You can call the college admissions office for information about campus tours. The admissions staff can answer most of your questions about campus visits.

Planning a Campus Visit

There are several possibilities. You can speak to your teachers and counselors to find out if your high school sponsors college campus visits. Alternatively, one of your high school or community clubs might be willing to plan a campus visit. Check with the college about group visits (they will need about three to six weeks' notice to plan for your group's visit). However, it is more common for a prospective student and her or his family to make plans and to visit colleges on their own. You should discuss this with your family. Make plans to visit as many colleges as you can during your junior year in high school.

It is a good idea to make appointments as far in advance as you can. Many families choose to travel during holidays or weekends, and most colleges prepare for a rush of visitors at these times. However, during a rush period you may not be able to get all the appointments that you want. On the other hand, at other times of the year you might be able to call at 8 A.M. and get some appointments for the same day.

A campus visit can be as inexpensive as you and your family want to make it. Expenses will include:

- transportation and parking (if you drive),
- meals,
- hotel (if you stay overnight; be aware that if you and your family plan to spend the night you must make your own hotel reservations).

If you cannot visit a campus, talk with a student from your high school who graduated and is now attending a college and has returned home for the holidays or summer.

Things to Do on Your Campus Visit

Admissions counselors are available on weekdays all year. At some colleges they may also be available on Saturdays. You can ask for a tour of the campus and a dormitory tour (residence halls). These tours are given by staff especially trained to provide information to prospective students. Residence staff often conduct tours of the dormitories, but they may require separate appointments.

With careful planning you can include additional activities in your campus visit. Academic program appointments or class visits can also be arranged. If you want to meet with someone in an academic program, you should mention your intended major when you speak or write to the admissions office. If you have time, you can sit in on a class or arrange to talk with students about their experiences.

If you have time to visit twice, the first visit could be an "anonymous" official tour and the second visit could include class visits and pre-arranged faculty conversations. This is a non-threatening approach.

MAKING YOUR FINAL SELECTIONS

There are many things to consider before you make your final selections. You can keep your options open by applying to more than one college. Keep in mind that admissions officers examine much more than grades and test scores in making admissions decisions. You could very well be admitted to a college that you (or family and friends) believed you didn't have a good chance of getting into. That would be a very pleasant surprise! Thus, it is advisable to apply to schools you like and to at least one college for each of three categories described under the heading "Types of Colleges." Begin by asking yourself the following question:

What do I think my chances are of being admitted to this college?
1. I am overqualified and I am very sure that I will be admitted.
2. I am qualified and I am sure that I will be admitted.
3. I almost qualify for admission, but I am not sure that I will be admitted.
4. I definitely do not qualify, and I am sure that I will not be admitted.

You should apply to all colleges that you are interested in and for which you answer 1 or 2 to the question above. You should also seriously consider applying to colleges for which you answered yes to number 3 (use the checklist in Figure 6). If you are not sure whether you should answer 3 or 4, have a discussion with a family member, an encouraging teacher, or a college representative or staff member. Even if you answer 3 or 4, the university may have programs designed for students like you. In other words, apply to colleges for which you might answer any of the first three responses above. (Remember there is an application fee to process your papers.)

Discuss with others, including the college recruiter, the decision to apply or not to a college that you only "almost qualify" for or a college that you do not qualify for. By applying to a college for which you have minimal qualifications, you give the college admissions staff the opportunity to admit you on the basis of student qualities that may be in short supply the year you apply! You also give the college the opportunity to offer you admission to programs designed for students like you. If you don't apply, you are in essence making the admissions decision for that college and possibly denying yourself an opportunity. Taking a chance may require some courage, but it may result in a pleasant surprise.

KEEPING TRACK OF INFORMATION

In making your college choices, you will definitely take into account the costs of going to college and the resources available to you. You should carefully research this matter. The next Step provides detailed information on costs and resources.

At the end of this Step are three checklists. You may want to make photocopies of them to use as many times as you need. The first checklist provides guidelines on the information you can collect on each college you are interested in (see Figure 5). Make a copy for each college that you do research on. Using a large envelope or a folder for each college will help you keep organized. Make brief notes about your impressions of each college. You can make these notes in a notepad, on index cards, or in a computer file. Add your personal notes to your collection of information for each college.

The second checklist will help you keep track of the general questions and topics to discuss (see Figure 6). These include information about yourself, personal and family priorities, and things that you want in a college.

The third checklist includes a list of things you might want to do if and when you visit college campuses (see Figure 7). Again, you can make copies for each campus you might visit. Make brief notes on an index card for each campus visit and add them to your files.

Lastly, to help you get started in contacting a college or university you may be interested in attending, we are providing a sample letter you can use to help you write your own letter (see Figure 8).

Figure 5
Checklist of Information to Collect on Each College

Do you have information about each college that you are interested in? Your high school and public libraries, the Internet Web pages of each college, and college recruiters are all good sources.

First, list the college and obtain contact information for the admissions office.

- ❑ College/University   _____
- ❑ telephone number   _____
- ❑ e-mail address   _____
- ❑ admissions office address   _____
  _____
  _____

Second, contact the college or university and ask for informational materials.

- ❑ Packages for prospective students that include
  - ❑ admission requirements = guidelines used by college admissions officers
  - ❑ application materials
  - ❑ financial aid and scholarship materials
- ❑ Information on programs
  - ❑ in all the areas of study you are interested in
  - ❑ for first-generation college students
  - ❑ for students from low-income families

Third, obtain important deadlines and mark the dates on your calendar.

- ❑ admissions test dates (if required)
- ❑ deadline for signing up for the admissions test(s)
- ❑ admissions application deadlines
  - ❑ benefits of applying early
- ❑ housing application deadlines
  - ❑ benefits of applying early

Figure 5 (continued)

Fourth, look over the materials for this college and review your interests and self-assessment. Answer the following questions.

Does this college have most of the things I am looking for in a college?

❑   Yes

❑   No

If you answered "Yes" to the question above: What do I think my chances are of being admitted to this college?

❑   1. I am over-qualified. I am very sure that I will be admitted.

❑   2. I am qualified. I am sure that I will be admitted.

❑   3. I almost qualify for admission, but I am not sure that I will be admitted.

❑   4. I definitely do not qualify. I am sure that I will not be admitted.

Note: If you checked 1, 2, or 3, you should consider applying to this college. If you are not sure whether you should check 3 or 4, you should have a discussion with a family member, an encouraging teacher, or a college representative or staff member. Even if you check 3 or 4, the university may have recruitment programs designed with you in mind!

Final thoughts: general impression of the college and/or other questions.

_____

_____

_____

Figure 6
Checklist of Questions and Topics to Consider

Have you thought about and discussed the following questions and topics? A bit of space is available for you to make a brief note.

❑ Self and Family
   ❑ Your own and your family's expectations

_____

     ❑ Personal priorities

_____

     ❑ Your family's priorities

_____

     ❑ Other priorities

_____

Notes

_____
_____
_____

     ❑ Educational interests and goals

_____

     ❑ A.A. or B.A. degree?

_____

     ❑ Graduate school, sooner or later?

_____

     ❑ Vocational interests and goals

_____

Notes

_____
_____
_____

   ❑ Self-Assessment
     ❑ Educational Strengths

_____

     ❑ Non-Academic Achievements

_____

     ❑ Unique Qualities

_____

Notes

_____
_____
_____

Figure 6 (continued)

❑ Window-shopping: Things to know about colleges and universities

    ❑ Types of Colleges

_____

    ❑ Campus life and reputation

_____

    ❑ Facilities: classrooms, library, cafeterias, snack bars, meal plans, handicap-accessible features

_____

Notes

_____
_____
_____

❑ For each college you are interested in: What do I think my chances are of being admitted to this college?

    ❑ 1. I am overqualified and I am very sure that I will be admitted.

    ❑ 2. I am qualified and I am sure that I will be admitted.

    ❑ 3. I almost qualify for admission, but I am not sure that I will be admitted.

    ❑ 4. I definitely do not qualify, and I am sure that I will not be admitted.

❑ Notes (other information to obtain and things to consider)

_____
_____
_____
_____
_____

Figure 7
Checklist for Campus Visits

❑ Will you visit college campuses? Even if you do not, you can still make notes from the information you gather.

❑ Things to do on your campus visit
    ❑ meet with admissions officers
    ❑ tour the campus
    ❑ tour the residence halls (dormitories)
    ❑ visit a class
    ❑ talk to student(s) at the college
    ❑ meet with advisors or professors in the academic programs that interest you
    ❑ determine accessibility for handicapped individuals

❑ Campus climate:
    _____ number of Latino students
    _____ graduation rate of Latinos
    _____ number of Latino faculty and staff
    _____ kinds of Latino student organizations

❑ Your impressions of your campus visit

_____
_____
_____
_____
_____

Figure 8
Sample Letter to a College Recruiter or Admissions Officer

March 4, 2002

Jarintzi Gutierrez
1524 Sacramento Dr.
Joliet, IL 60435

Office of Admissions
University of Illinois
Urbana, IL 61801

Dear Ms. or Sir,

I am writing to request information and application materials. I am a junior at Central High School and will be graduating on June 17, 2003.

I am interested in attending your university and would like information about the academic programs and majors offered, and applications for admissions, housing, and financial aid. Please include materials on financial and academic programs for minority students. Send the materials to:

> Jarintzi Gutierrez
> 1524 Sacramento Dr.
> Joliet, IL 60435

Thank you for your assistance.

Sincerely,

Jarintzi Gutierrez

Jarintzi Gutierrez

What Does College Cost and Where Can I Find Financial Aid?

RONALD S. MARTINEZ
Director of Student Financial Aid, University of New Mexico

For the 1999–2000 academic year, the average tuition charged by public four-year colleges and universities in the United States was $3,356.[1] This is a 3.4 percent increase over the previous year. Private four-year college tuition increased by 4.6 percent, to an average of $15,380. By region, the Southwest, where the greatest number of Latinos are, offers the lowest tuition rates at both public ($2,536) and private ($11,275) four-year colleges. New England, where there are the fewest Latinos, has the highest tuition rates, averaging $4,727 at four-year public and $20,171 at four-year private colleges. Two-year public (where most Latinos are enrolled) and private colleges are charging an average tuition of $1,627 and $7,182, respectively. The average surcharge for out-of-state or out-of-district students at public institutions is $3,191 at two-year colleges and $5,350 at four-year colleges. Room and board charges average $4,730 at four-year public and $5,959 at four-year private colleges.

More than half the students attending four-year colleges pay less than $4,000 in tuition and fees, and almost three-quarters face tuition charges of less than $8,000. For most U.S. citizens, including Latinos, college remains accessible. That is not to say it will be easy, but achieving the dream is possible—especially with the availability of more than $64 billion in student financial aid. Enrollment in education beyond high school rose for all income groups in the 1990s. Yet an individual's chances of entering and completing college remain closely correlated with economic background and circumstance. Wide gaps in opportunity exist between those at the bottom of the income ladder and those at the top. There are ways to improve your chances of getting the financial help you need to become a college graduate. That is the purpose of this Step.

WHAT DOES COLLEGE REALLY COST?

The real cost of college is sometimes difficult to identify because many colleges and universities only publish the expenses you might pay directly to the school. However, this need not be a complex problem. College costs usually include tuition and fees, books and supplies, room and board (food), transportation, and personal expenses. Generally a computer is required as well; this may become a cost to you if the college does not have reasonable access to computers for its students (and most colleges do not have sufficient numbers of computers). If you have a physical disability, you might also incur additional costs for specialized equipment. It is advisable to contact the college's financial aid office for specific information on these expenses and on computer access for students. Financial aid office staff will gladly provide information regarding a reasonable amount to budget for each of the above items. Most colleges also have a Web site providing cost information.

Do not disregard any of the above expenses. For example, if you plan on living with your parents, you might think it won't be necessary to budget for food because you can eat at home. However, there still might be a food cost for which to budget. Why? Because you'll be in a new and different environment, and unless you live very close to campus it will not be possible to eat all meals at home. And don't plan to skip too many meals. It's difficult to study when you're hungry.

Living and eating in the college's facilities is usually a good value and helps you connect to the campus community, but it might also be very different from the tasty, spicy *comida* to which you may be accustomed. And you may simply want to eat out occasionally to get the tastes you desire. If you are going away to college, be sure to budget expenses for at least one round-trip back home per year. You'll want to be home for major holidays.

WHAT TYPES OF FINANCIAL AID ARE AVAILABLE?

In 2000–2001 there is over $64 billion in financial assistance available nationally to help students attend college and pay college expenses. Consider this Step as the Latino student's guide for learning to maximize the opportunity to receive a fair share of these funds. There are three general categories of financial aid available: (1) grants and scholarships, (2) employment opportunities, and (3) educational loans.

Grants and Scholarships

Grants and scholarships are similar in that each is free money given to you to attend college. Grants and scholarships do not have to be repaid unless you withdraw early in the academic term. A grant is provided to you on the basis of your "financial need." A scholarship is awarded on the basis of your academic merit or performance in a specific field. For example, a scholarship may be awarded for ability or performance in art, music, theatre, or athletics as well as for excellence in other academic fields. A scholarship provides the recipient with a monetary award as well as recognition for achieving a high level of excellence. Usually, there are scholarships by local groups designated for Latinos. Inquire at your high school to find out about them.

Where Can I Find Scholarships to Help Pay College Costs?

Do not pay to have a personal scholarship search done for you. There are some good scholarship search companies in operation, but with broad access to the Internet you can conduct your own scholarship search for free, with just a little bit of time and effort. Also explore options for scholarships with your teachers, high school guidance counselors, or librarians. Also check local civic organizations and the Web sites of the colleges you are interested in attending. If there is a college near where you live, contact its financial aid office for help as well, even if you are not thinking of attending that school.

Start your search at the Web site of the Hispanic Scholarship Fund. Another good Web-based resource to get you started on a scholarship search is FastWeb. Both Web addresses are listed below:

- *http://www.hsf.net*
- *http://www.fastWeb.com*
- *http://www.fastWeb.com/fastsearch/college*

The last address listed above will allow you to find the Web sites of most colleges and universities in the United States. The search is conducted by state and is very easy to use. You can find most information you need on a college's Web site, including information about scholarships offered to students. Get started today! Conduct a Web site search frequently. If you don't have a computer, go to your local public library. You can use the computers there for free.

Employment Opportunities

Employment opportunities are provided at most colleges to help students earn funds to pay for college expenses and keep the cost of borrowing to a minimum. These opportunities are generally provided in two formats. The first is college employment, whereby the employing office or department pays 100 percent of your wages for work performed. The second is through a college work-study program (CWSP), which may be federally or state funded. The beauty of the CWSP is that up to 75 percent of the wages may be paid for by the CWSP, and the employing office or department may pay as little as 25 percent of your wages. This makes you a very inexpensive and desirable employee. It should be easy for you to secure work.

However, should you need assistance in locating a job, make an appointment to discuss options with the student employment office at the college you will attend. The staff will explain their system for helping students find meaningful work.

College work-study programs are usually need-based financial aid, but some states also offer a no-need option of CWSP. These employment opportunities may or may not be related to your program of study and may be offered both on campus and in the local community. Work-study jobs are real employment, and it is expected that you will perform duties as assigned. They are not opportunities to receive pay for studying!

It is generally recommended that as a new student, you seek only *on-campus* employment in your first two years at college. An on-campus job will help you to connect with faculty, staff, and student members of the college community and will facilitate your transition to this new, dynamic environment to which you now belong.

Should I Work While Attending College Full-time?

Work is good for developing valuable skills and for earning money, but it is important to remember the primary reason you are in college: to learn and to earn a degree. Too much employment can be detrimental to your main goal. Between fifteen and twenty hours of employment per week is reasonable. Beyond twenty hours of employment, academic performance tends to deteriorate quickly. When you are first starting college you may want to work only ten to fifteen hours a week until you can measure your capacity to handle work and college studies at the same time.

Student employment is more than a way to finance part of your education. It will help you gain a sense of responsibility. Students learn a great deal on the job and are often able to test their academic knowledge in their work. Student employment can foster good citizenship, responsibility, and a sense of community. You may even secure a community service job that will help you to give something back to your growing middle class Latino community. And you are also developing skills desired by employers all over the world. Educated employees with good work experience are highly valued in today's economy. Seize every opportunity to learn new skills as you gain a higher education.

Educational Loans

Educational loans are the primary source of financial aid funding in the United States. The largest provider of these loans is the federal government. Loans must be repaid in the future, usually after you graduate or cease to be enrolled on at least a half-time basis. Need-based loans are subsidized, meaning you don't have to make payments or accrue interest on the loans while you are enrolled at least half-time, as defined by each college. Non-subsidized loans are also available, but the interest is your responsibility and it must (1) be paid while you are enrolled, or (2) be capitalized (that is, added to your total amount to be repaid). Interest rates on most federal student loans are variable but do not exceed 8.25 percent.

There is often reluctance on the part of Latino students and their parents to borrow for a college education. However, most students who borrow receive such a significant return on their investment in a higher education that student loan debt is a manageable burden. The long-term economic benefits of a college education continue to far outweigh the burden of paying off student loans.

According to the U.S. Census Bureau, the median annual earnings in 1997, for Latino men age 25–34 years, were $20,617 for high school graduates as opposed to $31,635 for Latino men with a Bachelor's degree. Over a forty-year working lifetime this difference is over $440,000! The comparable median annual earnings in 1997 for Latina women age 25–34 years, who were high school graduates, were $14,747. Latina women with a Bachelor's degree earned an average of $28,550 in 1997. This difference over forty years of working exceeds $550,000—over half a million dollars!

The average undergraduate student at a public, four-year college borrows approximately $13,500 by graduation, requiring a manageable monthly payment of about $160 for ten years. *This is a very good investment in your future!* Learn to manage borrowing. You will be borrowing for major purchases for most of your life.

WHAT IS NEED-BASED FINANCIAL AID?

Financial aid from most student aid programs is awarded on the basis of financial need. When you apply for federal student aid, the information you report is used in a formula established by the U.S. Congress. The formula determines your Expected Family Contribution (EFC), an amount you and your family are expected to contribute toward your education based on your family's income and assets. For very low income students the EFC is often zero.

Financial aid applicants are classified as dependent or independent, for financial aid purposes, because eligibility for federal student aid programs is based on the concept that students and their parents (or spouse, if applicable) have the *primary* responsibility for paying for their college education.

Dependency

When you apply for federal student aid, your answers to certain questions will determine whether you're considered a dependent of your parents or independent for financial aid purposes. If you are considered a dependent of your parents, you must report their income and assets as well as your own on the Free Application for Federal Student Aid (FAFSA). The FAFSA is a standard financial aid application form printed by the U.S. Department of Education. You can get one from any high school guidance counselor or college financial aid office. If you are independent, you report only your own income and assets (and those of your spouse, if you're married).

If you are considered a dependent, you should know that in order to fill out the FAFSA you will need copies of your parents' IRS filing forms from last year. Similarly, information about assets and any bank loans still outstanding (e.g., notes not paid off yet), will have to be provided. Lastly, if your parents do not handle the English language very well, especially concerning technical questions, you should find a person in the community (e.g., your high school counselor) or someone at a local community college who speaks Spanish to help guide your parents through the forms and to answer any question that they may have. They may feel more comfortable in completing the required FAFSA forms when dealing with a Spanish speaker.

For application year 2000–2001, you are considered an independent student, for financial aid purposes, if at least one of the following applies to you:

- you were born before January 1, 1977;
- you are married (at the time you complete the FAFSA);
- you are enrolled in a graduate or professional program beyond a Bachelor's degree (such as law or medicine);
- you have legal dependents other than a spouse;
- you are an orphan or were a ward of the court until age 18; or
- you are a veteran of the U.S. Armed Forces.

If you think you have unusual circumstances that would make you independent, even though none of the above criteria apply to you, talk to your aid administrator. She or he can change your status if she or he believes your circumstances warrant it, based on documentation you provide. The financial aid administrator is not required to do this. That decision is based solely on his or her professional judgment, and it's final.

Eligibility Criteria

Eligibility for federal student aid is determined on the basis of financial need and on several other criteria listed here. However, there may be additional criteria, which can vary by state and college. For example, to receive an award whose funding is coming from a state government, the student usually has to be considered a resident of that state.

Generally, to receive federal financial aid you must:

- have financial need (not required for all loans);
- have (or expect to receive) a high school diploma or GED certificate or pass a test approved by the U.S. Department of Education;
- be working toward a degree or certificate;
- be enrolled in an eligible academic program;
- be a U.S. citizen or eligible non-citizen;
- have a valid Social Security number;
- register with the Selective Service, if male (you can do this on the FAFSA); and,
- maintain satisfactory academic progress once enrolled in college.

If your Expected Family Contribution (EFC) is low, you may be eligible for a federal Pell grant, assuming you meet all other eligibility requirements. The amount of a Pell grant varies based on the college's cost of attendance and the student's EFC. For the 2000–2001 school year, the maximum Pell grant is $3,300.

There is not a maximum EFC that defines eligibility for other financial aid programs. Instead, your EFC is used in an equation to determine your financial need. In determining your need for aid from other programs, the financial aid administrator must consider other aid you're expected to receive. The formula to determine need is simple:

(Cost of College Attendance) − (Expected Family Contribution) − (Aid from Other Sources) = Financial Need

Special Circumstances

Although the process of determining a student's eligibility for federal student aid is basically the same for all applicants, there is some flexibility. Your financial aid administrator can adjust data used to calculate your EFC or adjust your cost of attendance, if he or she believes your circumstances warrant it, based on the documentation you provide. These circumstances could include a family's abnormally high medical costs or tuition expenses for children attending a private elementary or secondary school. Another example might be if you or your parents have become recently unemployed and have lost wages. If conditions such as these apply to you or your family, contact your financial aid administrator to discuss the possibility of revising the EFC calculation.

Remember, there have to be very good reasons for the financial aid administrator to make any adjustments, and you'll have to provide adequate proof to support the reasonableness of those adjustments. The financial aid administrator's decision is final and cannot be appealed to the U.S. Department of Education.

WHAT IS THE APPLICATION PROCESS FOR NEED-BASED FINANCIAL AID?

The basic financial aid application for most colleges is the Free Application for Federal Student Aid (FAFSA; see Appendix A at the end of this chapter). If you applied for federal student aid for the 1999–2000 school year, you probably will be able to file a Renewal Free Application for Federal Student Aid. If you qualify to use the Renewal FAFSA, you'll have fewer questions to answer.

If you have not previously applied for federal student aid, you may apply by completing and submitting *the appropriate school year's FAFSA*. There are several versions of the FAFSA. I have identified those that are the most user-friendly. You may submit a FAFSA:

- by using FAFSA on the Web;
- by mailing a paper FAFSA; or
- if admitted into a college, by having your college submit your FAFSA application data electronically.

FAFSA on the Web is a free U.S. Department of Education Web site where you can complete a FAFSA online and submit it via the Internet. I highly recommend this method of application if you have Internet access, because *you can apply on the priority date at your college and still meet the deadline*. In addition, there are edit checks built in that prevent you from making serious errors. You can use FAFSA on the Web on a personal computer (PC) or a Macintosh that is equipped with a supported browser. The Web site address is *http://www.fafsa.ed.gov.*

You may also apply by mailing a paper FAFSA. You can get one from your local high school or college or from the Federal Student Aid Information Center at 1–800–4–FED–AID (1–800–433–3243). You can get a *Spanish language (paper version)* FAFSA from the Federal Student Aid Information Center by calling 1–800–433–3243.

If you want your school to submit your application electronically, you must check directly with the financial aid staff at the college that interests you to make sure that the school is staffed to handle this option. Not all colleges support this option now that Internet access is readily available.

If you apply by mail, send your completed application in the envelope that came with it. It is already addressed, and using it will help ensure that your application reaches the correct address.

If you are not near a school or college but have access to the Internet, you can download a Portable Document Format (PDF) FAFSA from the Internet at *http://www.ed.gov/offices/OPE/express.html*. After you download, you must print the FAFSA, complete it, and mail it to the address provided.

Caution: Read the instructions carefully when you complete the FAFSA or the Renewal FAFSA. Most mistakes are made because students don't follow instructions. Pay special attention to questions on income, because most errors occur in this area. An extra hour to re-check instructions and responses (before sending) could save you many weeks of frustration and anxiety later.

Be sure also to make a photocopy of your application (or print out a copy of your FAFSA on the Web application) before you submit it. This way, you have a copy of the data you submitted for your own records.

Save copies of all materials used in completing the FAFSA. You may need them later to prove that the information you reported is correct. If data verification is required and you don't provide the documentation requested, you won't be eligible to receive any federal financial aid.

Approximately 35 percent of FAFSA applications are flagged for data verification by the processing center for the U.S. Department of Education. The actual data verification is performed by the college's financial aid staff (for the federal government) using the documentation you provide, such as federal income tax returns.

Will I Need to Fill Out Other Forms, in Addition to the FAFSA, to Receive Aid?

For most of the federal student aid programs, the FAFSA is the only form you need to file. To receive a federal direct or federal family education (FFEL) Stafford loan, you will need to complete additional forms, such as a promissory note for the lender. (In the direct loan program, the federal government is the lender.) In the FFEL Stafford loan program, the lenders are private institutions such as banks or credit unions. Which loan program you borrow from is dependent on the program in which your college participates. *Loan amounts and interest rates are the same in both programs.* Your college financial aid office can tell you what additional forms you will need to fill out.

Applying for federal student aid is *free*. However, to be considered for non-federal aid (aid from the college), you may have to fill out additional forms and possibly pay a processing fee. Check with your college to determine if a non-federal application is necessary. It is mostly private, independent colleges that require a non-federal financial aid application. The most commonly used non-federal financial aid application is the Financial Aid Profile.

When Should I Apply?

Apply as soon *after* January 1, of each year, as possible. It's easier to complete the application when you (and your parents) have already completed the previous year's federal income tax returns. *Do not sign, date, or send your FAFSA prior to January 1* (that is too early; it will be rejected). If you are in danger of missing an application priority deadline at your college, you may complete the FAFSA using estimated income and taxes. You can then update the FAFSA after you or your parents file federal income tax returns.

Note: You must reapply for federal aid every year. Also, if you change colleges, your financial aid does not automatically go with you. Check with your new college to find out what steps you must take to continue receiving aid.

What Happens after I Apply?

After your completed application is received by the federal processing center, the processor will produce a Student Aid Report (SAR; see Appendix B at the end of this chapter). The SAR will report the information from your FAFSA. If there are no questions or problems with your application, your SAR will report your Expected Family Contribution (EFC). The results will be sent to you and to the colleges that you list on your FAFSA application.

If you apply using FAFSA on the Web, your data will be processed when your completed FAFSA is received by the processing center. In some cases, you'll have to mail in a signature page before your application can be processed. You'll receive a SAR in the mail approximately one week after your completed application, including a signature (if required), is received.

If you have a college financial aid administrator submit your application electronically, on your behalf, your FAFSA data will be processed and returned to the college in about a week. In addition to sending the results to your school electronically, the U.S. Department of Education will send you a SAR acknowledgment in the mail.

If you apply by mail, your application will be processed in approximately three to four weeks. Then, you'll receive a SAR in the mail. If it has been more than four weeks since you submitted your application and you have not heard anything, you can check on your application by contacting the

Federal Student Aid Information Center at 1–800–433–3243. If you applied using FAFSA on the Web, you can check on the status of your application through the FAFSA on the Web site.

If you submit a paper version of the FAFSA or the Renewal FAFSA that contains a postcard, you can use the postcard to track the processing of your application. You must fill in the postcard with the required information, attach a stamp to the postcard, and mail it with your application. When the federal processor receives your application, the postcard will be stamped with the date that it is received. You will receive the date-stamped portion of the postcard for your files. If you do not receive your SAR within four weeks of the date stamped on the postcard, you should contact the Federal Student Aid Information Center at 1–800–433–3243 and refer to the date stamped on the postcard.

What Happens after I Receive the SAR?

When you receive the SAR, you must review it carefully to make sure it is correct. If the data are correct and you do not need to make changes, you can receive financial aid on the basis of that information.

If changes are necessary, you can make corrections on Part 2 of the SAR and return it to the address given at the end of Part 2. If you applied through your school electronically and would like to make corrections to your information by mail, you must request a copy of your SAR from the Federal Student Aid Information Center. Also, you can correct your FAFSA data through the Internet using Corrections on the Web. To access your FAFSA data electronically, go to the FAFSA on the Web address, enter your personal identification number (PIN), and click on "corrections." (Remember, your PIN number is assigned when you first apply online.) The electronic address is *http://www.fafsa.ed.gov*. Once into corrections, you simply locate the data element you want to correct and overlay it with the correct data, save, and submit. Remember to print a copy for your files before exiting the Web site.

If you want to have your application information sent to a college that is not listed on your SAR, you may update or correct your SAR to add the college. You may contact the Federal Student Aid Information Center at 1–800–433–3243 to have your FAFSA information sent to the school or give the new college's financial aid administrator (FAA) permission to request your information electronically. Provide the FAA with a photocopy of your SAR when making this request. If you ask the Federal Student Aid Information Center to send your information to a new college, you will need to provide your PIN. If your address changes after you receive your SAR, you should call the Federal Student Aid Information Center to change your address.

If you would like a duplicate copy of your SAR, you can call the Federal

Student Aid Information Center to request one. Be sure you have your full name, permanent address, Social Security number, PIN, and date of birth ready when you call. You'll receive the duplicate SAR in two to three weeks. Your duplicate SAR will be sent to the address you reported on your application.

Valuable Financial Information Sources on the World Wide Web

Funding your education—*http://www.ed.gov/prog_info/SFA/FYE*

FAFSA on the Web—*http://www.fafsa.ed.gov*

The Financial Aid Information Page—*http://www.finaid.org*

Financial Aid Office Web pages—*http://www.finaid.org/otheraid/fao.phtml*

Financial Aid Calculators—*http://www.finaid.org/calculators*

Financial Aid Calculators—*http://www.collegeboard.org*

General Scholarship Search—*http://www.fastWeb.com*

Hispanic Scholarship Fund—*http://www.hsf.net*

Hope Scholarship (tax credit)—*http://www.ed.gov/offices/OPE/PPI/HOPE*

My Future (military)—*http://www.myfuture.com/OUTPUT/moneycol.htm*

Federal School Codes (Needed to Complete the FAFSA)

http://www.ed.gov/offices/OSFAP/Students/apply/search.html

Receiving and Understanding Your Financial Aid Award Letter

Once you have cleared any edit and verification issues, your application is ready to be funded. You are generally notified, by the college's financial aid office, with an award notification letter. The award letter should identify you by name, address, Social Security number, and student I.D. number (if the college uses one). The award is for a single academic year, usually fall through spring. The award letter identifies the cost of attendance, the expected family contribution, and the total amount of your eligibility for financial aid. Next comes the actual award. The award letter should identify each financial aid program offered by name, tell you its source (federal, state, college, etc.), and indicate the amount awarded for the year (and for each term).

Each college generally awards federal aid first, followed by state aid and then any funds available from the college itself until it meets your need or exhausts its available options. If you are fairly needy, applied by the college's financial aid application deadline, and indicated you wanted loans and work, then you have maximized your opportunity to receive grants, loans, and work-study. You are well positioned.

Many colleges, but not all, also require that you notify them whether you will accept the award, by a specified date. *If you do not reply on time, the award may be cancelled and offered to the next student applicant. Don't let this happen to you!* Read your award letter carefully. Determine if you need to take any action to reserve your financial aid.

Usually included with the award letter is additional information regarding the award you have just received. For example, if the award includes a loan, there may be a promissory note to sign and other instructions to explain the terms of the loan. *Follow instructions closely and return any signed documents by the date specified.* Take the time to read and understand this information well before you arrive on campus. If you do not understand something in the packet, contact the college's financial aid office for clarification.

WHAT DO I NEED TO DO TO RETAIN ELIGIBILITY FOR FINANCIAL AID?

There are really only two things you need to do at most colleges and universities to retain eligibility for financial aid. First, re-apply to establish your eligibility each year by the application priority date set by the college. As you might realize, most four-year colleges and universities have a priority date, often in February or March, for receipt of the Free Application for Federal Student Aid. Also check with the college to see if there are other application requirements. Second, perform well in the classroom. You must maintain satisfactory academic progress toward a degree or certificate to retain eligibility for financial aid. Each college has a Satisfactory Academic Progress Policy specifying the academic requirements for continued eligibility for financial aid. These requirements include a minimum grade point average (GPA) and a specific number of credit hours to be satisfactorily completed each term or academic year for continued eligibility. In addition, the policy specifies the length of time you may continue to receive financial aid at each degree or certificate level. You are now ready and armed with the information you need to finance your college degree.

Best wishes for success. Please share this information to help others to succeed. Together we can make a significant difference in the college attendance rates of Latino students. *Adelante!*

NOTE

1. Financial figures quoted in this introduction are from *Trends in College Pricing 1999* (New York: The College Board, 1999).

Appendix A
Sample Free Application for Federal Student Aid (FAFSA)

Free Application for Federal Student Aid

OMB 1845-0001   **July 1, 2000 — June 30, 2001 school year**

Use this form to apply for federal and state* student grants, work-study, and loans.

You can also apply over the Internet at **http://www.fafsa.ed.gov** instead of using this paper form. In addition to federal student aid, you may also be eligible for a Hope or a Lifetime Learning income tax credit, both of which you claim when you file your taxes. For more information on these tax credits, this application, and the U.S. Department of Education's student aid programs, look on the Internet at **http://www.ed.gov/studentaid** You can also call 1-800-4FED-AID (1-800-433-3243) Monday through Friday between 8:00am and 8:00pm eastern time. TTY users may call 1-800-730-8913.

Your answers on this form will be read by a machine. Therefore,

- use black ink or #2 pencil and fill in ovals completely, like this: ●

- print clearly in CAPITAL letters and skip a box between words: `1 5` `E L M` `S T`

- report dollar amounts (such as $12,356.00) like this: $ `1 2` , `3 5 6` (no cents)

- write numbers less than 10 with a zero (0) first: `0 7`

Pink is for students and purple is for parents.

- If you are filing a **1999 income tax return,** we recommend that you fill it out before completing this form. However, you do not need to file your income tax return with the IRS before you fill out this form.
- After you complete this application, make a copy of it. Then send the original of pages 3 through 6 in the attached envelope or send it to Federal Student Aid Programs, P.O. Box 4015, Mt. Vernon, IL. 62864-8615.
- We must receive your application—pages 3 through 6—no earlier than **January 1, 2000, and no later than July 2, 2001.**
- You should hear from us within four weeks. If you do not, please call 1-800-433-3243.
- If you or your family has **unusual circumstances** (such as loss of employment) that might affect your need for student financial aid, submit this form and consult with the financial aid office at the college you plan to attend.
- You may also use this form to apply for **aid from other sources, such as your state or college.** The deadlines for states (see below) or colleges may be as early as January 2000 and may differ. You may be required to complete additional forms.

Now go to page 3 and begin filling out this form. Refer to the notes as needed.

Deadline dates for state aid. Generally, state aid comes from your state of legal residence. **Check with your high school guidance counselor** or the financial aid administrator at your college about state and college sources of student financial aid. State deadlines are below.

AZ June 30, 2001 *(date received)*
*^ CA March 2, 2000 *(date postmarked)*
DE April 15, 2000 *(date received)*
* DC June 24, 2000 *(date received by state)*
FL May 15, 2000 *(date processed)*
HI March 1, 2000
IL First-time applicants – September 30, 2000
  Continuing applicants – June 30, 2000
  (date received)
^ IN For priority consideration – March 1, 2000
  (date postmarked)
^ IA June 1, 2000 *(date received)*
* KS For priority consideration – April 1, 2000
  (date received)
KY For priority consideration – March 15, 2000
  (date received)
^ LA For priority consideration – April 15, 2000
  Final deadline – June 30, 2000
  (date received)

ME May 1, 2000 *(date received)*
MD March 1, 2000 *(date postmarked)*
^ MA For priority consideration – May 1, 2000
  (date received)
MI High school seniors – February 21, 2000
  College students – March 21, 2000
  (date received)
MN June 30, 2001 *(date received)*
MO April 1, 2000 *(date received)*
MT For priority consideration – March 1, 2000
  (date postmarked)
NH May 1, 2000 *(date received)*
^ NJ June 1, 2000 if you received a
  Tuition Aid Grant in 1999-2000
  All other applicants
  – October 1, 2000, for fall and spring terms
  – March 1, 2001, for spring term only
  (date received)
*^ NY May 1, 2001 *(date postmarked)*

NC March 15, 2000 *(date received)*
ND April 15, 2000 *(date processed)*
OH October 1, 2000 *(date received)*
OK April 30, 2000 *(date received)*
OR May 1, 2001 *(date received)*
* PA All 1999-2000 State grant recipients and all
  non-1999-2000 State grant recipients in
  degree programs – May 1, 2000
  All other applicants – August 1, 2000
  (date received)
PR May 2, 2001 *(date application signed)*
RI March 1, 2000 *(date received)*
SC June 30, 2000 *(date received)*
TN May 1, 2000 *(date processed)*
*^ WV March 1, 2000 *(date received)*

Check with your financial aid administrator for these states: AL, AK, *AS, AR, CO, *CT, *FM, GA, *GU, ID, *MP, *MH, MS, *NE, *NV, *NM, *PW, *SD, *TX, UT, *VT, *VI, *VA, WA, WI, and *WY.

* *Additional form may be required*   ^ *Applicants encouraged to obtain proof of mailing.*

Appendix A (continued)

Notes for questions 14–15 (page 3)

If you are an eligible noncitizen, write in your eight or nine digit Alien Registration Number. Generally, you are an eligible noncitizen if you are: (1) a U.S. permanent resident and you have an Alien Registration Receipt Card (I-551); (2) a conditional permanent resident (I-551C); or (3) an other eligible noncitizen with an Arrival-Departure Record (I-94) from the U.S. Immigration and Naturalization Service showing any one of the following designations: "Refugee," "Asylum Granted," "Indefinite Parole," "Humanitarian Parole," or "Cuban-Haitian Entrant." If you are in the U.S. on only an F1 or F2 student visa, or only a J1 or J2 exchange visitor visa, or a G series visa (pertaining to international organizations), you must fill in oval c. If you are neither a citizen nor eligible noncitizen, you are not eligible for federal student aid. However, you may be eligible for state or college aid. You should check with your financial aid administrator at your school before completing this form.

Notes for questions 18–22 (page 3)

For undergraduates, full time generally means taking at least 12 credit hours in a term or 24 clock hours per week. 3/4 time generally means taking at least 9 credit hours in a term or 18 clock hours per week. Half time generally means taking at least 6 credit hours in a term or 12 clock hours per week. Provide this information about the college you plan to attend.

Notes for question 31 (page 3) — Enter the correct number in the box in question 31.

Enter 1 for 1ˢᵗ bachelor's degree
Enter 2 for 2ⁿᵈ bachelor's degree
Enter 3 for associate degree (occupational or technical program)
Enter 4 for associate degree (general education or transfer program)
Enter 5 for certificate or diploma for completing an occupational, technical, or educational program of less than two years

Enter 6 for certificate or diploma for completing an occupational, technical, or educational program of at least two years
Enter 7 for teaching credential program (nondegree program)
Enter 8 for graduate or professional degree
Enter 9 for other/undecided

Notes for question 32 (page 3) — Enter the correct number in the box in question 32.

Enter 1 for 1st year undergraduate/never attended college
Enter 2 for 1st year undergraduate/attended college before
Enter 3 for 2nd year undergraduate/sophomore
Enter 4 for 3rd year undergraduate/junior

Enter 5 for 4th year undergraduate/senior
Enter 6 for 5th year/other undergraduate
Enter 7 for graduate/professional or beyond

Notes for questions 38 c. and d. (page 4) and 72 c. and d. (page 5)

If you filed or will file a foreign tax return, use the information from your foreign tax return to fill out this form. Convert all figures to U.S. dollars, using the exchange rate that is in effect today.

If you filed or will file a tax return with Puerto Rico, Guam, American Samoa, the Virgin Islands, the Marshall Islands, the Federated States of Micronesia, or Palau, use the information from these tax returns to fill out this form.

Notes for questions 39 (page 4) and 73 (page 5)

In general, a person is eligible to file a 1040A or 1040EZ if he or she makes less than $50,000, does not itemize deductions, does not receive income from his or her own business or farm, and does not receive alimony or capital gains. The person is not eligible if he or she itemizes deductions or receives self-employment income, alimony, or capital gains.

Notes for questions 42 (page 4) and 76 (page 5) — only for people who filed a 1040EZ or Telefile

On the 1040EZ, if a person answered "Yes" on line 5, use EZ worksheet line F to determine the number of exemptions ($2750 equals one exemption). If a person answered "No" on line 5, enter 01 if he or she is single, or 02 if he or she is married.

On the Telefile, use line J to determine the number of exemptions ($2750 equals one exemption).

Notes for questions 49–51 (page 4) and 83–85 (page 5)

Net worth means current value minus debt.

Investments include real estate (other than the home you live in), trust funds, money market funds, mutual funds, certificates of deposit, stocks, bonds, other securities, Education IRAs, installment and land sale contracts (including mortgages held), commodities, etc. Investment value includes the market value of these investments. Do not include the value of life insurance and retirement plans (pension funds, annuities, non-Education IRAs, Keogh plans, etc.) or the value of prepaid tuition plans. Investment debt means only those debts that are related to the investments.

Business value includes the market value of land, buildings, machinery, equipment, and inventory. Business debt means only those debts for which the business was used as collateral.

Notes for question 59 (page 4)

Answer **"Yes"** (you are a veteran) if (1) you have engaged in active service in the U.S. Armed Forces (Army, Navy, Air Force, Marines, and Coast Guard), or were a cadet or midshipman at one of the service academies, and (2) you were released under a condition other than dishonorable. Also answer "Yes" if you are not a veteran now but will be one by June 30, 2001.

Answer **"No"** (you are not a veteran) if (1) you have never served in the U.S. Armed Forces, or (2) you are currently an ROTC student, a cadet or midshipman at a service academy, or a National Guard or Reserves enlistee (and were not activated for duty). Also answer "No" if you are currently serving in the U.S. Armed Forces and will continue to serve through June 30, 2001.

Page 2

Appendix A (continued)

Free Application for Federal Student Aid

OMB 1845-0001 *July 1, 2000 — June 30, 2001 school year*

Step One: For questions 1-36, leave blank any questions that do not apply to you (the student).

	1. LAST NAME	2. FIRST NAME	3. M.I.
1-3. Your full name (as it appears on your Social Security card)			

	4. NUMBER AND STREET (INCLUDE APARTMENT NUMBER)
4-7. Your permanent mailing address	

	5. CITY (AND COUNTRY, IF NOT U.S.)	6. STATE	7. ZIP CODE

8. Your Social Security Number [ ] - [ ] - [ ]

9. Your date of birth MONTH / DAY / YEAR 1 9

10. Your permanent telephone number   AREA CODE [ ] - [ ]

11. Do you have a driver's license?   Yes ○ 1   No ○ 2

12-13. Driver's license number and state   12. LICENSE NUMBER   13. STATE

14. Are you a U.S. citizen? Pick one. **See Page 2.**
a. Yes, I am a U.S. citizen. .... ○ 1
b. No, but I am an <u>eligible noncitizen</u>. **Fill in question 15.** ○ 2   **15.** ALIEN REGISTRATION NUMBER   A
c. No, I am not a citizen or <u>eligible noncitizen</u>. .... ○ 3

16. Marital status as of today
I am single, divorced, or widowed. ○ 1
I am married. ○ 2
I am separated. ○ 3

17. Month and year you were married, separated, divorced, or widowed   MONTH / YEAR

For each question (18 - 22), please mark whether you will be <u>full time</u>, <u>3/4 time</u>, <u>half time</u>, less than half time, or not attending. Mark "Full time" if you are not sure. See page 2.

18. Summer 2000	Full time ○ 1	3/4 time ○ 2	Half time ○ 3	Less than half time ○ 4	Not attending ○ 5
19. Fall semester or quarter 2000	Full time ○ 1	3/4 time ○ 2	Half time ○ 3	Less than half time ○ 4	Not attending ○ 5
20. Winter quarter 2000-2001	Full time ○ 1	3/4 time ○ 2	Half time ○ 3	Less than half time ○ 4	Not attending ○ 6
21. Spring semester or quarter 2001	Full time ○ 1	3/4 time ○ 2	Half time ○ 3	Less than half time ○ 4	Not attending ○ 5
22. Summer 2001	Full time ○ 1	3/4 time ○ 2	Half time ○ 3	Less than half time ○ 4	Not attending ○ 5
23. Highest school your father completed	Middle school/Jr. High ○ 1	High school ○ 2	College or beyond ○ 3	Other/unknown ○ 4	
24. Highest school your mother completed	Middle school/Jr. High ○ 1	High school ○ 2	College or beyond ○ 3	Other/unknown ○ 4	

25. What is your state of legal residence?   STATE

26. Did you become a legal resident of this state before January 1, 1995?   Yes ○ 1   No ○ 2

27. If the answer to question 26 is **"No,"** give month and year you became a legal resident.   MONTH / YEAR

28. If you have **never** been convicted of any illegal drug offense, enter "1" in the box and go to question 29. A drug-related conviction does not necessarily make you ineligible for aid; call 1-800-433-3243 or go to http://www.fafsa.ed.gov/q28 to find out how to fill out this question.

29. Most male students must register with Selective Service to get federal aid. Are you male?   Yes ○ 1   No ○ 2

30. If you are male (age 18-25) and not registered, do you want Selective Service to register you?   Yes ○ 1   No ○ 2

31. What degree or certificate will you be working towards during 2000-2001? **See page 2** and enter the correct number in the box.

32. What will be your grade level when you begin the 2000-2001 school year? **See page 2** and enter the correct number in the box.

33. Will you have a high school diploma or GED before you enroll?   Yes ○ 1   No ○ 2

34. Will you have your first bachelor's degree before July 1, 2000?   Yes ○ 1   No ○ 2

35. In addition to grants, are you interested in student loans (which you must pay back)?   Yes ○ 1   No ○ 2

36. In addition to grants, are you interested in "work-study" (which you earn through work)?   Yes ○ 1   No ○ 2

Page 3

Appendix A (continued)

Step Two: For 37-51, if you (the student) are now married (even if you were not married in 1999), report both your and your spouse's income and assets. Ignore references to "spouse" if you are currently single, separated, divorced, or widowed.

37. For 1999, have you filed your IRS income tax return or another tax return listed in **question 38**?

    a. I have already filed. ○ ₁   **b.** I will file, but I have not yet filed. ○ ₂   **c.** I'm not going to file. **(Skip to question 44.)** ○ ₃

38. What income tax return did you file or will you file for 1999?

    a. IRS 1040 .... ○ ₁   **c.** A foreign tax return. **See Page 2.** .... ○ ₃

    b. IRS 1040A, 1040EZ, 1040Telefile ...... ○ ₂   **d.** A tax return for Puerto Rico, Guam, American Samoa, the Virgin Islands, the Marshall Islands, the Federated States of Micronesia, or Palau. **See Page 2.** ...... ○ ₄

39. If you have filed or will file a 1040, were you <u>eligible to file a 1040A or 1040EZ</u>? See page 2.   Yes ○ ₁ No/^{don't}_{know} ○ ₂

For questions 40-53, if the answer is zero or the question does not apply to you, enter 0.

40. What was your (and spouse's) adjusted gross income for 1999? Adjusted gross income is on IRS Form 1040–line 33; 1040A–line 18; 1040EZ–line 4; or Telefile–line I. $ ⬚⬚⬚,⬚⬚⬚

41. Enter the total amount of your (and spouse's) income tax for 1999. Income tax amount is on IRS Form 1040–line 49 plus 51; 1040A–line 32; 1040EZ–line 10; or Telefile–line K. $ ⬚⬚⬚,⬚⬚⬚

42. Enter your (and spouse's) exemptions. Exemptions are on IRS Form 1040–line 6d, or on Form 1040A–line 6d. For 1040EZ or Telefile, **see page 2.**   ⬚⬚

43. Enter your Earned Income Credit from IRS Form 1040–line 59a; 1040A–line 37a; 1040EZ–line 8a; or Telefile–line L. $ ⬚⬚⬚,⬚⬚⬚

44-45. How much did you (and spouse) earn from working in 1999? Answer this question whether or not you filed a tax return. This information may be on your W-2 forms, or on IRS Form 1040–lines 7, 12, and 18; 1040A–line 7; or 1040EZ–line 1. Telefilers should use their W-2's.   **You (44)** $ ⬚⬚⬚,⬚⬚⬚   **Your Spouse (45)** $ ⬚⬚⬚,⬚⬚⬚

46. Go to page 8 of this form; complete the column on the left of **Worksheet A**; enter student total here. $ ⬚⬚⬚,⬚⬚⬚

47. Go to page 8 of this form; complete the column on the left of **Worksheet B**; enter student total here. $ ⬚⬚⬚,⬚⬚⬚

48. Total current balance of cash, savings, and checking accounts $ ⬚⬚⬚,⬚⬚⬚

For 49-51, if net worth is one million or more, enter $999,999. If net worth is negative, enter 0.

49. Current <u>net worth</u> of <u>investments</u> (<u>investment value</u> minus <u>investment debt</u>) **See page 2.** $ ⬚⬚⬚,⬚⬚⬚

50. Current <u>net worth</u> of business (<u>business value</u> minus <u>business debt</u>) **See page 2.** $ ⬚⬚⬚,⬚⬚⬚

51. Current <u>net worth</u> of investment farm (Don't include a farm that you live on and operate.) $ ⬚⬚⬚,⬚⬚⬚

52-53. If you receive veterans education benefits, for **how many months** from July 1, 2000 through June 30, 2001 will you receive these benefits, and **what amount** will you receive per month? Do not include your spouse's veterans education benefits.   **Months (52)** ⬚⬚   **Amount (53)** $ ⬚⬚⬚

Step Three: Answer all six questions in this step.

54. Were you born before January 1, 1977? .... Yes ○ ₁ No ○ ₂

55. Will you be working on a degree beyond a bachelor's degree in school year 2000-2001? ...... Yes ○ ₁ No ○ ₂

56. As of today, are you married? (Answer yes if you are separated, but not divorced.) .... Yes ○ ₁ No ○ ₂

57. Answer **"Yes"** if: (1) You have children who receive more than half of their support from you; **or** (2) You have dependents (other than your children or spouse) who live with you and receive more than half of their support from you, now and through June 30, 2001. .... Yes ○ ₁ No ○ ₂

58. Are you an orphan or ward of the court or were you a ward of the court until age 18? .... Yes ○ ₁ No ○ ₂

59. Are you a <u>veteran</u> of the U.S. Armed Forces? **See page 2.** .... Yes ○ ₁ No ○ ₂

If you (the student) answer "No" to every question in Step Three, go to Step Four.

If you answer "Yes" to any question in Step Three, skip Step Four and go to Step Five.

(If you are a graduate health profession student, you may be required to complete Step Four even if you answered "Yes" to any question in Step Three.)   **Page 4**

Appendix A (continued)

Step Four: Complete this step if you (the student) answered "No" to all questions in Step Three. Please tell us about your parents. **See page 7 for who is considered a parent.**

60. Parents' marital status as of today? (Pick one.) Married ○ 1 Single ○ 2 Divorced/Separated ○ 3 Widowed ○ 4

61-62. Your father's Social Security Number and last name
61. FATHER'S/STEPFATHER'S SSN [   ] – [ ] – [   ]
62. FATHER'S/STEPFATHER'S LAST NAME [   ]

63-64. Your mother's Social Security Number and last name
63. MOTHER'S/STEPMOTHER'S SSN [   ] – [ ] – [   ]
64. MOTHER'S/STEPMOTHER'S LAST NAME [   ]

65. How many people are in your <u>parents' household</u>? **See page 7.** [ ]

66. How many in question 65 (**exclude your parents**) will be <u>college students</u> between July 1, 2000, and June 30, 2001? **See page 7.** [ ]

67. What is your parents' state of legal residence? STATE [ ]

68. Did your parents become legal residents of the state in question 67 before January 1, 1995? Yes ○ 1 No ○ 2

69. If the answer to question 68 is "No," give the month and year legal residency began for the parent who has lived in the state the longest. MONTH [ ] / YEAR [   ]

70. What is the age of your older parent? [ ]

71. For 1999, have your parents filed their IRS income tax return or another tax return listed in **question 72**?
a. My parents have already filed. ○ 1
b. My parents will file, but they have not yet filed. ○ 2
c. My parents are not going to file. **(Skip to question 78.)** ○ 3

72. What income tax return did your parents file or will they file for 1999?
a. IRS 1040 .... ○ 1
b. IRS 1040A, 1040EZ, 1040Telefile ..... ○ 2
c. A foreign tax return. **See Page 2.** .... ○ 3
d. A tax return for Puerto Rico, Guam, American Samoa, the Virgin Islands, the Marshall Islands, the Federated States of Micronesia, or Palau. **See Page 2.** ...... ○ 4

73. If your parents have filed or will file a 1040, were they <u>eligible to file a 1040A or 1040EZ</u>? **See page 2.** Yes ○ 1 No/don't know ○ 2

For 74 - 85, if the answer is zero or the question does not apply, enter 0.

74. What was your parents' adjusted gross income for 1999? Adjusted gross income is on IRS Form 1040–line 33; 1040A–line 18; 1040EZ–line 4; or Telefile–line I. $[   ],[   ]

75. Enter the total amount of your parents' income tax for 1999. Income tax amount is on IRS Form 1040–line 49 plus 5I; 1040A–line 32; 1040EZ–line 10; or Telefile–line K. $[   ],[   ]

76. Enter your parents' exemptions. Exemptions are on IRS Form 1040–line 6d or on Form 1040A–line 6d. For Form 1040EZ or Telefile, see page 2. [ ]

77. Enter your parents' Earned Income Credit from IRS Form 1040–line 59a; 1040A–line 37a; 1040EZ–line 8a; or Telefile–line L. $[   ],[   ]

78-79. How much did your parents earn from working in 1999? Answer this question whether or not your parents filed a tax return. This information may be on their W-2 forms, or on IRS Form 1040–lines 7, 12, and 18; 1040A–line 7; or 1040EZ–line 1. Telefilers should use their W-2's.
Father/Stepfather (78) $[   ],[   ]
Mother/Stepmother (79) $[   ],[   ]

80. Go to page 8 of this form; complete the column on the right of **Worksheet A**; enter parent total here. $[   ],[   ]

81. Go to page 8 of this form; complete the column on the right of **Worksheet B**; enter parent total here. $[   ],[   ]

82. Total current balance of cash, savings, and checking accounts $[   ],[   ]

For 83–85, if net worth is one million or more, enter $999,999. If net worth is negative, enter 0.

83. Current <u>net worth</u> of <u>investments</u> (<u>investment value</u> minus <u>investment debt</u>) See page 2. $[   ],[   ]

84. Current <u>net worth</u> of business (<u>business value</u> minus <u>business debt</u>) See page 2. $[   ],[   ]

85. Current <u>net worth</u> of investment farm (Don't include a farm that your parents live on and operate.) $[   ],[   ]

Now go to Step Six.   Page 5

Appendix A (continued)

Step Five: Complete this step only if you (the student) answered "Yes" to any question in Step Three.

86. How many people are in your (and your spouse's) <u>household</u>? **See page 7.**

87. How many in question 86 will be <u>college students</u> between July 1, 2000, and June 30, 2001? **Do not include your parents. See page 7.**

Step Six: Please tell us which schools should receive your information.

For each school (up to six), please provide the federal school code and your housing plans **(enter "1" for on campus, "2" for off campus, and "3" for with parents).** Look for the federal school codes on the Internet at **http://www.ed.gov/studentaid,** at your college financial aid office, at your public library, or by asking your high school guidance counselor. If you cannot get the federal school code, write in the complete name, address, city, and state of the college.

Federal school code	OR Name of college	College street address and city	State	Housing Plans
88. FIRST SCHOOL CODE				89.
90. SECOND SCHOOL CODE				91.
92. THIRD SCHOOL CODE				93.
94. FOURTH SCHOOL CODE				95.
96. FIFTH SCHOOL CODE				97.
98. SIXTH SCHOOL CODE				99.

Step Seven: Please read, sign, and date.

By signing this application, you agree, if asked, to provide information that will verify the accuracy of your completed form. This information may include a copy of your U.S. or state income tax form. Also, you certify that you (1) will use federal and/or state student financial aid only to pay the cost of attending an institution of higher education, (2) are not in default on a federal student loan or have made satisfactory arrangements to repay it, (3) do not owe money back on a federal student grant or have made satisfactory arrangements to repay it, (4) will notify your school if you default on a federal student loan, and (5) understand that **the Secretary of Education has the authority to verify income reported on this application with the Internal Revenue Service.** If you purposely give false or misleading information, you may be fined $10,000, sent to prison, or both.

100. Date this form was completed.

MONTH   DAY   / / 2000 ○ or 2001 ○

101. **Student** signature   (Sign in box)

Parent signature (one parent whose information is provided in Step Four.)   (Sign in box)

If this form was filled out by someone other than you, your spouse, or your parent(s), that person must complete this part.

Preparer's Name and Firm _____

Address _____

102. Social Security #

OR

103. Employer ID #

SCHOOL USE ONLY
D/O ○ ¹   Federal School Code

FAA SIGNATURE
¹

104. Signature and Date ¹ _____

MDE USE ONLY
Special Handle

Page 6

Appendix A (continued)

Notes for questions **60–85** (page 5) **Step Four:** Who is considered a <u>parent</u> in this Step?

If your parents are both living and married to each other, answer the questions about them. (You will be providing information about two people.)

If your parent is widowed or single, answer the questions about that parent. (You will be providing information about one person.) If your widowed parent has remarried as of today, answer the questions about that parent and the person whom your parent married. (You will be providing information about two people.)

If your parents have divorced or separated, answer the questions about the parent you lived with more during the past 12 months. If you did not live with one parent more than the other, give answers about the parent who provided more financial support during the last 12 months, or during the most recent year that you actually were supported by a parent. (You will be providing information about one person.) If this parent has remarried as of today, answer the questions on the rest of this form about that parent and the person whom your parent married. (You will be providing information about two people.)

Notes for question **65** (page 5)

Include in your <u>parents' household</u>:

- yourself and your parents, and
- your parents' other children if (a) your parents will provide more than half of their support from July 1, 2000 through June 30, 2001 or (b) the children could answer "No" to every question in Step Three, and
- other people if they now live with your parents, your parents provide more than half of their support and will continue to provide more than half of their support from July 1, 2000 through June 30, 2001.

Notes for questions **66** (page 5) and **87** (page 6)

Count yourself as a <u>college student</u> even if you will attend college less than half time in 2000-2001. **Do not include your parents.** Include others only if they will attend at least half time in 2000-2001 in a program that leads to a college degree or certificate.

Notes for question **86** (page 6)

Include in your (and your spouse's) <u>household</u>:

- yourself (and your spouse, if you have one), and
- your children, if you will provide more than half of their support from July 1, 2000 through June 30, 2001, and
- other people if they now live with you, and you provide more than half of their support from July 1, 2000 through June 30, 2001.

Information on the Privacy Act and use of your Social Security Number.

We use the information that you provide on this form to determine if you are eligible to receive federal student financial aid and the amount that you are eligible to receive. Section 483 of the Higher Education Act of 1965, as amended, gives us the authority to ask you and your parents these questions, and to collect the social security numbers of you and your parents.

State and institutional student financial aid programs may also use the information that you provide on this form to determine if you are eligible to receive state and institutional aid and the need that you have for such aid. Therefore, we will disclose the information that you provide on this form to each institution you list in questions 88–99, state agencies in your state of legal residence, and the state agencies of the states in which the colleges that you list in questions 88–99 are located.

If you are applying solely for federal aid, you must answer all of the following questions that apply to you: 1–9, 14–16, 25, 28–30, 33–34, 37–41, 43–51, 54–60, 65–67, 70–75, 77-87, and 100–101. If you do not answer these questions, you will not receive federal aid.

Without your consent, we may disclose information that you provide to entities under a published "routine use." Under such a routine use, we may disclose information to third parties that we have authorized to assist us in administering the above programs; to other federal agencies under computer matching programs, such as those with the Internal Revenue Service, Social Security Administration, Selective Service System, Immigration and Naturalization Service, and Veterans Administration; to your parents or spouse; and to members of Congress if you ask them to help you with student aid questions.

If the federal government, the U.S. Department of Education, or an employee of the U.S. Department of Education is involved in litigation, we may send information to the Department of Justice, or a court or adjudicative body, if the disclosure is related to financial aid and certain conditions are met. In addition, we may send your information to a foreign, federal, state, or local enforcement agency if the information that you submitted indicates a violation or potential violation of law, for which that agency has jurisdiction for investigation or prosecution. Finally, we may send information regarding a claim that is determined to be valid and overdue to a consumer reporting agency. This information includes identifiers from the record; the amount, status, and history of the claim; and the program under which the claim arose.

State Certification.

By submitting this application, you are giving your state financial aid agency permission to verify any statement on this form and to obtain income tax information for all persons required to report income on this form.

The Paperwork Reduction Act of 1995

The Paperwork Reduction Act of 1995 says that no one is required to respond to a collection of information unless it displays a valid OMB control number, which for this form is 1845-0001. The time required to complete this form is estimated to be one hour, including time to review instructions, search data resources, gather the data needed, and complete and review the information collection. If you have comments about this estimate or suggestions for improving this form, please write to: U.S. Department of Education, Washington DC 20202-4651.

Page 7

PLEASE FOLD AND TEAR ALONG DOTTED LINE

Appendix A (continued)

Worksheets – Even though you may have few of these items, check carefully.

Do not mail these worksheets in with your application. Keep these worksheets with a copy of your application.

_____ **Worksheet A** _____

For question **46:** Enter and add together all of the following that apply to you (and your spouse) in the column on the left. Enter the total amount in question 46 on page 4.

For question **80:** Enter and add together all of the following that apply to your parents in the column on the right (if you are required to complete Step 4 of the application). Enter the total amount in question 80 on page 5.

For question 46 Student (and spouse)	Calendar Year 1999	For question 80 Parent(s)
$	Payments to tax-deferred pension and savings plans (paid directly or withheld from earnings), including amounts reported on the W-2 Form in Box 13, codes D, E, F, G, H, and S. Include untaxed portions of 401(k) and 403(b) plans.	$
$	Deductible IRA and/or Keogh payments: IRS Form 1040–total of lines 23 and 29; or 1040A–line 15	$
$	Child support **received** for all children. Don't include foster care or adoption payments.	$
$	Welfare benefits, including Temporary Assistance for Needy Families (TANF). Don't include food stamps.	$
$	Tax exempt interest income from IRS Form 1040–line 8b; or 1040A–line 8b	$
$	Foreign income exclusion from IRS Form 2555–line 43; or 2555EZ–line 18	$
$	Untaxed portions of pensions from IRS Form 1040–(line 15a minus 15b) plus (16a minus 16b); or 1040A–(line 10a minus 10b) plus (11a minus 11b) excluding rollovers	$
$	Credit for federal tax on special fuels from IRS Form 4136–line 9 – nonfarmers only	$
$	Social Security benefits received that were not taxed	$
$	Housing, food, and other living allowances paid to members of the military, clergy, and others (including cash payments and cash value of benefits)	$
$	Workers' Compensation	$
$	Veterans noneducation benefits, such as Death Pension or Dependency & Indemnity Compensation (DIC)	$
$	Any other untaxed income and benefits, such as VA Educational Work-Study allowances, untaxed portions of Railroad Retirement Benefits, Black Lung Benefits, Refugee Assistance, etc. Don't include student aid, educational WIA (formerly JTPA) benefits, or benefits from flexible spending arrangements, e.g., cafeteria plans.	$
$	Cash **received**, or any money paid on your behalf, not reported elsewhere on this form	XXXXXXXXX
$ _____ (Enter this amount in question 46.) **Student (and spouse) total**	(Enter this amount in question 80.)	$ _____ **Parent(s) total**

_____ **Worksheet B** _____

For question **47:** Enter and add together all of the following that apply to you (and your spouse) in the column on the left. Enter the total amount in question 47 on page 4.

For question **81:** Enter and add together all of the following that apply to your parents in the column on the right (if you are required to complete Step 4 of the application). Enter the total amount in question 81 on page 5.

For question 47 Student (and spouse)	Calendar Year 1999	For question 81 Parent(s)
$	Education credits (Hope and Lifetime Learning Tax Credits) from IRS Form 1040-line 44; or 1040A-line 29.	$
$	Child support **paid** because of divorce or separation. Do not include support for children in your (or your parents') household, as reported in question 86 (or question 65 for your parents).	$
$	Taxable earnings from Federal Work-Study or other need-based work programs	$
$	AmeriCorps awards — living allowances only	$
$	Student grant and scholarship aid (in excess of the tuition, fees, books, and supplies) that was reported to the IRS in question 40 for students and 74 for parents	$
$ _____ (Enter this amount in question 47.) **Student (and spouse) total**	(Enter this amount in question 81.)	$ _____ **Parent(s) total**

Appendix B
Sample Student Aid Report (SAR) Paperwork

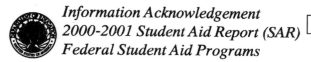

Information Acknowledgement
2000-2001 Student Aid Report (SAR)
Federal Student Aid Programs

OMB No. 1845-0008
Form Approved
Exp. 12/31/2001

123-45-6789
ST 99 DRN: 1234

Do not use this form to make corrections. See your Financial Aid Administrator.

000117C041

ABCDEFGHI J. ABCDEFGHIJKLMNOP
1234 ABCDEFGHIJKLMNOPQRSTUV
ABCDEFGHIJKLMNOPQ, AB 12345

March 17, 2000
EFC: 00979*C

BA DEG REC'D

We have processed the electronic Application for Federal Student Aid, Renewal Application for Federal Student Aid, or correction that you submitted through your school. On the back of this page we have printed the information we received and a summary of the results of processing that information. You should review this information and contact your Financial Aid Administrator (FAA) if any corrections need to be made. Based on the information you provided, we may have assumed certain information to calculate your eligibility for Federal student aid. We printed the assumption we made and the word "assumed" for those items on the back of this page. If these assumptions are not correct, contact your FAA to make the necessary corrections.

We have applied a formula to the information from the form you submitted. The result of this formula will be used by your school to determine your eligibility for most types of Federal student aid. See your FAA to determine what types of student aid you may be able to receive. Based on the information you gave us, you are not eligible for a Federal Pell Grant.

Your application has been selected for review in a process called verification. You must submit to your school signed copies of certain 1999 financial documents. Contact your FAA to find out which documents are required.

You must contact your FAA to determine if you meet all of the eligibility requirements to receive Federal financial aid.

123-45-6789 ST 01

Appendix B (continued)

This section contains information from your student aid application (shaded items display parents' information, if provided). If you need to make corrections, see the financial aid administrator at your school.

#	Field	Value		#	Field	Value
1.	LAST NAME	ABCDEFGHI.JKLMNOP		53.	MONTHLY VA EDUCATION BENEFITS AMOUNT	$ (123 ASSUMED)
2.	FIRST NAME	ABCDEFGHI		54.	BORN BEFORE 1-1-1977?	(YES ASSUMED)
3.	MIDDLE INITIAL	A		55.	WORKING ON DEGREE BEYOND BACHELOR'S?	(BLANK)
4.	PERMANENT STREET ADDRESS	12345 ABCDEFGHIJKLMNOPQ		56.	ARE YOU MARRIED?	(YES ASSUMED)
5.	CITY	ABCDEFGHIJKLMNOPQ		57.	HAVE DEPENDENTS OTHER THAN SPOUSE?	(YES ASSUMED)
6.	STATE ABBREVIATION	AB		58.	ORPHAN OR WARD OF COURT?	(BLANK)
7.	ZIP CODE	12345		59.	VETERAN OF U.S. ARMED FORCES?	(BLANK)
8.	SOCIAL SECURITY NUMBER	123-45-6789		60.	PARENT(S) MARITAL STATUS	(MARRIED ASSUMED)
9.	DATE OF BIRTH	JANUARY 01, 1961		61.	YOUR FATHER'S SOCIAL SECURITY NUMBER	123-45-6789
10.	PERMANENT HOME PHONE NUMBER	(999) 999-9999		62.	YOUR FATHER'S LAST NAME	ABCDEFGHIJKLMNOP
11.	DO YOU HAVE A DRIVER'S LICENSE?	YES		63.	YOUR MOTHER'S SOCIAL SECURITY NUMBER	123-45-6789
12.	DRIVER'S LICENSE NUMBER	A-1234-456-789-012-34		64.	YOUR MOTHER'S LAST NAME	ABCDEFGHIJKLMNOP
13.	DRIVER'S LICENSE STATE ABBREVIATION	AB		65.	NUMBER OF FAMILY MEMBERS IN 2000-2001	(02 ASKED)
14.	CITIZENSHIP STATUS	(ELIG. NON-CIT ASSUMED)		66.	NUMBER IN COLLEGE IN 2000-2001	ASSUMED)
15.	ALIEN REGISTRATION NUMBER	123456789		67.	PARENT(S) STATE OF LEGAL RESIDENCE	AB
16.	MARITAL STATUS	(MARRIED ASSUMED)		68.	LEGAL RESIDENT BEFORE JANUARY 1, 1995?	(BLANK)
17.	DATE OF MARITAL STATUS	JANUARY 1992		69.	DATE PARENT(S) BECAME LEGAL RESIDENT	DECEMBER 1941
18.	ENROLLMENT STATUS SUMMER TERM 2000	LESS THAN 1/2 TIME		70.	AGE OF OLDER PARENT	99
19.	ENROLLMENT STATUS FALL SEM/QTR 2000	LESS THAN 1/2 TIME		71.	PARENT(S) FILED 1999 INCOME TAX RETURN	WILL FILE
20.	ENROLLMENT STATUS WINTER QTR 2000-2001	LESS THAN 1/2 TIME		72.	TYPE OF 1999 TAX FORM USED	U.S. TRUST TERRITORY
21.	ENROLLMENT STATUS SPRING SEM/QTR 2001	LESS THAN 1/2 TIME		73.	ELIGIBLE TO FILE A 1040A OR 1040EZ?	(BLANK)
22.	ENROLLMENT STATUS SUMMER TERM 2001	LESS THAN 1/2 TIME		74.	ADJUSTED GROSS INCOME FROM IRS FORM	$ (-123,456 ASSUMED)
23.	FATHER'S EDUCATIONAL LEVEL	COLLEGE OR BEYOND		75.	U.S. INCOME TAX PAID	$ (123,456 ASSUMED)
24.	MOTHER'S EDUCATIONAL LEVEL	COLLEGE OR BEYOND		76.	EXEMPTIONS CLAIMED	00
25.	STATE OF LEGAL RESIDENCE ABBREVIATION	AB		77.	EARNED INCOME CREDIT	$ (12,345 ASSUMED)
26.	LEGAL RESIDENT BEFORE JANUARY 1, 1995?	(BLANK)		78.	FATHER'S INCOME EARNED FROM WORK	$ (123,456 ASSUMED)
27.	DATE YOU BECAME A LEGAL RESIDENT	JANUARY 1961		79.	MOTHER'S INCOME EARNED FROM WORK	$ (123,456 ASSUMED)
28.	DRUG CONVICTION ELIGIBILITY?	INELIGIBLE/DON'T KNOW		80.	AMOUNT FROM WORKSHEET A	$ (12,345 ASSUMED)
29.	ARE YOU MALE?	(BLANK)		81.	AMOUNT FROM WORKSHEET B	$ (12,345 ASSUMED)
30.	REGISTER YOU FOR SELECTIVE SERVICE?	(BLANK)		82.	CASH, SAVINGS, AND CHECKING	$ 123,456
31.	TYPE OF DEGREE/CERTIFICATE	1ST BA		83.	NET WORTH OF INVESTMENTS	$ 123,456
32.	GRADE LEVEL IN COLLEGE IN 2000-2001	1ST PREVIOUSLY ATTENDED		84.	NET WORTH OF BUSINESS	$ 123,456
33.	HIGH SCHOOL DIPLOMA OR GED?	(BLANK)		85.	NET WORTH OF INVESTMENT FARM	$ 123,456
34.	FIRST BACHELOR'S DEGREE BY 7-1-2000?	(BLANK)		86.	NUMBER OF FAMILY MEMBERS IN 2000-2001	(02 ASSUMED)
35.	INTERESTED IN STUDENT LOANS?	(BLANK)		87.	NUMBER IN COLLEGE IN 2000-2001	(2 ASSUMED)
36.	INTERESTED IN WORK-STUDY?	(BLANK)		88.	FIRST COLLEGE NAME	0123456789012345678901234567890123456
37.	FILED 1999 IRS INCOME TAX RETURN	WILL FILE		89.	FIRST HOUSING PLANS	WITH PARENT(S)
38.	TYPE OF 1999 TAX FORM USED	U.S. TRUST TERRITORY		90.	SECOND COLLEGE NAME	0123456789012345678901234567890123456
39.	ELIGIBLE TO FILE A 1040A OR 1040EZ?	(BLANK)		91.	SECOND HOUSING PLANS	WITH PARENT(S)
40.	ADJUSTED GROSS INCOME FROM IRS FORM	$ (-123,456 ASSUMED)		92.	THIRD COLLEGE NAME	0123456789012345678901234567890123456
41.	U.S. INCOME TAX PAID	$ (12,345 ASSUMED)		93.	THIRD HOUSING PLANS	WITH PARENT(S)
42.	EXEMPTIONS CLAIMED	00		94.	FOURTH COLLEGE NAME	0123456789012345678901234567890123456
43.	EARNED INCOME CREDIT	$ (12,345 ASSUMED)		95.	FOURTH HOUSING PLANS	WITH PARENT(S)
44.	STUDENT'S INCOME EARNED FROM WORK	$ (123,456 ASSUMED)		96.	FIFTH COLLEGE NAME	0123456789012345678901234567890123456
45.	SPOUSE'S INCOME EARNED FROM WORK	$ (123,456 ASSUMED)		97.	FIFTH HOUSING PLANS	WITH PARENT(S)
46.	AMOUNT FROM WORKSHEET A	$ (12,345 ASSUMED)		98.	SIXTH COLLEGE NAME	0123456789012345678901234567890123456
47.	AMOUNT FROM WORKSHEET B	$ (12,345 ASSUMED)		99.	SIXTH HOUSING PLANS	WITH PARENT(S)
48.	CASH, SAVINGS, AND CHECKING	$ 123,456		100.	DATE COMPLETED	JANUARY 1, 1999
49.	NET WORTH OF REAL ESTATE/INVESTMENTS	$ 123,456		101.	SIGNED BY	STUDENT AND PARENT
50.	NET WORTH OF BUSINESS	$ 123,456		102.	PREPARER'S SOCIAL SECURITY NUMBER	REPORTED
51.	NET WORTH OF INVESTMENT FARM	$ 123,456		103.	PREPARER'S EIN	REPORTED
52.	HOW MANY MONTHS RECEIVE VA BENEFITS?	00		104.	PREPARER'S SIGNATURE	SIGNED

Processing Results

Record Type:	X	Expected Family Contribution: Primary	00000	Dependency Status Model:	X
Verification Flag:	X	Secondary	00000	Dependency Override:	X
Application Receipt Date:	mm/dd/ccyy	Automatic Zero EFC Flag:	X	Duplicate Request Indicator:	X
Transaction Process Date:	mm/dd/ccyy	Formula Type:	X	Hold Code:	X
Transaction Receipt Date:	mm/dd/ccyy	Simplified Needs Test Flag:	X	Subsequent Application Flag:	X
System Generated Indicator: X		FAA Adjustment	X	Pell Eligible Flag:	X

SSN Match Flag: X	Selective Service Registration Flag: X	Selective Service Match: X
INS Match Flag: X	INS Verification #: 9999999999999	SSA Citizenship Code: X
NSLDS Match Flag: X	NSLDS Results Flag: X	NSLDS Transaction Number: 99
VA Match Flag: X	PRIS Match Flag: X	

Reject Code(s): 01 02 03 04 05 06 07
Comment Codes: 001 002 003 004 005 006 007 008 009 010

000117C041

Appendix B (continued)

2000-2001 Student Aid Report (SAR)
Federal Student Aid Programs
Part 1 - Information Summary

OMB No. 1845-0008
Form Approved
Exp. 12/31/2001

123-45-6789
AB-01 DRN: 1234

IMPORTANT: Read **ALL** information in Part 1 to find out what to do with this Report.

000117C041

ABCDEFGHI J. ABCDEFGHIJKLMNOP
1234 ABCDEFGHIJKLMNOPQRSTUV
ABCDEFGHIJKLMNOPQ, AB 12345

March 17, 2000
EFC: 00979*C
BA DEG REC'D

Read this letter carefully and review each item on Part 2 of this Student Aid Report (SAR). Follow the instructions at the top of Part 2 and in the Free Application for Federal Student Aid (FAFSA) instruction booklet to help you make corrections. If all of the information on your SAR is correct, you do not need to return it to the Federal Student Aid Programs. For additional help with your SAR, contact the Financial Aid Administrator (FAA) at your school or the Federal Student Aid Information Center at 1-800-4FED-AID (1-800-443-3243).

If all the information on this SAR is correct, you may be eligible to receive a Federal Pell Grant and other Federal student aid in 2000-2001. Your FAA will determine whether you meet all eligibility requirements to receive aid. The amount of aid will depend on the cost of attendance at your school, your enrollment status (full-time, three-quarter-time, half-time, or less than half-time), Congressional budget restrictions, and other factors.

HERE IS WHAT YOU NEED TO DO NOW: Review the information on Part 2. If any of the information is incorrect, follow the instructions at the top of Part 2 to make corrections. IF ALL THE INFORMATION IS CORRECT, you do not have to submit the SAR to the schools you listed. All of your schools will receive the information electronically.

Based on the information provided on your application, we had to assume certain information to calculate your eligibility for Federal Student Aid. We printed the assumption we made and the word "Assumed" in the "You Told Us" column for each of these items. If these assumptions are correct, do not change them.

Be sure to review the items in boldface type on Part 2 or your SAR and make any corrections if necessary.

It appears you reported the same income value more than once. Review the income items in boldface type on Part 2 of your SAR. If these items are correct, do not change them.

To resolve your Perkins overpayment, call the U.S. Department of Education at 1-800-621-3116, or write to the U.S. Department of Education, Atlanta Service Center, 61 Forsyth Street, Room 19T89, Atlanta, Georgia 30303.

Appendix B (continued)

(letter continued)

Your application cannot be processed until you have resolved a prior year verification overpayment. Contact the U.S. Department of Education by calling 202-708-4601, or by writing to: U.S. Department of Education, Student Financial Assistance Programs, Analysis and Forcasting Division, Grants Analysis Branch, 7th and D Streets, SW, ROB-3, Room 4613, Washington, DC 20202-5451. Include with your letter a copy of this SAR and your current address and telephone number (including the area code).

FOR FAA USE ONLY

This information will be used by your Financial Aid Administrator to determine your eligibility for student aid.

Agency Source: x
Record Source Type: x
Record Type: x
Verification Flag: x
Model: x

Duplicate Copy: x
SysGen: x
Dependency Override:
Special Handling: x
Early Analysis Flag: x

FAA Adjustment: x
Reject Reasons: 01 02 03 04 05 06 07
Application Receipt Date mm/dd/ccyy
Transaction Receipt Date: mm/dd/ccyy
Subsequent Application Flag: mm/dd/ccyy
Reprocessing Code: 99

MONTHS:	1	2	3	4	5	6	7	8	9	10	11	12
PRIMARY EFC:	00000	00000	00000	00000	00000	00000	00000	00000	00000	00000	00000	00000
SECONDARY EFC:	00000	00000	00000	00000	00000	00000	00000	00000	00000	00000	00000	00000

INTERMEDIATE COMPUTE VALUES:
TI: 999999999   ATI: 999999999   STX: 999999999   EA: 999999999   STI: 999999999
IPA: 999999999   AI: 999999999   CAI: 999999999   DNW: 999999999   FTI: 999999999
APA: 999999999   PCA: 999999999   AAI: 999999999   TPC: 999999999
TSC: 999999999   PC: 999999999   SIC: 999999999   SCA: 999999999

Auto Zero EFC Flag: x   SNT Flag: x   Pell Eligible Flag: x

MATCH FLAGS:
SSN Match Flag: x   Selective Service Registration Flag: x   Selective Service Match: x
INS Match Flag: x   INS Verification #: 999999999999999   SSA Citizenship Code: x
NSLDS Match Flag: x   NSLDS Results Flag: X   NSLDS Transaction Number: 01
VA Match Flag: X   PRIS Match Flag: X

COMMENTS: 001 002 003 004 005 006 007 008 009 010 011 012 013 014 015 016 017 018 019 020

123456789012   PAGE N OF N   123-45-6789 ST 01

Appendix B (continued)

JOHNNY E. STUDENT
123-45-6789

2000-2001 Student Aid Report (SAR)
FINANCIAL AID HISTORY

Processed: 03-17-2000

This page contains your previous financial aid information, which is contained in the National Student Loan Data System (NSLDS). Your Financial Aid Administrator will use it to determine your eligibility.

#Overpayment:	Contact:	#Discharged: N	#Defaulted Loans: Y	#Loan Sat. Repayment: Y	#Active Bankruptcy: N	#Post Screening Reason: 5
Pell: Y	05					
FSEOG: Y	Access NSLDS					
Perkins: Y	12345678					

Aggregate Amount

	Outstanding Principal Bal.:	Pending Disbursements:	Total:
#FFELP/Direct Loans: Subsidized Loans:	$123,456	$123,456	$123,456
Unsubsidized Loans:	$123,456	$123,456	$123,456
Combined Loans:	$123,456	$123,456	$123,456
FFEL Consolidation Loans:	$123,456		$123,456

#Perkins Loans:
Outstanding Principal Bal.: $123,456   Current Year Loan Amount: $123,456

#2000-2001 Pell Payment Data:

Sch.Code:	Tran:	Sch.Amt:	Award Amt:	Disb.Amt:	Rem.Amt:	% Sch.Used:	As of:	EFC:	Ver.Flag:
76543210	01	$1234	$1234	$1234	$1234	100.00	01/15/99	12345	X
12345678	01	$1234	$1234	$1234	$1234	100.00	01/15/99	12345	X
12345678	01	$1234	$1234	$1234	$1234	100.00	01/15/99	12345	X

Access NSLDS for additional Pell data.

Loan Detail:

	Net Loan Amount	Loan Begin Date	Loan End Date	GA Code	School Code	Grade Level	Contact	Contact Type
#FFEL Stafford Unsubsidized Status Code DA as of 01/05/99 Outstanding Bal. $123,456 as of 02/02/99	$123,456	01/01/97	05/01/97	719	00132100	01	719	GA
#FFEL Stafford Subsidized Status Code FB as of 09/01/99 Outstanding Bal. $123,456 as of 02/07/99	$123,456	01/01/96	01/01/97	736	00132600	02	736	GA
#Direct Stafford Subsidized Status Code ID as of 09/06/99 Outstanding Bal. $123,456 as of 02/03/99	$123,456	01/01/96	01/01/97	N/A	00132700	03	SV0101	DLS
#Direct Consolidation Subsidized Status Code DL as of 12/06/99 Outstanding Bal. $123,456 as of 01/01/99	$123,456	08/01/95	05/10/96	N/A	00132100	04	SV0101	DLS
#Supplemental Loan (SLS) Status Code DX as of 05/01/99 Outstanding Bal. $123,456 as of 02/02/99	$123,456	01/01/95	04/01/95	701	00132600	05	N/A	N/A
#Perkins Expanded Lending Option Status Code DU as of 06/05/99 Outstanding Bal. $123,456 as of 01/01/99	$123,456	09/02/94	06/02/95	N/A	00132100	06	00132100	SCH
#FFEL Stafford Unsubsidized Status Code ID as of 09/01/99 Outstanding Bal. $123,456 as of 09/02/96	$123,456	09/01/94	12/01/94	734	00132100	07	830906	LEN
#Federal Perkins Status Code DL as of 01/01/96 Outstanding Bal. $123,456 as of 02/01/99	$123,456	09/01/93	01/01/94	N/A	00132300	07	00132300	SCH
#FFEL Stafford Subsidized Status Code RP as of 02/01/99 Outstanding Bal. $123,456 as of 02/01/99	$123,456	01/04/93	12/01/93	620	00132800	07	620	GA
#Federal Perkins Status Code DB as of 09/01/99 Outstanding Bal. $123,456 as of 02/01/99	$123,456	01/01/88	05/26/88	N/A	00132500	07	00132500	SCH
#FFEL Stafford Non-Subsidized Status Code DT as of 09/01/99 Outstanding Bal. $123,456 as of 02/01/99	$123,456	N/A	N/A	555	00132900	07	05	EDR
#FFEL Stafford Unsubsidized Status Code DB as of 05/01/99 Outstanding Bal. $123,456 as of 02/02/99	$123,456	N/A	N/A	555	00132700	07	04	EDR

Access NSLDS for additional loan records.

R4NDN00015   PAGE N OF N   123-45-6789 ST 01

Appendix B (continued)

2000-2001 Student Aid Report
Federal Student Aid Programs
Part 2 - Information Review Form

OMB No. 1845-0008
Form Approved
EXP. 12/31/2001

Processed: 03-21-2000
EFC: 99999 *C
BA DEG REC'D

- Pay special attention to any items in **BOLDFACE TYPE**; they may need to be corrected.
- To correct any item, print the correct answer in the boxes to the right of the item in question.
- To delete a preprinted answer in the "YOU TOLD US" column, draw a line completely through the previous answer and through the answer boxes or ovals to the right of the item.
- Use the code information on the Instructions and Codes page if you need to correct items 28 and/or 31.
- If you make corrections, sign and send BOTH pages of Part 2 to the address on the last page of Part 2.
- Do not attach tax returns or other documents.
- If an answer is zero, write in "0".
- Report dollar amounts (such as $12,356.00) like this: **SAMPLE** ➡ $ | 1 | 2 |, | 3 | 5 | 6 | (no cents)
- If you need to correct an item that contains an oval ○, completely fill in the oval as follows: ● . Do not ⊗ or ⊘ ovals. Erase or white-out mistakes completely.
- Print corrections neatly in answer boxes: **SAMPLE** ➡ | 1 | 5 | | E | L | M | | S | T |

123-45-6789
ST-01   DRN: 1234

Step One: YOU (THE STUDENT)

YOU TOLD US	WRITE IN INFORMATION FOR NEW OR CORRECTED ITEMS ONLY.
1. Last Name STUDENT	
2. First Name JOHNNY	3. Middle Initial E.
4. Permanent Street Address 123 SOUTH MAIN STREET	
5. City NORTH LIBERTY	
6. State Abbreviation IA	7. ZIP Code 52317
8. Social Security Number 123-45-6789	
9. Date of Birth AUGUST 03, 1963	/	1	9	Use MM/DD/CCYY format (e.g., 05/01/1980)
10. Permanent Home Phone Number (319) 555-1234	
11. Do you have a Driver's License? YES	Yes ○ 1 No ○ 2
12. Driver's License Number ST17983-IA-000123008	
13. Driver's License State Abbreviation IA	
14. Citizenship Status (BLANK) (EILG. NON-CIT. ASSUMED)	U.S. Citizen ○ 1 Eligible Non-Citizen ○ 2 Neither ○ 3
15. Alien Registration Number (BLANK)	A
16. Marital Status (BLANK) (MARRIED ASSUMED)	Single, Divorced or Widowed ○ 1 Married ○ 2 Separated ○ 3
17. Date of Marital Status OCTOBER 1997	/ Use MM/CCYY format (e.g., 05/1996)

Appendix B (continued)

YOU TOLD US	WRITE IN INFORMATION FOR NEW OR CORRECTED ITEMS ONLY.				
18. Summer Term 2000 FULL TIME	Full time ○ 1	3/4 time ○ 2	Half time ○ 3	Less than half time ○ 4	Not attending ○ 5
19. Fall Semester or Quarter 2000 3/4 TIME	Full time ○ 1	3/4 time ○ 2	Half time ○ 3	Less than half time ○ 4	Not attending ○ 5
20. Winter Quarter 2000-2001 HALF TIME	Full time ○ 1	3/4 time ○ 2	Half time ○ 3	Less than half time ○ 4	Not attending ○ 5
21. Spring Semester or Quarter 2001 LESS THAN HALF TIME	Full time ○ 1	3/4 time ○ 2	Half time ○ 3	Less than half time ○ 4	Not attending ○ 5
22. Summer Term 2001 NOT ATTENDING	Full time ○ 1	3/4 time ○ 2	Half time ○ 3	Less than half time ○ 4	Not attending ○ 5
23. Father's Educational Level HIGH SCHOOL	Middle school/Jr. High ○ 1	High school ○ 2	College or beyond ○ 3	Other/unknown ○ 4	
24. Mother's Educational Level COLLEGE OR BEYOND	Middle school/Jr. High ○ 1	High school ○ 2	College or beyond ○ 3	Other/unknown ○ 4	

YOU TOLD US			
25. State of Legal Residence Abbreviation MD		32. Grade Level in College in 2000-2001?	
26. Did you become a legal resident of this state before January 1, 1995? YES	Yes ○ 1 No ○ 2		1st Never Attended ○ 1
		1ST PREVIOUSLY ATTENDED	1st Previously Attended ○ 2
27. If you answered "No" to question 26, date you became a legal resident. OCTOBER 1978	Use MM/CCYY format (e.g., 05/1980)		2nd/Sophomore ○ 3
			3rd/Junior ○ 4
			4th/Senior ○ 5
			5th or More ○ 6
28. Drug Conviction Eligibility? ELIGIBLE/DON'T KNOW	Enter Code from Instructions		Graduate/Professional ○ 7
29. Are you male? YES	Yes ○ 1 No ○ 2	33. High School Diploma or GED? YES	Yes ○ 1 No ○ 2
30. If you are male, 18-25, not registered, do you want Selective Service to register you? YES	Yes ○ 1 No ○ 2	34. First Bachelor's Degree by 7-1-2000? YES	Yes ○ 1 No ○ 2
		35. Interested in Student Loans? YES	Yes ○ 1 No ○ 2
31. Type of Degree/Certificate 1ST BA	Enter Code from Instructions	36. Interested in Work-Study? YES	Yes ○ 1 No ○ 2

Step Two: 1999 STUDENT (AND SPOUSE) INCOME AND ASSETS

YOU TOLD US	WRITE IN INFORMATION FOR NEW OR CORRECTED ITEMS ONLY.	YOU TOLD US	WRITE IN INFORMATION FOR NEW OR CORRECTED ITEMS ONLY.
37. Filed 1999 Income Tax Return WILL FILE	Have already filed ○ 1 / Will file, have not yet filed ○ 2 / Not going to file. ○ 3	44. Student's Income Earned from Work $ (BLANK) (999,999 ASSUMED)	$,
38. Type of 1999 Tax Form Used U.S. TRUST TERRITORY	A. IRS 1040 ○ 1 / B. IRS 1040A, 1040 EZ, 1040 Telefile ○ 2 / C. A foreign tax return ○ 3 / D. A tax return for Puerto Rico, Guam, American Samoa, the Virgin Islands, the Marshall Islands, the Federated States of Micronesia, or Palau ○ 4	45. Spouse's Income Earned from Work $ (BLANK) (999,999 ASSUMED)	$,
		46. Amount from Worksheet A $ 12,345	$,
		47. Amount from Worksheet B $ 12,345 (00,000 ASSUMED)	$,
		48. Cash, Savings, and Checking $ 123,456	$,
39. If you filed or will file a 1040, were you eligible to file a 1040A or 1040EZ? YES	Yes ○ 1 No/don't know ○ 2	49. Net Worth of Investments $ 123,456	$,
40. Adjusted Gross Income from IRS Form $ 000,000 (999,999 ASSUMED)	$,	50. Net Worth of Business $ 123,456	$,
41. U.S. Income Tax Paid $ (BLANK) (00,000 ASSUMED)	$,	51. Net Worth of Investment Farm $ 123,456	$,
42. Exemptions Claimed 02		52. How many Months Receive VA Education Benefits? 02	
43. Earned Income Credit $ -12,345 (+12,345 ASSUMED)	$,	53. Monthly VA Benefits Amount $ 123	$

PAGE N OF N   2V   123-45-6789 ST 01

Appendix B (continued)

DRN: 1234

Step Three: STUDENT STATUS

YOU TOLD US	WRITE IN INFORMATION FOR NEW OR CORRECTED ITEMS ONLY.
54. Born Before 1-1-1977? NO (YES ASSUMED)	Yes ⚪ 1 No ⚪ 2
55. Working on a degree beyond a bachelor's degree in 2000-2001? NO	Yes ⚪ 1 No ⚪ 2
56. Are You Married? (BLANK) (MARRIED ASSUMED)	Yes ⚪ 1 No ⚪ 2
57. Have Dependents Other Than Spouse? (BLANK) (12 ASSUMED)	Yes ⚪ 1 No ⚪ 2

YOU TOLD US	WRITE IN INFORMATION FOR NEW OR CORRECTED ITEMS ONLY.
58. Orphan or Ward of Court? NO	Yes ⚪ 1 No ⚪ 2
59. Veteran of U.S. Armed Forces? NO	Yes ⚪ 1 No ⚪ 2

Step Four: 1999 PARENTAL INFORMATION

YOU TOLD US	
60. Parent(s) Marital Status (BLANK) (MARRIED ASSUMED)	Married ⚪ 1 Single ⚪ 2 Divorced/Separated ⚪ 3 Widowed ⚪ 4
61. Your Father's Social Security Number 123456789	[ ][ ][ ] – [ ][ ] – [ ][ ][ ][ ]
62. Your Father's Last Name FULLLASTNAMETEST	[ ][ ][ ][ ][ ][ ][ ][ ][ ][ ][ ][ ][ ][ ][ ][ ]
63. Your Mother's Social Security Number 123456789	[ ][ ][ ] – [ ][ ] – [ ][ ][ ][ ]
64. Your Mother's Last Name FULLLASTNAMETEST	[ ][ ][ ][ ][ ][ ][ ][ ][ ][ ][ ][ ][ ][ ][ ][ ]
65. Parent(s) number of family members in 2000-2001 (BLANK) (12 ASSUMED)	[ ]

	YOU TOLD US	WRITE IN INFORMATION FOR NEW OR CORRECTED ITEMS ONLY.
66. Parent(s) number of family members in college in 2000-2001 (BLANK) (2 ASSUMED)	74. Adjusted Gross Income from IRS Form $ 123,456	$ [ ][ ] , [ ][ ][ ]
67. Parent(s) state of legal residence MD	75. U.S. Income Tax Paid $ 123,456	$ [ ][ ] , [ ][ ][ ]
68. Parent(s) legal resident of the state before 1-1-1995? YES Yes ⚪ 1 No ⚪ 2	76. Exemptions Claimed 02	
69. If "No" to question 68, enter the date parent became legal resident. OCTOBER 1996 [ ] / [ ] Use MM/CCYY format (e.g., 05/1980)	77. Earned Income Credit $ 12,345	$ [ ][ ] , [ ][ ][ ]
70. Age of older Parent? 55	78. Father's Income Earned from Work $ 123,456	$ [ ][ ] , [ ][ ][ ]
71. Filed 1999 Income Tax Return WILL FILE	Have already filed ⚪ 1 Will file, have not yet filed ⚪ 2 Not going to file. ⚪ 3	79. Mother's Income Earned from Work $ 123,456	$ [ ][ ] , [ ][ ][ ]
		80. Amount from Worksheet A $ 12,345	$ [ ][ ] , [ ][ ][ ]

72. Type of 1999 Tax Form Used
 	
IRS 1040
	A. IRS 1040 ⚪ 1
	B. IRS 1040A, 1040 EZ,
	  1040 Telefile ⚪ 2
	C. A foreign tax return ⚪ 3
	D. A tax return for Puerto Rico,
	  Guam, American Samoa, the
	  Virgin Islands,
	  the Marshall Islands,
	  the Federated States
	  of Micronesia, or Palau ⚪ 4
		81. Amount from Worksheet B
		$ 12,345
			$ [ ][ ] , [ ][ ][ ]

		82. Cash, Savings, and Checking $ 123,456	$ [ ][ ] , [ ][ ][ ]
		83. Net Worth of Investments $ 123,456	$ [ ][ ] , [ ][ ][ ]
		84. Net Worth of Business $ 123,456	$ [ ][ ] , [ ][ ][ ]
73. If your Parent(s) filed or will file a 1040, were they eligible to file a 1040A or 1040EZ? NO Yes ⚪ 1 No/don't know ⚪ 2	85. Net Worth of Investment Farm $ 123,456	$ [ ][ ] , [ ][ ][ ]

123456789012   PAGE N OF N   3V   123-45-6789 ST 01

Appendix B (continued)

Step Five: STUDENT'S HOUSEHOLD INFORMATION

86. Number of Family Members in 2000-2001	87. Number in College in 2000-2001
02	2

Step Six: STUDENT'S SCHOOL INFORMATION

Housing Plans: 1 -- on-campus   3 -- with parent(s)   2 -- off-campus

YOU TOLD US	NEW/CORRECTED COLLEGE NAME, CITY, STATE	Enter Code From Above
88. First College Name, City and State		89. Housing Plans — WITH PARENT(S)
90. Second College Name, City and State		91. Housing Plans — ON-CAMPUS
92. Third College Name, City and State		93. Housing Plans — OFF-CAMPUS
94. Fourth College Name, City and State		95. Housing Plans — (BLANK)
96. Fifth College Name, City and State		97. Housing Plans — (BLANK)
98. Sixth College Name, City and State		99. Housing Plans — (BLANK)
100. Date Completed — FEBRUARY 15, 1998	DO NOT CORRECT	
101. Signed By?	DO NOT CORRECT	
102. Preparer's Social Security Number — REPORTED		
103. Preparer's EIN — REPORTED		
104. Preparer's Signature — SIGNED		

Application Receipt Date: 01/15/2000

Step Seven: PLEASE READ, SIGN, AND DATE

IF YOU MADE NO CHANGES
▶ Do NOT send your SAR to either address given on this page.
▶ Follow the instructions on Part 1 of your SAR. You may need to contact your school.

IF YOU MADE CHANGES
▶ Read and Sign the Certification statement to the right
▶ Send BOTH pages of Part 2 to:

Federal Student Aid Programs
P.O. Box 7020
Lawrence, KS 66044-7020

IF YOU NEED ANOTHER COPY OF YOUR SAR
▶ Write to:
Federal Student Aid Programs
P.O. Box 7021
Lawrence, KS 66044-7021
▶ Include your name, social security number, and signature.

CERTIFICATION

All of the information on this SAR is true and complete to the best of my knowledge. If I am asked, I agree to give proof that my information is correct. The proof might include a copy of the 1999 U.S. Income Tax Form filed by me or my family. I understand that if I purposely give false or misleading information on this SAR, I may be subject to a $10,000 fine, a prison sentence, or both.

Student Signature (sign in box below)
Student   Date

JOHNNY E. STUDENT
Parent Signature (one parent whose information is provided in Step Four.)
Parent   Date

School Use Only

Professional Judgment	D/O ○ 1 ○ 2	FAA Adjustment ○ 1

Federal School Code

FAA Signature

MDE Use Only

DE [ ]   Special Handle [ ]

Appendix B (continued)

2000 – 2001 SAR
INSTRUCTIONS AND CODES

HELPFUL HINTS:

Use the following checklist to ensure you've done everything necessary in order to apply for federal student aid.

☐ Read all the comments on Part 1 of your SAR. This will help you to correct any information we had questions about when we processed your financial aid application.

☐ Review ALL the items on Part 2 of your SAR to make sure that the information is correct. Follow the instructions at the top of Part 2.

☐ If you need to make corrections or respond to boldface items, contact your financial aid office to determine if your school can submit these corrections electronically. You may also submit your corrections, or make changes to your address or school through the Department of Education's web page (http://www.fafsa.ed.gov). You must use your PIN (formerly EAC) to access your record online.

☐ If you've made any corrections on this SAR that need to be processed, you (and your parent, if necessary) must sign the certifications located on the last page of this SAR and return your SAR to Federal Student Aid Programs, P.O. Box 7020, Lawrence, KS 66044-7020. Keep a copy of your SAR for your records.

☐ If you believe we entered your data incorrectly and you want us to make the changes for you over the phone, contact the Federal Student Aid Information Center on 1-800-4FED-AID (1-800-433-3243). The information specialist will determine if we made a data entry error. If so, the specialist may be able to correct your data over the phone.

☐ If you (and your family) have unusual circumstances, such as tuition expenses at an elementary or secondary school, unusual medical or dental expenses not covered by insurance, a family member who recently became unemployed, or changes in income or assets that affect your eligibility for financial aid, contact your financial aid office.

☐ Do not send any documentation (including tax forms) to the address next to your signature. This documentation will be discarded. If your financial aid administrator (FAA) requests documentation, send it directly to the financial aid office.

☐ If you only need to change your address or change the schools you have listed, you can make these changes over the telephone by calling 1-800-4FED-AID (1-800-433-3243) / TTY 1-800-730-8913. Only you (the applicant) can make this request and you must have the Data Release Number (DRN) that is printed on Part 1 and Part 2 of your SAR when you call.

CODES FOR QUESTION 28: DRUG CONVICTION ELIGIBILITY

1   Eligible
2   Part-year eligibility
3   Ineligible/don't know

WARNING: If you are convicted of drug distribution or possession, your eligibility for Title IV student financial aid is subject to suspension or termination.

NEED HELP?

If you do not know how to answer a question, want further assistance correcting your SAR, want to know the status of the submission of your application, need general information concerning student financial aid, or do not understand what to do next, you have several options:

➤ Refer to the instructions that came with your application;
➤ Call 1-800-4FED-AID (1-800-433-3243); (TTY = 1-800-730-8913);
➤ Write to Federal Student Aid Programs, P.O. Box 84, Washington, DC 20044-0084;
➤ Contact the financial aid office at the school you plan to attend; or
➤ Visit our website at www.ed.gov/finaid.html

ATTENTION: Did you know that you could file your *FAFSA* or *RENEWAL FAFSA on the Web*? When you apply next year, you can file your form electronically by going to:

http://www.fafsa.ed.gov

THE OFFICE OF MANAGEMENT & BUDGET WANTS YOU TO KNOW:

↳ According to the Paperwork Reduction Act of 1995, no persons are required to respond to a collection of information unless it displays a valid OMB control number. The valid OMB control number for this information collection is 1845-0008. The time required to complete this information collection is estimated to be an average of 15 to 30 minutes, including the time to review instructions, search existing data resources, gather the data needed, and complete and review the information collected. If you have any comments concerning the accuracy of the time estimate(s) or suggestions for improving this form please write to: U.S. Department of Education, Washington, DC 20202-4651. If you have any comments or concerns regarding the status of your individual submission of this form, write directly to: Federal Student Aid Information Center, P.O. Box 84, Washington, DC 20044.

↳ By answering questions 88 through 99, and signing the Free Application for Federal Student Aid, you gave permission to the U.S. Department of Education to provide information from your application to the college(s) listed in Step 6. You also agreed that such information is deemed to incorporate by reference the certification statement in step 7 of the financial aid application.

CODES FOR QUESTION 31: TYPE OF DEGREE/CERTIFICATE

1   1st Bachelor's degree
2   2nd Bachelor's degree
3   Associate degree (occupational or technical program)
4   Associate degree (general education or transfer program)
5   Certificate or diploma for completing an occupational, technical, or educational program less than two years
6   Certificate or diploma for completing an occupational, technical, or educational program of at least two years
7   Teaching credential program (non-degree program)
8   Graduate or professional degree
9   Other/Undecided

On Campus

Your First Year of College: How to Know about Available Services

SILAS ABREGO

Associate Vice President for Student Affairs, California State University, Fullerton

Your high school graduation celebrations have quickly faded into the past and you anxiously wait for the first day of college. You are looking forward to it, but you are not entirely sure what to expect. As a result, you are rather apprehensive about college life. Most likely, you are the first person in your family to go to college and everything appears intimidating: immense buildings, thousands of other students, the pressure to excel academically, and your newfound freedom. You realize that none of your friends will be with you, and the only thing you are certain about is your desire to prepare for a career and become self-reliant. Also, you want to succeed, because of your family's and community's high expectations.

You have certainly heard stories about students who did not succeed in college. You wonder if you have the financial resources or the academic readiness necessary to compete at this level. You may be one of only a handful of Latinos on campus, and the institution you will be attending may be unfamiliar with your educational needs and learning style. You can rest assured that college life will be challenging. On the way to achieving your goals, you may face many disappointments. You will need plenty of courage to rebound from each setback or crisis. Your success will require personal sacrifice, unfailing determination, and an ability to recognize obstacles as temporary opportunities to formulate solutions.

How you manage the first year and, more specifically, the first semester—the study habits you develop, the attitudes you cultivate, and the support networks you nurture—will establish a foundation upon which you will base multiple academic and personal achievements. Take advantage of your summer and prepare for the first semester by becoming familiar with your future alma mater. The more you know about the university and its procedures, policies, and resources, the better prepared you will be to achieve your goals. When you finally find yourself on campus as a new college student, make use of the resources you discovered through your summer research.

PREPARING FOR DAY ONE

Your apprehension about attending college will be greatly diminished if you do some homework during the summer. Most fears can be attributed to a lack of knowledge about the college experience. This is particularly true if you are a first-generation college student. You may have had very little or no exposure to higher education. Remember that many of your fears can be addressed prior to the first day of classes. So, with a college catalog in hand, let us begin addressing your concerns.

College Catalogs

Each university issues an excellent source of information: the general undergraduate catalog. You should become familiar with this publication, because it is the school's contract with its students. (Many colleges also print annual student handbooks, which contain similar information.) Everything you read in a college catalog will serve you well. The information will be indispensable, not only in developing your first-year survival plan but also in setting long-term goals. You can obtain a copy of the catalog from the university's admissions office or purchase one from the college bookstore. The Internet is also an excellent resource; many universities' Web sites contain copies of their catalogs. Do not be discouraged by the intimidating size of catalogs! They contain a wealth of information that will help you plot a survival strategy and aid you as you negotiate the institutional maze.

Institutions of higher education are complex and multifaceted. The curricula are often not presented in a manner that is easily understood. Nevertheless, it is imperative that you have a proper understanding of the purpose of higher education and, in particular, the mission of your college or university. On one of the first pages of the catalog, you will find the institution's mission statement. This statement describes the primary goals the university is striving to achieve. Virtually all curricula and administrative policies are developed with the intent of meeting the institution's mission. Pay particular attention to the goals concerning you as a learner. By doing so, you will understand how the sequence of your courses and the degree requirements and objectives relate to the mission. Moreover, this activity will broaden your viewpoint and help you focus on accomplishing your personal and academic goals. Do not just concentrate on earning a Bachelor's degree. Be sure to consider all your educational options.

Another important topic concerns university policies and regulations, especially those dealing with enrollment, attendance, and grading. Here, you will find a variety of information that may affect you during registration periods:

- What does it mean to attend college "full-time"? Remember that most financial aid awards require full-time attendance.
- When can a class be dropped? Is there a deadline for changing class schedules without penalty, or can classes be dropped at any time during the semester? Bear in mind that many students carry F's on their transcripts because they were not aware of deadlines for permissible course changes.
- What is an "incomplete"? If you overextend yourself during the semester, you may want to use this option for your own benefit.
- What happens when you receive a final grade of an F? Will you be able to eventually have that grade removed from your transcript? Bear in mind that classes may be repeated for credit.
- Can low grade point average (GPA) place your enrollment in jeopardy? Remember that continued college enrollment depends on meeting a minimum GPA required by the university.

Be certain not to omit the critical section describing academic dishonesty, paying special attention to the discussion of plagiarism (copying someone else's work and passing it off as your own). Regardless of your major, you will most definitely be required to write academic papers, and plagiarism (intentional or unintentional) carries severe penalties.

When you turn eighteen, you acquire a new set of rights. As a college student you have rights as well. The catalog section dedicated to student rights contains useful information. You will learn about appeal procedures (especially useful when you need to appeal a semester grade). You will also find a discussion of your rights concerning sexual harassment and racial discrimination. Finally, you may have questions regarding privacy of personal information or academic records. The section on student rights will have a statement concerning the privacy rights of students. Read it and you will know what course of action to take if your privacy rights are jeopardized.

There are many other issues of interest covered in the general catalog, so be sure to sit down and devote time to look it over. The time you spend reading the catalog will pay off in the future.

Financial Aid

Financial aid is a frequent concern for many Latino students, be they low income or otherwise. Lack of financial resources is perhaps the single most prevalent reason for leaving school. So, learn as much as you can on how to finance your education. Read the catalog section dedicated to financial aid. Also, remember that the offices of financial aid exist primarily to provide students with access to funds to ease the burden of attending college. These offices deal with many types of assistance ranging from scholarships to grants and loan programs to employment. Become familiar with all your options.

An important step involves making an appointment to see a financial aid counselor. He or she will help determine your eligibility for assistance in available aid programs. Aside from understanding federal and state aid requirements, it is very useful to be aware of the many scholarships offered by individual universities. Also, it is important to cultivate a long-term relationship with your financial aid counselor. Your financial needs will most likely change over the course of your college career. A personal contact in the financial aid office will prove valuable when you suddenly find that your financial circumstances have changed. To learn more about financial aid, refer to Step 3.

Part-Time Employment

Statistics indicate that 80 percent of undergraduate students work at some point while attending college. Working part-time while completing college can yield many benefits, especially if you are employed on campus. Most universities have career planning and placement offices. These centers post employment openings for each school year and summer. At the first available opportunity, visit the university student employment office and look over the job postings. As a new student, you may need to start near the bottom of the pay scale. Don't let this discourage you from accepting on-campus employment. There are many advantages to working for your university.

Campus employers understand that because you are a student your top priority is your education. That realization translates into flexibility. Most on-campus employers are happy to work around your class schedule. Keep in mind that class schedules change with every term. When you have an important test conflicting with your job schedule, you will find a better chance of arranging for time off with an on-campus employer. This is something off-campus businesses are less willing to accommodate. On-campus employment eliminates commute time because you can work directly before or after classes. Before applying for any job, be sure to consider the number of hours you will be able to devote to employment. As a full-time student, you should not work more than fifteen hours per week. Your education should always be your priority.

Perhaps the greatest benefit of on-campus employment for Latino students is getting further connected with campus life: meeting other students, networking with staff and faculty, and developing relationships with those who know the university experience first-hand. Many benefits will emerge from relationships you foster with the members of your network. Over time, your colleagues and peers may even become a part of your extended family. Good supervisors will take an interest in you as a student and as a person and will help you develop work-related skills. Your supervisors may discuss your classes with you and keep track of your academic progress. When you need someone to cut through administrative red tape that may be slowing your progress, contact your supervisor. He or she may know the right person to assist you.

Your supervisor can also act as your mentor: someone with whom you can discuss personal issues, goals, and aspirations; someone who can provide you with guidance. Do not forget that recommendations can open doors. Positive recommendations are a result of diligent effort and high-quality work performed while attending college. Being a productive employee and nurturing a positive work relationship with your supervisors will pay off. So, be sure to weigh the benefits of university employment before you accept a job off-campus.

Academic Advisement

As your registration date approaches, whether it is early in the summer or just before classes begin, be sure to schedule an appointment with an academic advisor. Some schools require all new students to meet with an advisor to ensure that all students have access to experienced assistance in planning their class schedules. If you are not obligated to meet with a counselor, do so anyway—especially if you are a first-generation college student. Such meetings are crucial in developing long-term learning goals. It is a good idea to get in the habit of meeting with an academic counselor before every registration period each semester or quarter. Some students change their majors at least once during their academic career. Your advisor will guide you through these changes, so that you will not delay your graduation by accumulating unnecessary credits. However, keep in mind that identifying a major early enhances your academic progress and stability.

Advisement offices have access to a variety of resources that can aid students in search of a major. If your high school provided limited exposure to career and educational opportunities, be sure to visit the college's student advisement center, which may also be known as the career planning and placement center. The office will have information sheets with descriptions of each major including suggested course patterns, information about professors, and potential job opportunities. Advisement centers can also provide counseling and testing services to help you evaluate your own interests, skills, and life goals. The staff will often be able to connect you with someone in your chosen profession. This will give you first-hand experience regarding your chosen career. Again, remember that one of your goals during your academic career should involve building a support network consisting of students, staff, faculty, and the community at large.

Campus Tour and Orientation

Latino students, especially those who are first in their families to attend college, may find it difficult to adjust to university life, so attending a campus orientation is a practical way to begin your first academic year. Make sure to arrange a visit to your campus prior to the beginning of classes, so that you can participate in an orientation meeting along with a campus tour. You will most likely meet in a large classroom, which will give you the opportunity to become accustomed to rooms that accommodate more than 100 students. During the orientation you will also have a chance to walk around the campus and hear about various services offered by your university.

The orientation meeting will introduce you to the history and mission of the institution. You are likely to learn more about university learning goals, registration procedures, financial assistance, and campus resources such as the library. You will be given many opportunities to attend workshops addressing these and other topics, such as student clubs, government, and activities. You will certainly meet other students who are just as apprehensive as you about their new college careers. If you have not yet had an opportunity to speak with an academic advisor, you will be able to schedule an appointment at this time.

Many students do not place enough value on participating in new student orientations. Many do not realize that attending campus tours and orientations plays an essential role in adjusting to new surroundings. During the first week or two of classes, every student encounters issues that require visiting specific departments or knowing what department to contact. You may want to inquire about financial aid, support services, or health insurance. Consider this most frustrating question: Where do I go for guidance when I do not know who can help me? Take the time to attend a new student orientation and become familiar with the geography, buildings, and culture of your new university.

It is always a good idea to have your parents attend a campus orientation, particularly if you are a first-generation college student. It is crucial that they have a sense of the demands you will be facing. The more they understand about the challenges you will come up against, the stronger their support will be, especially if you are still residing at home. Even though you are an adult now, your parents should still be at the top of your support group. Be sure to consult them frequently—they are a source of strength and one of your greatest assets.

THE FIRST SEMESTER—FINALLY

You made it! You are no longer a high school graduate. You are now a new college student. How exhilarating, liberating, and . . . frightening! So many people are wandering around looking at registration receipts and campus maps. Where am I going? Will I make it to my class on time? Will I have to buy all the books required for each course? Where can I get lunch? Did I park in the right place or will I get a ticket? Are there still on-campus jobs available? There will be so many questions requiring immediate answers. But, unlike some of the other students, you will be able to focus your energy on academic endeavors because you attended the campus orientation. You have already obtained most of the information necessary to make your first college days successful.

Becoming a Successful Student

To get the most out of a class, you have to *prepare for it*. This means preparing beforehand. Do not put a good grade at risk by falling behind. Completing assignments before class will enable you to gain much more from class materials. Having read and prepared assigned homework will enable you to ask questions in class, thereby participating in discussions and making yourself known by coming to the instructor's attention. Completing assignments prior to attending class will also reinforce your newfound knowledge, which will improve your understanding and retention of class materials.

To get the most out of a class, you have to *attend it*. Instructors spend lecture time explaining, expanding on, and highlighting the content of class materials. Do not think that you can be a successful student merely by relying on assigned textbooks. Attending class is an integral part of your education. During your college career you will often come across professors whose excitement and enthusiasm for a class will motivate and inspire you. You can only benefit by attending all your classes.

Attending class is not like watching television. Interactivity and lively exchange, rather than passivity, should characterize your classroom behavior. You will learn faster and retain more when your mind is actively engaged in a class lecture or discussion. Ask questions, answer questions, request clarification and illustrations, and challenge the instructor. All these activities will make class time exciting and rewarding. If you are not critically working with and manipulating your newfound knowledge, creating links between concepts and comparing ideas, class time will become like a chore rather than an opportunity to learn.

An excellent way to engage with course content and reinforce concepts is to *take notes* during class and then *review them* afterwards (you should also take notes on your reading). Doing so is an effective way to *integrate* what you hear in class with what you read in your textbooks. You will improve your memory, create links between concepts, and develop questions. Furthermore, when you prepare for final exams your notes will help you remember things the instructor said weeks or months earlier.

Another method by which to process new learning is to supplement your instruction. Do not depend on your textbooks and assignments alone. Supplement your instruction by reading other books and pertinent articles. If you can, join student study groups. By studying with others you can share opinions, test out ideas, and clarify points with which you are having difficulty. You have to take the responsibility for your own learning.

Sometime during your first semester, you should consider participating in a workshop on note taking. Every student has taken notes at some point in his or her academic career, but few know how to do it efficiently. Contact your learning center advisor and request attendance in such a workshop. Being a successful student in college is much more difficult than it was in high school. Take the time to refine and upgrade your study skills, and you will acquire the tools needed to succeed.

Tracking Your Academic Progress

Many college classes have "mid-term" and "final" exams, which often determine your course grade. In addition, on a periodic basis throughout the term you are likely to receive grades on assignments, such as homework, chapter tests, and book reports. At the end of the term, your instructor will give you a grade that is meant to represent your overall performance for the semester. Considering the importance of receiving good grades, it is unfortunate that many students hamper their own success by relying on the instructors to track their progress and by focusing only on the mid-term and final exams.

Make sure that you are aware of your academic standing throughout the semester. For example, you need to know that by week four you have taken one test and turned in six assignments. What if you know that you have completed all the assignments, but you do not know your grade? This should lead you straight to that most important of all class documents, the syllabus.

On the first day of class, every instructor distributes a copy of the course syllabus. You may think the syllabus is something to stash away in the back of your notebook. Do not make that mistake! Keep the syllabus handy at all times during the semester. In it, you will find indispensable information: course schedule, reading assignments, exam dates, the instructor's office hours, and his or her grading policy. Some instructors may inundate students with multiple assignments: daily quizzes, weekly book reports, monthly tests, a mid-term and a final, as well as a term paper. Others may only have a mid-term and a final. Some students have a tendency to focus on only the two major assignments. Make sure that you give your time and attention to the small assignments as well. They are equally important.

The professor may count quiz grades as a mere 10 percent of your grade and participation as another 10 percent. If you are quiet and do not participate in class and you tend not to prepare for quizzes, you may discover before you have even taken your first exam that obtaining an A in the class is already impossible. Now the best you can hope for is a B, *assuming that you "ace" everything else.* Imagine that you are sick one day and miss a test, then you get a C on a couple of book reports, and then B's and C's on a couple of quizzes. Suddenly, all your assignments point to a final grade of C. Do not ignore small tasks. And remember that instructors appreciate students who make a good effort, who complete all assignments on time, and who show an active interest in the class.

Become familiar with the instructor's grading policy, so that you can calculate your grade and immediately know your own academic standing. By computing individual grades on a periodic basis, you will always know what needs to be done to achieve your academic goals. By being aware of your standing and by tracking your progress, you will be able to recognize when you need assistance. You will be ready to seek help.

Updating Your Academic Toolbox

You just graduated from high school, and your mind is still packed with all sorts of scholarly information. Over the past twelve years, you have spent countless classroom hours listening to teachers and memorizing information. How much time have you spent acquiring skills necessary to be an independent learner? What about techniques to reduce tension brought on by an upcoming test? How are your typing and word processing skills? What about research skills? Do you know how to use the library for research? Can you efficiently produce high-quality work by using presentation software? Would you like to improve your ability to retain information? Would you like to upgrade your writing skills? How about learning to efficiently manage time? As you know, many high schools attended by Latino students face multiple financial challenges and, as a result, can provide only limited learning opportunities. If you haven't acquired the necessary skills in high school, it is essential that you do so now to avoid falling behind in your academic studies.

Most universities have learning centers or academic student support services that can help you become a more competent, efficient, and resourceful student. You will find workshops on note taking, test taking, reducing anxiety, time management, improving computer skills, study skills, critical thinking, research skills, and instruction in basic computer applications. You will also find group or individual tutoring and study sessions. The typical learning assistance center will provide you with a variety of diagnostic tools to help you identify your academic strengths as well as possible obstacles to learning.

At some point in their college career, everyone encounters a deficiency in academic skills. Do not hesitate to take advantage of campus resources to help you overcome learning difficulties. Too many students wait until they are at risk of being put on academic probation (when your GPA falls below a certain point set by the college, usually 2.0) before they seek help. Take the initiative, be proactive, and ask for assistance early. In fact, if you want to increase your level of achievement, use the campus learning center regardless of your academic circumstances. When you use the learning center, you will strengthen your skills, thereby creating opportunities that might otherwise be unavailable. If you are a low-income, first-generation college student, enroll in retention programs such as the Educational Opportunity Program and Student Support Services.

Developing a Support Network

As a Latino or a Latina college student, you may sometimes feel alienated, discouraged, or overwhelmed. In fact, you may feel that you don't belong in college because you haven't had many educational or financial advantages. The first year of college can also be a very lonely time, particularly if you are reserved or reticent about meeting people. Attempting to handle multiple pressures of attending college on your own can become a heavy burden. If you cannot avoid these pressures, be prepared for them by proactively identifying peers and mentors who can become part of your support network. Learning to network is a valuable skill. It will serve you well not only in college but also in your future career.

While in college, you will need friends on campus with whom you can share concerns and socialize. On every campus there are individuals who are dedicated to guiding and assisting you. Some of these people have already had similar experiences, so they know first-hand about the obstacles and challenges you face. They can help you identify solutions.

At some campuses, particularly those that welcome students of diverse backgrounds, it will be fairly easy to identify these peers—for example, in ethnic studies departments, student clubs, and so on. At other schools, it may be more difficult because they might work outside of your major or in a non-mainstream office. Regardless of where they are located, seek them out because they have the experience and knowledge you will need during the first year of college. Your mentors will become crucial links between your very first day on campus and the day of your graduation.

Scanning the college catalog for programs designed to assist students of diverse backgrounds is a good way to identify potential members of your support network. Check to see if the campus has an ethnic studies department or program. Staff and faculty members in ethnic studies departments are well aware of programs and services that may be of interest to you. Moreover, these professors teach courses that will familiarize you further with Latino history and culture. Many of these classes may count toward the general education requirements. These departments also hire student assistants who can inform you about student activities and groups. Determine if your campus offers a mentoring program, peer mentoring, and/or tutoring labs. There, you will find staff and experienced students willing to assist you.

Many of these offices are staffed year round, so take the initiative and make an appointment to visit them during the summer. Introduce yourself to staff members and let them know that you are a new student. Ask about financial aid and student employment counselors. Inquire about faculty members, tutoring programs, student organizations, and support networks. Having a variety of information about the institution and its players will most likely reduce your anxiety.

Other channels for building a support network include joining Latino student organizations, participating in campus multicultural centers, and becoming involved with student government. Your connections to any of these groups will give you the strength to achieve and the belief that you belong on campus. Do not get so caught up in your academic pursuits that you omit forming a support network that will aid you while on campus and smooth your transition out of the university once you graduate.

Understanding That There Is More to College Than Academics

As a college student your first priority is to address each course, regardless of the quality of teaching or its perceived relevance to your future. Performing well in your coursework is critical to your future success. Do not regard your college classes as a set of hoops through which you quickly jump. Each course and each year of study builds a foundation for the next class or phase of life. Academic success can be a guarantee for lifelong success. The combination of natural talent, desire, hard work, and a good education is difficult to duplicate. Your life will be forever changed for the better when you succeed academically. In order to make your education more rounded, participate in extracurricular activities. A well-rounded and fulfilling college experience should be punctuated with complementary pursuits. Seek them out, enjoy them, and learn from them.

Participate in student organizations, leadership institutes, intercollegiate and athletic competitions, student government, and retreats or internships. You should make these events an integral part of your college experience. At any college, you are bound to find at least one organization that will spark your interest. By joining one, you will meet great people, learn new skills, and have fun.

Participating in student government is an excellent way to develop leadership skills and experience. You will learn how institutions work, practice the art of politics, run meetings, and campaign for office. There are few better or more enjoyable ways to prepare for a career.

If you are taking a full load of classes, working ten to twenty hours per week, and studying two hours for every hour of class time, you will definitely be a very busy person. However, after participating in a time management workshop, you will have the skills and discipline to free up the time necessary to pursue extracurricular activities sponsored by your college.

Encountering and Overcoming Discrimination

You will experience mixed emotions when faced with racism or discrimination for the first time in college. Latina women may encounter both gender and ethnic discrimination. Even though colleges and universities are committed to providing an institutional climate conducive to learning, discrimination still exists. If you encounter it, let's hope your encounter will be an isolated event or an expression of individual ignorance, rather than a reflection of institutional culture.

There is no doubt that some faculty will think you have been admitted because of your ethnicity rather than your academic achievements. In classroom discussions concerning Latino topics, others may assume that you are an expert. There is no denying that racial slurs and stereotypes exist on college campuses. If you think that remarks are made out of ignorance, bring it to the attention of the involved person. If racial slurs are frequent and you are certain you are being discriminated against, bring the matter to the attention of the appropriate campus administrator who is responsible for diversity programs. In addition, to help you handle any hostile feelings of your own, seek out a minority faculty or staff member who will listen to you or who can refer you to helpful counsel. Most important, always remember that you belong in an educational setting. Regardless of any hostile and racist attitudes you may encounter, you will achieve your goals.

SUMMARY

How you approach and negotiate your first year of college will indicate much about your success during subsequent years. Following the advice in this Step and this book will provide you with a strong foundation for success. Achieving success is never easy, but proper planning will go a long way in making your educational journey a rewarding one. Always appreciate that you, as a Latino or Latina student, add richness to the university. Also, never fail to appreciate the diversity of students you encounter, especially those from different cultures and those holding different value systems. Do not lose sight of your purpose, and do not be deterred from achieving your educational goals. Rely on your support group to help you move beyond your baccalaureate degree and into graduate schools or programs. Also, remember and appreciate the support of your family and community.

SUGGESTED READINGS

Flores, Judith Le Blanc. "Facilitating Postsecondary Outcomes for Mexican Americans." 1994. ERIC ED 372903.

Isaac, Alicia. *The African American Student's Guide to Surviving Graduate School.* Thousand Oaks, CA: Sage Publications, 1998.

Lopez, Edward M. "Challenges and Resources of Mexican American Students within the Family, Peer Group, and University: Age and Gender Patterns." *Hispanic Journal of Behavioral Sciences* 17 (1995): 499–508.

Velasquez, Patrick M. "The Integration and Persistence of Chicano Students in Higher Education: Student and Institutional Characteristics." 1996. ERIC ED 394423.

First Semester Strategies for Academic Success (Or, How to Meet Your Academic Responsibilities)

A. REYNALDO CONTRERAS

Professor, San Francisco State University

As a Latino college student in your first semester, you have successfully graduated from high school against great odds. Yours has been a struggle to negotiate boundaries among what is important to your family, to your friends, and to your school. These struggles have posed challenges to your academic success. For you as a Latino student, the demands of college are significantly different from those of high school but no less intimidating. The academic curriculum, the rigors of academic expectations and evaluations, the resources available, your particular course of study, and your performance in high school are all factors that will influence your transition from high school to college. Your job in college is to become a successful Latino student. To do this you will need to develop your strategies for academic success. The purpose of this Step is to provide you with strategies to enhance your academic success in the first semester of college.

Strategies for academic success constitute a broad topic that actually includes many separate skills: time management, concentration, memory, text reading, listening and note taking, and test taking, to name a few. In addition, your motivation and attitude toward college studies affect your application of these skills.

UNDERSTANDING THE ACADEMIC ENVIRONMENT

School . . . Books . . . Reading . . . Writing . . . 'Rithmetic . . . Homework . . . Bells . . . Attendance . . . Detention . . . Tests . . . Grades . . .

To incoming Latino college students, the above words often bring associations and images tied to their high school days. Some memories of those days are good, and others we would rather not recall. The academic environment of college is quite different from that of high school. No bells, no detention—nothing to make school a "punishment." From kindergarten to high school, most of us are told we must go to school. But for college, we make the choice to come. As a Latino student, you are there because you want to be. No matter what your reasons are for attending college, as a Latino student you will find it a very rewarding experience.

Getting to Know the Campus

Like many other Latino students, you may be one of the first members in your family to go to college. Hence, you have little familiarity with a college campus. Therefore, to help you become acquainted with your college campus the following suggestions are offered.

The Library

- Familiarize yourself with the campus. Locate the nearest appropriate library. Walk your route to and from classes before the semester begins.
- Learn to use the library. Attend a library orientation at the beginning of the semester. They are offered regularly. Walk through the library once to get your bearings, when you're not feeling pressured to get an assignment done. Rely on reference librarians for help in finding materials and access to electronic networks and information databases.

Advising

- The dean's office of the college you're enrolling in is an important contact point. Be sure to use the academic advisors in the dean's office to assist you in degree plans and course selections.
- Get to know other students, especially other Latino students, who have been there for a while. Seek them out for advice. Graduate students in your field who are studying to get a master's or doctoral degree can be a good source of information.

Academics

- Keep in mind that in college, as a Latino student, you will be expected to perform with high standards of quality.
- From the course catalog, write down on your calendar the deadlines for dropping classes or changing some other aspect of your academic program. Set priorities among your courses in case you decide to drop one. As the deadlines approach, evaluate your performance with your professors and, if possible, discuss your options with an advisor.

- Make it a point to talk with at least four other people in each of your classes. You can get a feel for how others view the course, assignments, grades, and so on. Talking to fellow students helps to reduce the feeling that "you're the only one."
- Try hard not to fall behind in your studying. Most professors give comprehensive exams at the end of the semester.
- Most review sessions for each of the classes you are enrolled in are extremely valuable; be sure to check them out.

College Administration

- When you telephone an administrative office, always get the name and the telephone and extension number of the person you are speaking with. This will assist you if you are transferred from one office to another.
- Make copies of all documents you turn in so you will have one in case the original is lost.
- For really important issues, get decisions in writing or obtain a copy of the document. This will help you maintain some measure of continuity, because a staff member you talk to one semester may not be there the next.
- Be friendly to secretaries. They can be a valuable source of information. On the other hand, don't let anyone refuse you information. If you can't get the information you are seeking, ask to be referred to someone who can help.
- Always ask questions and continue until you get an answer. Don't give up!

EFFECTIVE LISTENING AND NOTE TAKING

"Effective listening requires the expenditure of energy."

You can think about four times faster than a lecturer can speak. Effective listening requires the expenditure of energy; to compensate for the rate of presentation, you have to actively intend to listen. Note taking is one way to enhance listening. A systematic approach to the taking and reviewing of your notes can add immeasurably to understanding and remembering the content of lectures.

Before Class

- Develop a mind-set geared toward listening.
- Test yourself on content of the previous lecture while waiting for the next one to begin.
- Skim relevant reading assignments to acquaint yourself with main ideas and new technical terms.
- Enhance your physical and mental alertness: eat a snack before class, sit in the front and/or center of the room, and focus your attention on the speaker.

- Choose electronic (laptop) or paper notebooks that will enhance your systematic note taking.

During Class

- Listen for the structure and information in the lecture.
- Resist distractions, emotional reactions, or boredom.
- Pay attention to the speaker for verbal, postural, and visual clues to what is important.
- Label important points and organizational clues: main points, examples.
- If the lecturer has an accent you find hard to understand or has distracting mannerisms, relax and attend even more carefully to the content of the lecture.
- When possible, translate the lecture into your own words; but if you can't, do not let it worry you into inattention.
- Be consistent in your use of form and abbreviation.
- If you feel you don't take enough notes, divide the page into five sections and try to fill each part every ten minutes (or work out your own formula).
- Ask questions if you don't understand.
- Instead of closing your notebook early and getting ready to leave, listen carefully to information given at the end of class: summary statements may be of particular value in highlighting main points, and there may be possible quiz questions.

After Class

- Clear up any questions raised by the lecture by asking either the teacher or classmates.
- Fill in missing points or misunderstood terms from text or other sources.
- Edit your notes, labeling the main points and adding recall clues and questions to be answered. Key points in the notes can be highlighted with different colors of ink.
- Make note of your ideas and comments, keeping them separate from those of the speaker.

Periodically

- Review your notes: glance at your recall clues and see how much you can remember before rereading the notes.
- Look for the emergence of themes, main concepts, and methods of presentation over the course of several lectures.
- Make up and answer possible test questions.

Become an Active Learner

One way to increase your learning potential as a Latino student is to become an active learner. This means participating in your learning. It means engaging in the process of learning by:

- asking questions about what you've read,
- using your own words to summarize what you've learned,
- linking what you've learned to what you already know, and
- reviewing continually your course notes.

By doing the above, the material to be learned will become more meaningful to you. The more meaningful it is, the easier it will be to retain and recall for an upcoming test or paper. Passive learners tend to approach learning as remembering and memorizing. They read their textbook, copy their notes from the textbook, and memorize these notes for later recall. To be an active learner, you must do more than read and memorize. Active learning is thinking! The following tips are suggested to help you become an active learner.

Ask questions about what you are reading. Asking questions about the material you are reading or studying will help you identify what you need to learn. These questions can be broad (Why does the instructor want me to read this material?) or specific (How does this idea relate to the ideas I read in the previous chapter?). The better you can identify what you are to learn, the better you will be able to determine what to look for as you review or skim over the material. Being able to make this distinction will save time and help you learn material with less frustration.

Discover the purpose behind your assignments. You need to know what you are to do on assignments and why. You can determine your purpose by asking these questions:

- Why does the instructor want me to read this chapter? book? handout? essay? What ideas am I to learn? How do these ideas relate to other course ideas and objectives?
- What is the purpose of the writing assignment? What am I to communicate to the professor? How will my ideas relate to the ideas or concepts in the course? How can I best express what I know?
- What am I to gain from this activity? How does this assignment help me better understand the objectives of the course? What course concepts am I applying or exploring?

By asking questions such as these, you are making connections between the material you read or write about and the learning objectives of the course. When you make these types of connections, you are giving a purpose to what you do. This purpose will help you begin to understand the "big picture" of the course.

Determine what the main concepts and objectives of the course are and how the smaller assignments contribute to these learning goals. By making connections between what you do in the assignments and what the professor wants you to learn, you will be able to make sense of all the seemingly unrelated ideas and principles you encounter in the course.

If you can take an idea, concept, or principle in a textbook and relate it to a situation or event in your own experience (or in the experiences of others), then you are making that "textbook idea" more meaningful to you personally. You are finding a way to help yourself understand, remember, and even evaluate the concept. The more meaningful the information is to you, the easier it will be to retain for a test or to express in an essay.

Use as many avenues as possible to take in information. Being an active learner means using as many senses as possible in your learning process. Reading is just a first step in an active learning process. You should also write about what you have read by taking notes on your reading. The best kind of notes are those that restate the main ideas in your own words. No matter what type of notes you take—informal outlines, summary paragraphs, lists of key ideas, concept maps—your aim is to put the material into your words. If you cannot restate the ideas in your own words, then you do not yet understand the material and will need to return to the reading to figure it out. If you can restate the ideas accurately, then you are on your way to learning the material. Writing about it becomes a second way and second time that you (your mind, actually) process, or learn, the material. Tell others about what you have read. When you do this, you put the ideas into your own words. This reprocessing of information helps you better understand and retain the material. Speaking aloud can be a wonderful technique for reviewing material. So, find a quiet spot and start talking to yourself! "Telling others" is an excellent opportunity for you to connect what you have learned with what you have experienced or already know.

Listen for the ideas you've read about in the professor's lecture. By purposefully listening for the ideas you have been reading about, you will be able to make connections between what you have read and what the professor says about the topic in the lecture. You will also have the added benefit of building your concentration for the lecture topic because you will be listening for the ideas you've already read about. Remember, learning is thinking; it is an active process by which you question, select, sort, and prioritize the many ideas presented to you in the textbook, lectures, and discussions. An active learner can distinguish what is important from what is not. An active learner saves time in the long run. There is no need for end-of-the-term cramming because the active learner is reviewing and reinforcing his or her learning throughout the term. Learning is not always equated with performance on a test. A test measures what you know at a given moment and under a specific set of circumstances. True learning results in being able to apply what you know in various circumstances and over a lifetime of experiences.

BUILDING SUPPORT SYSTEMS FOR ACADEMIC SUCCESS

"Communicating with others is the key to success!"

Similar to many other Latino students, your decision to go on to college and to obtain a degree adds an entirely unknown component to your life. Even though your college experience will be personally and professionally rewarding, it will also at times be very challenging, stressful, and demanding. As a minority student, you will be challenged to excel beyond expectations with little established support for Latino students on campus. In order to survive and be successful so that you can achieve your goals, it's very important that you establish support networks. The following are some tips for setting up a support system.

Build support networks with immediate others. It's very important to talk with those closest to you—family and friends—about your decision to go to college and to give them a sense of what is ahead for you. Without some understanding of why you are doing what you are doing, those close to you—your parents, brothers, sisters, and close friends—can become resentful and angry with you for the time you will need to be away. To build your support network at home, you need to inform those closest to you of your reasons and goals for going to college.

Build support networks with your peers. Probably just as important as gaining your family's support is building a support network of your peers. Your fellow students, many of whom are Latinos, will offer you more support, encouragement, and strategies for survival than will your family or your advisors and professors because they understand what you are going through. You share so many concerns and goals with your peers that they are a gold mine of resources. If you can,

- get to know others in your classes early in the term.
- find a study partner or buddy—someone to call when you have a question, need a pat on the back, or desire a sympathetic ear.
- participate in study sessions, end-of-term gatherings, and lunchtime chats. You need to be with others who understand your complaints about and praises of your teachers and classmates. Your peers will listen to you, tell you when to stop whining, and remind you that "you can do it!"
- remember that perhaps the best advice is that which comes from a fellow Latino student who's "been there, done that."

TIME MANAGEMENT

"It's not easy to stop and smell the roses when class assignments need to be done!"

Too often Latino college students declare, "I have too much to do and not enough time!" Yes, college is demanding; it is, after all, an academic environment. At the same time, you need not give up your life or become a slave to school to survive. Time management strategies can help you use time productively and efficiently so that you still have some time for yourself, your friends, and your family.

What do we sacrifice in our search for time? Typically, we count on those nearest us to be the most forgiving and the most supportive of our need for more time. Cutting back on the things that we like to do—such as "hanging out" with friends, or playing baseball and soccer—is usually the first step in gaining more time.

Sometimes we begin to take short-cuts in classes in order to regain the time spent at home or at work. This eventually leads to falling behind and performing inadequately in classes, which again increases stress and anxiety. Your college experience need not become frantic, anxious, and stressful. What follows are strategies for using time wisely. These tips are not written in stone, so be open-minded and try some. If they don't work for you, modify them so they better fit your situation and circumstances, or abandon them and try some others.

Get yourself organized. Use an electronic or paper planner/organizer to get organized. You need something that will give an overview of your time use. For instance, a week-by-week or month-by-month view of what's ahead is more useful than a daily sketch because you need to know "what's ahead" as well as "what's on tap for today." By knowing upcoming demands, you can make plans accordingly and prevent problems, such as not having time to meet a deadline.

Know how to find study time. What does "finding time" mean? It means you need to analyze how you currently use your time. To analyze your time use, follow these steps:

- Create a weekly plan to see how you use your time. A weekly plan is nothing more than a time-sheet sketch of how you currently use your time. It gives you a visual picture of what you do and when you do it.
- Modify your weekly plan to gain time. Once you have made a schedule, find places in the schedule that can be modified or changed to give you more time. For instance, give up an evening of television—use this time to study. Also, listen to tape-recorded notes while walking or jogging.

Finding time does not always mean sacrificing something for study time. But it does mean making a careful analysis of your current use of time and finding ways to make it more productive.

Learn to maximize your time. Maximizing your time means getting the most out of it. This involves creating a routine study process. You should establish a regular time to study, such as most evenings from 9 to 10 P.M., or after dinner from 6 to 8 P.M., or early in the morning from 5 to 7 A.M. Once you establish a consistent time for studying, then when that time comes you should sit down and study. You will find it easy to focus on your study tasks because you've subconsciously told your mind and body that "this is the time for academic work."

Find an appropriate place to study. You need to find a place where you can attend to your coursework efficiently. Ideally this place needs:

- a relatively quiet setting (not in a high traffic area),
- all of your materials handy (a corner desk is useful for this purpose),
- a comfortable (but not too comfy!) chair, and
- good lighting (you don't want to harm or strain your eyes).

All these factors will help you pay attention to the task at hand—studying, writing, or reading. Also, when you take breaks you should physically leave the area, so you will feel as if you really are taking a break.

Spread your learning over the week and break your tasks into small, manageable units. Spending nine hours on Saturday or Sunday to complete all your homework may be necessary once in a while, but it is not a good use of time to study like this regularly. Not only will you lose your focus after an hour or so, causing all the material you review after the first few hours to be a blur, but you won't engage in "learn-relearn" activities that occur when you divide learning into smaller, more manageable tasks. To spread your learning over the week, try doing the following:

- Break your assignments into smaller chunks. Use the textbook's headings to divide the chapter into smaller reading and note-taking chunks.
- Preview the chapter (5 minutes), then read a section of the chapter (15 minutes), then write your notes (10 minutes). In this manner you are building your comprehension of and familiarity with the material each time you approach it.
- When writing papers and reports, break the task into stages: prewriting (outline), planning (review of references), drafting, revising, and editing.
- By breaking the learning into manageable units and spreading them over the week, you will increase your retention of the material. This re-thinking is a form of review of the material. It helps build your familiarity with the information and increases your understanding of the "why and how" behind what you were doing.

Don't misuse your time. Ineffective reading, study, and writing approaches can waste tremendous amounts of time. Be sure to use effective and efficient study approaches in your courses. One step toward learning efficiently is to become an active learner. Be flexible, evaluate your strategies, and make needed changes. Remember that the learning strategies you use successfully in one course may not work as well in another course. Successful students examine their strategies periodically. Get into the habit of asking yourself what is working, what isn't, and what modifications need to be made in your current approach so that you can perform at the level you want. Always remember that your situation is unique. What works for you may not work for others. You need to find the reading, writing, and study approaches that fit your own time schedule, learning style, and learning needs. Then, remember to monitor these approaches and make changes when necessary.

Be flexible. Your strategies are your tools and resources for success. Remember that you have to find the right tool for the job; thus, you will constantly modify and change your learning tools as you encounter new courses and new challenges. Being able and willing to make changes is the key to success.

KNOW HOW TO ELIMINATE STRESS

"Being aware of common sources of stress that can plague you as a student is the first step toward preventing stress attacks!"

Some common sources of stress experienced by Latino students include (1) trying to do it all at one time; (2) lacking time to study or having an inadequate place to study; and (3) experiencing feelings of guilt concerning their new relationship (due to college attendance) to parents, siblings, relatives, and friends.

You're not superhuman, so do not try to act like it. Too often, Latino students begin to think it is possible to accomplish all the goals all at once. However, this is not possible. It is even okay to ask for help. Some ways to achieve your goals while minimizing stress include:

- prioritizing tasks and goals,
- delegating tasks and responsibilities,
- taking a realistic view of your situation,
- being realistic about your expectations, and
- being flexible and allowing for times when your expectations won't and can't be met.

Your time is very precious; don't misuse it. Use study time wisely so you won't have to take time away from family or self. Assess time needed for school, and seek opportunities within your schedule to accomplish the work.

When you begin to feel anxious and frustrated, identify the sources of your stress. Ask yourself, What is causing me to feel anxious? What has changed recently that is causing me to feel frustrated? Once identified, you can determine why these things are sources of stress and begin to find solutions to reduce or eliminate them. Sometimes you may only have to adjust the way you perceive the source of stress. Ask yourself, Does the source really deserve the priority I am giving it?

Be kind to yourself. This means that you should:

- be patient and adjust unrealistic expectations.
- continue to pursue your interests. You may need to cut back while in college, but you need not end your other pursuits.
- eat healthy foods and continue to exercise. Don't forget the body while you're feeding your mind and soul.
- take catnaps (use an alarm clock). Napping can have many benefits. It relaxes the eyes, the body, and the mind.
- make time for yourself, even if it is only a few minutes each day.

Relax and enjoy this part of your life. If you relax, you will find that you are in classes with a terrific group of individuals, other students who are struggling with many of the same issues that you are. Talk to them. They can offer you a variety of strategies for reducing stress. Also, you will find that your classmates (Latinos and others) are a very diverse bunch, and in this diversity are many interesting life stories, a whole lot of life experience, and much camaraderie. Getting to know your classmates in this environment will definitely enhance your education.

GOAL SETTING

"Success is transforming a specific dream into reality."

Sometimes people hesitate because their goals are not in line with their intentions. In order to understand your hesitating habit, it is important to become more aware of what is important to you. Ask critical questions about your goals: Do these goals reflect my interests and values? Am I willing to make these goals a priority? Unless your goal has a high priority in your life, you probably will not devote sufficient attention and effort to succeed in it.

It is helpful to define your goals in behavioral terms. Make each goal an action or behavior you can accomplish. Take time to write out these goals. Separate them into three categories: life goals, college goals, and semester goals. For example:

1. Life goals:
    1.1. Life goal: To become successful as a professional.
        - Action and deadline to accomplish life goal: I will be successful as a lawyer within five years of being employed by a legal firm.

2. College goals:

  2.1. College goal: To become a competitive candidate for a successful law school.

    • Action and deadline to accomplish college goal: By the end of my fourth academic year I will complete with high grades all requirements for admission into a law school.

3. Semester goals

  3.1. Semester goal: To complete the English writing requirement.

    • Action and deadline to accomplish semester goal: By the end of the second semester of college I will complete the English writing requirement with an "A" grade.

Once you have listed goals in each category, number the top three in each category. Now you have nine prioritized goals. Under each goal, list the actions you must take to achieve it. Select the top three actions and put them on your schedule to do. Be realistic about timelines, but do adhere to them.

STUDYING ENVIRONMENT

"A major obstacle for students is to create an effective study place."

When managing your place to study, you might do the following. Although some of these tips may seem minor, they contribute to building an effective studying environment.

Keep a record of your goal achievement. This step will not take any time at all. However, it can be extremely effective. It may put just the slightest bit of pressure on you, enough so that your study behavior will become instantly more efficient. Keep goal sheets as a record of your study efficiency. Try setting slightly higher goals in successive evenings. Don't try to make fantastic increases in rate. Just increase the goal a bit at a time.

If your mind wanders, stand up. Don't sit at your desk staring into a book and mumbling about your poor will power. If you do, your book soon becomes associated with daydreaming and guilt. If you must daydream—and we all do so occasionally—get up and turn around. Don't leave the room; just stand by your desk, daydreaming while you face away from your assignment. The physical act of standing up helps bring your thinking back to the job. Try it! You'll soon find that just telling yourself "I should stand up now" will be enough to get you back on track.

Stop at the end of each page and count to ten slowly when you are reading. This may extend your study time, but it will be quite useful if your mind is wandering.

Don't start any unfinished business just before the time to start studying. Most people tend to think about jobs they haven't finished or obligations they have to fulfill much more than things that they have already done and gotten out of the way. Uncompleted activities tend to be remembered much longer than completed ones. Thus, it's no surprise that uncompleted activities and obligations are likely to crop up as a source of daydreaming. Therefore, when you know you're about to start studying, don't get involved in long discussions or projects. Make a habit of studying at pre-set times, and be careful what you do before you start studying. This can improve your ability to concentrate.

Set small, short-range objectives for yourself. Divide your assignment into subsections. Set a time when you will have finished the first page of the assignment, the second page, and so on. If you are doing math, set a time objective for the solution of each problem. In other words, break the assignment into small units. Set time objectives for each one. You will find that this is a way to increase your ability to study without daydreaming.

Keep a reminder pad. Another trick that enhances the ability to concentrate is to keep pencil and paper by your notebook. If while you're studying you happen to think about something that needs to be done, jot it down. Having written it down, you can go back to studying. After studying, when you look at the note pad, you will be reminded of the things you have to do. It's worrying about forgetting the things you have to do that might be interfering with your studying.

HOW TO TALK TO YOUR PROFESSOR

"Instructors are important learning facilitators that you need to make use of."

Make sure you get to know your professors and teaching assistants. Don't be afraid of what following through on this advice might mean. Not only do some instructors appear unapproachable, but you've also heard stories to back up your instincts: instructors are important, busy, highly intelligent people who couldn't care less about your progress in class, right? As a Latino student you may anticipate little attention or guidance from instructors or teaching assistants who may expect less than what is desirable from you. Therefore, you assume there is little value in getting to know your instructors and seeking their guidance. It is true that not all instructors welcome students during office hours, but if you follow these simple guidelines, you are likely to find most conversations with your instructors to be helpful as well as pleasant.

• Visit your instructor during posted office hours or a scheduled appointment.

- Visit your instructor when you have justifiable issues to discuss: for example, you honestly cannot understand why you performed poorly on a test, paper, or other assignment.
- Prepare before going to see your instructor. What specifically do you want your professor to know? Write it down before meeting. Think of the best way to state your concerns.
- Visit your instructor with an open, friendly attitude.

Although these suggestions won't necessarily cover every interaction you have with your professors, they will make a real difference in many cases. Remember, professors themselves are mothers, fathers, daughters, sons, sisters, and brothers (they're human). Many are unaware that their students feel uncomfortable in approaching them, so relax. Be yourself—open, friendly, and academically curious. Make sure you leave the office with a clear plan for your future studies and assignments, and return for another visit only if necessary. The relationships you form with your professors can be instrumental to opening opportunities for success.

Consult your advisor when you are having difficulty in a course, particularly when you feel as if you are in a "deep hole and can't find the ladder to climb out"; then you should contact your advisor as well as your professor. Many times, your advisor can give very helpful direction and even suggest strategies for improving your performance in a course. But most of all, your advisor can be a comforting ear to your concerns. Don't hesitate to talk to your advisors. They are there to help, support, and guide you.

TAKING TESTS

"Tests measure how you are doing in a course."

Usually test scores are the key determinants of your course grade. Doing well on tests requires test-taking skills, a purposeful positive attitude, strategic thinking, planning, and, naturally, a solid grasp of the course content. The following suggestions apply to all types of tests.

Familiarize yourself with the test. Ask the professor how long it will be and what kind of questions will be on it. Find out which concepts are most important, which chapters to focus on, and what you will have to do on the test. Also, ask for some sample test questions and whether there is a copy of a similar test on file in the library. Look over the tests you have already taken in the course to predict what you will need to prepare for. Your aim is to determine both the content of the questions and the type of memory and intellectual skills you will be asked to use. Examples of these skills include:

- remembering specific facts, details, terms, and definitions;
- comparing, contrasting, and otherwise interpreting meaning in the information;
- applying principles and theories to solve problems (which may not have been covered explicitly in the course);
- predicting possible outcomes given a set of variables; and
- evaluating the usefulness of certain ideas, concepts, or methods for a given situation.

Review all the work to be done and schedule time to do it. On the basis of your familiarity with the test, make a list of all the tasks you must complete to prepare for it. Assign priorities to your study tasks according to the topics you expect to be most important on the test. In scheduling your test preparation, try to stick to your own routines.

Review actively. Integrate notes, text, and other information onto summary sheets by diagramming, charting, outlining, categorizing in tables, or simply writing summaries. Try to create a summary sheet for each study session, for each main idea, or for each concept. Use all your senses as well as your sense of humor when writing summary sheets to make them meaningful.

Practice what you will be doing on the test. Answer unassigned problems and questions in the text or anticipate test questions by saying, "If I were making up this test, I would probably ask . . ." and then answer your own question. Remember that the best way to prepare for any test is to practice doing what you will have to do on the test.

Study with other well-prepared students. Attend review sessions. These sessions are intended to clarify the material; don't expect them to repeat lectures or give additional information.

Get into the test-taking frame of mind. Be prepared emotionally and physically as well as intellectually. Get into a "fighting" attitude, emotionally ready to do your best. Stay away from others right before the test, because anxiety is highly contagious. Focus on what you know rather than what you do not know; reinforce your strengths and do not dwell on your weaknesses. Get adequate rest the night before the test, eat well-balanced meals, and exercise regularly—in other words, prepare your brain for optimum functioning by keeping your physical resources well maintained. Avoid fasts. Also, do not take any stimulants you are not used to, and if you are used to them (e.g., coffee or soft drinks), keep within moderate amounts.

Upon entering the test-taking setting, do the following:

- Get organized. Select a seat where the lighting is best (frequently in the front of the room) and where your view of other students will be minimal.

- Get started. When you receive your copy of the test, use the back to jot down all the information you might forget, but first ask whether you can write on the test form.
- Preview the whole test before trying to answer any questions. Make sure your copy has no missing or duplicate pages. Ask the instructor or proctor to clarify any ambiguities. Read the directions carefully.
- Plan your time. Allow the most time for the questions that offer the most points, and leave time at the end to review.
- Start with what is easy. The easy questions build confidence and gain time for harder questions. Work the entire test, and put down an answer for each question even if you must guess.
- Read each question as is. Avoid overanalyzing or oversimplifying, or you will end up answering a question that exists only in your mind. Answer the question stated. Interpret the test within the scope of the course.

WRITING A PAPER

"Writing a paper requires being creative and critical."

Students often put off a writing assignment, considering it a chore too formidable to approach until the last minute. Writing is not a talent reserved for a select few, it is a skill that can be learned. Planning and organization are its essentials. With knowledge of these, any student can improve his or her writing ability through effort and practice. Suggested here are steps to *organized writing* for writing assignments, essay questions, and term papers. Writing requires that you expend two different types of energy: creative and critical.

Creatively choose a topic. If you are allowed to choose your own topic, select one that interests you. Choose something you know about, either your own experience or something you can learn about quickly with the available resources. To find ideas, check the index of your textbook. Ponder possibilities as you read and think. Jot down ideas as they occur to you, and keep them in one place. If your instructor assigns the topic, be sure you understand it. If you're not completely sure, get clarification from the instructor, a teaching assistant, or another student in the class. If you're not interested in the topic, develop an interest by finding a good (personal) reason for doing the assignment.

Critically narrow your topic. Write about something whose scope is limited enough that you can be detailed about it within the space you have. This may occur as you read and write. For example, narrow your topic from "History of Music" to "History of Music from 1900 to 1950" to "History of Jazz from 1900 to 1950" to "Comparison of Ragtime Music and Creole Music in American Jazz, 1900 to 1950."

Creatively collect your ideas. To collect ideas from reading materials, ask a librarian for help in locating source materials. Keep notes about separate ideas from your reading on electronic "note cards" or 3 × 5 index cards. Include author, title, and page number on each note card; make a separate bibliography card for each source. To generate more ideas, recall your own experiences. Daydream about them; follow your thoughts. Brainstorm: write down as quickly as you can any ideas that might be connected to your topic; don't worry about order, wording, or even whether or not you'll finally include these ideas in your paper. You can sort these out later. Talk to other people for more ideas.

Critically organize your ideas. Make an outline. This is essential. There is no better way. Browse through your collected notes until you detect a pattern in them, and then put similar ideas together. Or shuffle your note cards: How many ways can you see to relate these ideas? Arrange the groups of notes to reflect how they are related. If no suitable pattern occurs, go away for a while and then try again. Ignore the data; make up an outline about how you want things to be, and see if you can fit your data into it. Make a thesis statement. Write a paragraph or two summarizing what you want to say. Use this like a bull's eye: be sure that each paragraph you write is directed toward developing the thesis.

Creatively get your ideas on paper. Gather all materials you need: notes, paper, pencils, typewriter or computer. Allow yourself some time, and start writing. Allow yourself no excuses and work quickly. Don't worry about exact word choice or refinements of grammar; you can edit and revise later when you have something to work with. Write down main ideas, details, examples, and explanations in the order you've already determined in the outline. Remember, you are simply putting into one draft the notes and ideas you've already formulated. If you freeze up, "talk" your ideas to someone real or imagined or to a tape recorder. Explain as simply and clearly as you can what you want to say. Then type into an electronic file or paper what you've said. Alternatively, write out your ideas very quickly. Do this several times until you feel easier about putting words on paper or on the screen. If you are fearful that your paper won't be long enough, ask yourself what you can do to guarantee that your ideas have been accurately and thoroughly explained. Could you explain more carefully or give an example?

Critically revise your rough draft. Complete your rough draft several days or at least twenty four hours before the due date. Review organization. Does one paragraph follow another logically? Provide transitions. Cut paragraphs out and rearrange them like pieces of a puzzle. Examine for unity. Do all the paragraphs develop the thesis? Is the thesis clearly stated somewhere (usually at the beginning or end of the paper)? Is each paragraph unified around a stated or clearly implied topic sentence? Survey sentence structure. Are sentences grammatically correct? Are sentences varied in length and structure, designed to emphasize key ideas? Do they indicate relationships clearly and express ideas economically? Are they punctuated correctly? Inspect word choice. Are the words concrete and appropriate? Use a thesaurus for new ideas. Read the paper aloud, or tape-record it. Does it sound awkward? Have a friend read the paper to see if he or she can follow your train of thought. Make necessary changes.

Type a final draft and turn it in.

SUGGESTED READINGS

Hamachek, A. L. *Coping with College: A Guide for Academic Success*. Boston, MA: Allyn & Bacon, 1995.

Harvey-Smith, A. B. *Getting Real: Proven Strategies for Student Survival and Academic Success*. New York: Duncan and Duncan, 1999.

Reynolds, J. A. *Succeeding in College: Study Skills and Strategies*. Boston, MA: Allyn & Bacon, 1996.

Academic Support On and Off Campus

BALTAZAR ARISPE Y ACEVEDO JR.
Founding president of the Community College Without Walls in Houston, Texas

When you were growing up and went to family events such as birthday parties, weddings, and holiday celebrations, did you notice how many of your family or adult friends at these events had college degrees? How many of your parents' friends were lawyers, doctors, engineers, or teachers? In many cases very few of them had these kinds of occupations. Even though this may have been the case, it is not a reflection on their lack of ability or interest but rather on the lack of opportunities that were available to them to go to a college or university when they were your age. Many Latinos of your parents' and grandparents' age did not attend college; many of them did not even graduate from high school.

You are one of the few Latinos, of the over 35 million who live in America, who will attend a college or university. Most important to your family, to your grandparents, *tios, tias, hermanos, hermanas*, and other relatives and *amigos*, you will be one who will succeed and graduate with a college degree. This is what it is all about: your success as a young person, as a scholar, and as a Latino who is willing to meet the challenges of getting a college education and working hard to achieve your and your family's hopes and wishes for you as an adult.

Is there life after high school? By enrolling in a college program of study you have begun that life and are now involved in an academic experience that is more complex than high school was. *The key difference now is that it is all up to you.* You are now free to make many choices and to determine your own course of study. The most important fact to consider is that you are preparing yourself for a professional career that will require you to be competitive in your chosen field when you graduate.

The average college degree plan is set for a four-year calendar. You may be able to complete a Bachelor's degree in four years, if you attend college every semester and take a minimum load of fifteen hours of classes. You can also complete a degree in fewer than four years if you take courses during summers and during mini-semesters, which many colleges offer during the various holiday breaks. The key to success in your college career will depend on three factors: (1) how you use your time, (2) how you make use of collegiate support services and community resources, and (3) how well you learn to identify and access certain individuals as mentors and advocates during your college career. Also, please remember that you need not declare a major until the beginning of your junior year.

Success in college is very similar to the successful completion of a journey. In both instances you have a starting point and a destination. As a freshman, you are at the starting point and your destination is a Bachelor's degree. Before you can take a trip you must first decide where you plan to go, otherwise you may wind up going in circles and getting nowhere very fast. In this brief Step some helpful hints and resources are shared with you so that you will obtain your degree. Remember, you are not alone in your journey. There are many Latino professionals, community leaders, professors, counselors, and instructors who are ready and willing to assist you in reaching your academic goals.

DEVELOP A PERSONAL RESOURCE INVENTORY

Just before the semester begins, there are six things you should do to prepare yourself for a smooth start. By following these six simple steps, you will save time and prevent a lot of confusion and possible problems. These six steps have helped many college-going students.

1. Participate in freshman orientation. Review all handouts and brochures that are given out at these sessions.
2. Before the semester begins, become familiar with your schedule and conduct a trial run of locating all your classes throughout the campus.
3. Keep a log of how you spend the first two weeks of your first semester. Then set up a study skills schedule that allows for no less than one and a half hour per class for preparation time.
4. Identify and associate with classmates who seem to have a focus about their academics. Establish study groups with them. They will also be valuable resources for comparing notes and observations about your shared classes.
5. Check out your means of transportation, if you commute, and make sure that your vehicle is in good working order. Any breakdowns will affect your class attendance.

6. Find out if you have any friends at the college or university with whom you can carpool.

IDENTIFY CAMPUS-BASED ACADEMIC AND STUDENT SUPPORT SERVICES

Review and become thoroughly familiar with the college catalog or university handbook. You will receive one at orientation. Catalogs are also available at the office of the dean of students. A typical catalog provides the following information:

- the many services, activities, and policies of the institution,
- the names, telephone numbers, and Internet addresses of the different academic and student services offices,
- office hours of all departments,
- a current academic calendar, and
- the names and contact information for all student organizations.

Meet with a counselor at the academic advising center as soon as time permits. This step will help you to accomplish several important tasks. First, you will be able to review your course load and make sure that you are indeed enrolled in classes that will count toward graduation—or transfer to a senior institution, if you are enrolled in a community college.

Second, you will be able to acquire the names of academic advisors; it is usually best if you regularly meet with the same one and set up a file with that advisor.

Third, you can schedule an appointment to take a career interest inventory exam with the staff in the career services office. The most common career choice exam is the Myers-Briggs Type Indicator (MBTI), but there are other exams for the same focus. This exam will provide an assessment of your personality and your possible career interests. It is also a good reference for your academic advisor to have on file as you plan your career track.

Fourth, you will be able to inquire about career choice workshops. These workshops address topics such as (1) the high-tech job search (many professions nowadays involve a high-tech working environment), (2) writing a strong resumé, (3) practicing your interviewing skills, and (4) co-op and internship arrangements. You may have an opportunity to earn money and college credit by enrolling in work site–based assignments with professionals in some of the career areas that are of interest to you. This is a good way to gain exposure to the professional world of work while obtaining hands-on, career-related experience prior to graduation. However, it is advisable that you do not work during your first year of college unless you have to. Most students, even those with high GPAs, need to concentrate on their studies and learn what is expected of them in college, as opposed to high school.

IDENTIFY ALL ON-CAMPUS LEARNING SUPPORT SERVICES

Your study habits from high school may not be the most appropriate for some of your college courses. Also, the assignments and deadlines will be different because your class schedule will be varied and not sequential. In order to be prepared to complete your assignments, be aware that the following learning support services may be readily accessible.

Skill-building workshops provide activities that focus on:

note-taking techniques,

time management,

preparing for exams,

writing in the appropriate research style,

goal setting,

using your memory to the fullest,

test-taking strategies,

writing the right type of term paper,

individual learning styles: auditory, kinesthetic, or visual, and

reducing test anxiety.

Multimedia resource centers are becoming more evident in the libraries of most colleges and universities. These centers maintain materials for intensive practice and instruction using computers and video equipment as well as self-paced tutorials on the use of the library. Classes are usually offered on new software or updates on existing programs. In many instances all academic departments use the same operating system, PC or Mac, and the same word processing software such as WordPerfect, Lotus, or Microsoft Word. It is advisable to become proficient in the Lotus, Word, or WordPerfect platform with special emphasis on Excel and PowerPoint because these programs will facilitate the timely completion of your assignments.

Computer learning centers or labs are generally available in several locations such as dormitories and the student center. Because of this, accessibility to computers should not be a big problem for you.

Special services for eligible ethnic minority students are usually found in the office of the dean of students. These may include Talent Search, Services for Students with Disabilities, UpWard Bound, and Veterans' Services. Your eligibility for these services is usually determined by your financial aid status. You will need to stop by the office of student financial aid to request an updated assessment of your profile.

At some point in your studies you may find that you will require *tutorial assistance* to fully comprehend the content of some of your courses. Do not be disheartened; this happens to everyone. You are not supposed to know everything in every course you are taking; otherwise you would not be enrolled in college. The best place to start looking for tutoring support is in the office of the dean of students unless you have already determined your major, in which case you may need to go to your academic department. Both sites maintain extensive references about tutoring services. Some academic departments even offer an ongoing peer-tutoring program or maintain a list of students who are well versed in their discipline and provide tutoring to individual students for a small fee.

You must prepare to be tutored. This is done by:

- knowing your course syllabus thoroughly: be familiar with the requirements of the course and do not expect the tutor to know everything that you are supposed to turn in for a course grade.

- bringing all your class notes and books with you to each tutoring session.

- bringing specific questions about the class material; remember that tutors should not be expected to do your assignments or to teach you material that you have not studied.

- understanding that the role of the tutor is to provide supplemental learning assistance to help you through those parts of the subject material that are challenging you.

- always keeping your tutorial appointments and never asking for more than one hour's time for each course.

- following up each tutoring session with your own review to confirm what you have just learned.

USE THE INTERNET AS A LEARNING TOOL

The Internet can be both an aid and an impediment to your academic experience. The way that you use the Internet will influence the way that you search for data, access data, and apply data to your academic work. The Internet is an instrument, no more and no less. The following are some examples and shortcuts to using it as a supplement to the research resources that are readily available in your college or university and community.

1. Learn how to use the Internet. The following helpful resources can be purchased through *Amazon.com*: (1) Ned Snell, *Sams Teach Yourself the Internet in 24 Hours*, 2001 ed., ISBN 0672319667; (2) Adam C. Engst, Corwin S. Low, and Michael A. Simon, *Internet Starter Kit for Windows*, 2nd ed., ISBN 1568301774. In addition, the University of California at Berkeley has an outstanding online Internet tutorial. It is found at *www.berkeley.edu*.

2. Download the Adobe Acrobat Reader in your hard drive, or use those in the college's computer lab or multimedia center. Adobe is a software program that is used extensively by researchers and public institutions to write reports that go on the Web. The software is available for free and can be obtained by logging on to *www.adobe.com/acrobat.*

3. Experiment with different search engines such as AltaVista, Web-Crawler, MSN, SNAP, and others. Each search engine has different resources, and not all of them will lead you to the best sources of information. You will find a review of the capacities of search engines in the library. You can also ask your professors or teaching assistants which ones they use and why.

4. Use online learning resources that supplement those at your college and that can be accessed from your home or dorm. The following very good examples are found on the Internet through the courtesy of colleges and universities or individuals who have sound materials to share:

http://www.stclair.on.ca/stserv/library/research/study is a Web site maintained by the Technology Center at St. Clair College in Ontario, Canada. The site provides these resources:

- Guides to finding information on the WWW
- Info people guide to search tools, indexes, etc.
- Finding information on the WWW: A tutorial
- Searching tips
- Criteria for evaluating internet resources
- Evaluating WWW information [is it good data?]
- Why we need to evaluate what we find on the Web
- Library of Congress subject headings
- Guide to citing electronic information
- How to prepare an annotated bibliography
- MLA (Modern Language Association) style for citing Internet resources

http://www.eop.mu.edu/study/ is a Web site maintained by Marquette University in Milwaukee, Wisconsin. The site has an extensive Web-based inventory of study guides and test-taking strategies. It includes the following topics and links to other Internet sources:

- Test Taking: The True-False Test
- Test Taking: Multiple-Choice Questions
- How to Work through Matching Questions
- Sentence Completion Questions
- Taking the Short Answer Test
- Answering Essay Questions
- 6 Day Countdown for a Biology Exam
- Getting Ready for Your Math Final
- An Effective Model for Test Cramming
- Study Web (American Computer Resources, Inc.)
- Study Skills Self-Help Information (Virginia Tech)

- Study Guides and Strategies (University of St. Thomas)
- Study Skill Guides (Dartmouth College)
- Learning, Writing, and Subject-Specific Web Links (University of Guelph)
- The CalREN Project (University of California—Berkeley)
- Learning Strategies Database (Muskegon College)
- Chemicool Periodic Table (MIT)
- The Biology Project (University of Arizona)
- Nate Ziarek's Biology and Chemistry Resources (Marquette University EOP)

These introductory Internet resources and references will get you started as a sophisticated user of information from the digital age. There is much to be obtained from the Internet; you will learn from some of the tutorials how to evaluate good sources and unreliable ones.

IDENTIFY AND USE COMMUNITY-BASED SUPPORT SERVICES

You will find that the Latino community has much to offer to support your academic work. These services are usually found within your city's public library system and volunteer organizations. The League of United Latin American Citizens (LULAC; based in Washington, D.C.), the American GI Forum, and the National Council of La Raza (based in Washington, D.C.) have local affiliate agencies in cities throughout the country that provide academic and scholarship support to Latino students. The following are Web sites for these organizations that you can access easily through the Internet:

The Hispanic College Fund: *www.hispanicfund.org*

LULAC's National Educational Service Centers: *www.latino-net.org*

Mexican American Legal Defense and Educational Fund: *www.maldef.org*

The American GI Forum: *www.americangiforum.org*

There are other local, state, and regional community-based organizations that provide support services to Latino students. These can be found through Internet links with the organizations previously mentioned.

PERSONAL INITIATIVES

Your success in preparing for a career can also be impacted in a positive way through your involvement with mentors and successful graduates of your college. A mentor is an individual, usually older than you, who has been or is successful in a career. We all need mentors to provide us guidance, share their wisdom, and sometimes give constructive criticism. You can identify a possible mentor by visiting with faculty members or with community organizations that have an established mentorship program. Once you have identified a mentoring prospect, take time to schedule an interview to have a mutual exchange about common expectations. As a protégé you should also be prepared to introduce your mentor to your own worldview and experience as a young individual who is preparing to enter the world of work. In many instances mentors will be honored and more than willing to establish a mutually beneficial relationship with you.

Another way to gain insights about your academic and career choices is through interaction with successful graduates in the field that you are considering as a major. You can find the names of these graduates at the office of your college dean or the college's alumni center. You may want to write or call some of these former students and tell them of your interest and ask for their insights and advice about their careers now that they are out of college. The graduates who have been out of college for at least two or three years will have lots to share because they are now settling into their careers.

SUMMARY

College is not all about academics. It is also about having fun and developing social relationships with both peers and faculty members. At your college or university you will likely find many events and support services for Latino students. Among these will be clubs, associations, and service activities with organizations such as LULAC and the G.I. Forum that offer you an opportunity to serve the Latino community. Your Latino peers, as well as others, will become part of your post-college support network. Just as important will be Latino faculty and staff members who may become your mentors and guides during your college years. Even if this group is rather small at your university or college, you will find them to be eager and willing to contribute to your success. They will be crucial contacts who will provide you continuing assistance by becoming a resource for recommendations and references for future employers or graduate and professional schools. Indeed, these faculty and staff members may make a significant difference in your career. Take time to get to know them as both individuals and mentors who can become a critical part of your personal and professional life.

The last piece of advice is rather simple: never be intimidated or afraid to ask for help, and never think that your questions and inquiries may be viewed as foolish. The only foolish questions are those that are not asked. Be inquisitive and make use of every resource that is available at your college or university. In many instances, the major resources will be the Latino professionals at your institution who traveled the same road as you just a few short years ago.

STEP 7

Your Student Rights and What You Can Do If You Are Failing a Course

ROBERTO HARO
Professor of Ethnic Studies, San Francisco State University

American higher education continues to be challenged by different types of students and the concerns that they bring to the campus. From a historical perspective, campuses have always had to establish policies and practices to cope with student matters. Two related areas of special sensitivity are (1) students' rights, and (2) how students are able to secure due process on a campus. Most colleges and universities have used the concept of *in loco parentis*[1] to deal with matters involving student behavior and conduct, both in and out of the classroom. Prior to the 1940s, the office of the dean of students[2] was involved mainly with students as a surrogate parent. Consequently, many of the policies and procedures that governed student conduct, including pertinent aspects within the academic programs of the institution, had been established and monitored by an office in the division of student services. As a surrogate parent, particularly at residential colleges and universities, the deans of students often dealt with critical issues related to cheating, misconduct on and off the campus, and other infractions of policies and procedures by which students were expected to abide. There was, however, some lack of clarity in matters that involved faculty prerogatives, such as an instructor giving a student a failing grade, especially in questionable situations that may have involved non-academic factors. This continues to be a gray area for many student affairs administrators and faculty.

The literature in the field of student services is filled with case studies and articles that focus on specific issues in which students have encountered difficulties with colleges and universities. However, there is very little available in the professional literature about how any guidelines and formal policies should be interpreted by a college to ensure that Latino/as, as new types of students, know their rights and how to make certain they are able to get due process in disputes with the college or university. Much that has been written is dated or focuses on particular types of institutions with a perspective that views students as mainly a homogenous middle-class group. However, Latinos[3] are accounting for a larger percentage of America's college-age population. Because of their background and unique family experiences, Raza[4] do not seem to fit the traditional student image at many two- and four-year institutions. Consequently, it is necessary to adapt information from researchers and practitioners who work regularly with the areas of student rights and due process and interpret it for Latino communities.

To better understand and appreciate the situation a Latino student may encounter with academic matters on a campus, it is important to consider some of the policies and procedures that affect them. At many campuses, the limited dissemination (if any) of policies to ensure student rights and due process all but makes them unknown. Moreover, the campus officers designated to provide information about these rights and due process are often insensitive to the unique perspectives and needs of Latino students.

There are some critical parts of a student's academic requirements that govern how she or he is treated. The following issues will be discussed: attendance in class; the syllabus and course requirements; adding and dropping classes; request for incomplete grades; early withdrawal from a class; petitions for action; and fees for petitions or other actions that influence academic records.

ATTENDANCE IN CLASS

Attendance in class is a complicated issue. Many instructors, particularly at two-year colleges, take attendance early during the term to ensure that students who registered for the class are actually present. Other instructors, mainly at major research universities where some classes may have well over 200 students, are less interested in taking roll. However, where a student is assigned to a discussion section that is part of the course, teaching assistants responsible for such sections often take roll; part of the student's grade for the class may depend on participation at such sessions.

Latino students should realize that at some larger universities, the role of the teaching assistant is very important. Teaching assistants are usually graduate students completing their doctoral training and selected by the course instructor to assist her or him in teaching and working with the undergraduate students. In most cases, the teaching assistant will recommend a grade for the student, based on her or his performance, to the course instructor. Consequently, it is very important for a new student to attend any section she or he has been assigned to and learn to work with the teaching assistant as if that person were actually teaching the course.

Getting back to attendance, instructors in science and technology courses do place an emphasis on laboratory sections as part of the overall grade in the class. As a result, attending a computer or science laboratory is mandatory and the work performed there is an important part of a student's overall grade. So, a student should remember that attendance in class, even though the instructor does not take roll, is very important.

SYLLABUS AND COURSE REQUIREMENTS

When a student enrolls for a course, the instructor provides him or her with a course syllabus that usually includes the class requirements. A student should inquire of an instructor, if there is any uncertainty or lack of information, what constitutes the work required to satisfactorily pass the course. The syllabus is like a contract between the instructor and the student. Many instructors do not make paper copies of course syllabi, and instead they put these materials on their personal Web site or require students to access this information via a computer at a designated address. A student can demand that the instructor make a paper copy of the class syllabus, especially if the student does not have access to a computer and printer.

The class syllabus should contain the instructor's name, office number, telephone number and e-mail address, and times when she or he is available to meet with students. The syllabus also should contain the assignments for the course: these may include readings, laboratory and/or field work, and independent research. If the student is unclear on any assignment for the course, she or he should meet with the instructor immediately and seek clarification. The student should also find out from the instructor how grades are determined and the types of examination used in the class. If the class has a laboratory or field project, these should be explained and the part in the overall grade for the course made known. Where an instructor requires students to work in pairs or groups, the student should determine if she or he will be graded individually, or whether the instructor intends to give one grade to the entire group for their work or project. This can be a very troublesome issue, especially when students have not done cooperative projects before. If the Latino student has a form of language interference or lacks the appropriate academic experience for doing assignments in a collaborative mode, this needs to be made known to the instructor. For possible later use, it is most helpful if the student keeps a written record of this communication with the instructor.

Another significant aspect of the syllabus involves the type of examination(s) or projects that will determine the grade. The instructor must let the student know if she or he gives multiple choice or essay examinations.

Where projects are involved, the style and format for the report must be explained and reference made to one or more manuals or guidebooks that will provide examples of the format preferred by the instructor. The student should learn from the syllabus or the instructor directly what text will be required and used in the class to determine how much it will cost to take the class. Finally, the instructor should, in the syllabus or through another mode, let the students know what weight will be given to each examination and whether the final examination will be comprehensive or cover only the material assigned since the last mid-term.

ADDING AND DROPPING CLASSES

As a student begins to prepare her class schedule for a particular term, there are two steps that must be considered. First, most undergraduate students need to prepare a schedule of courses for each term in which they plan to enroll. This schedule of classes must be approved by an academic advisor. At many colleges a Latino student, especially in the freshman and sophomore years, will be assigned an advisor who may or may not be a faculty member. At large four-year universities, advisors are usually staff officers affiliated with a large division such as the college of letters and science or the general education program. Most advisors will assist a Raza student in selecting appropriate classes. Once a student has this schedule, she may encounter an enrollment practice known as the "add and drop" period. During this process a student may "shop around" for classes. At the beginning of each term, a student can attend classes selected before the term begins and determine if she will remain in one or more of the courses assigned or selected.

Second, Latino students should attend the classes scheduled and determine whether they feel prepared to take the courses, whether the expected work in the class is something they can do, and whether they feel comfortable with the instructor. During this add and drop period—usually about two or three weeks at the beginning of the term—the student can drop any classes and add others to replace the ones dropped. Once a student decides to drop and add classes, she must secure permission from the instructor of the course she needs to add. After that, she must make the changes in her schedule of classes for that term and have her advisor approve the change(s). If the student decides to make changes after the add and drop period, she will need permission from her advisor and may have to pay a fee to the registrar to make any changes.

REQUEST FOR INCOMPLETE GRADE; EARLY WITHDRAWAL

Once a student has enrolled and has filed her study list with the registrar, and the add and drop period has passed, there are two options in withdrawing from a course without a penalty: (1) petition to withdraw from the class, or (2) petition the instructor to be assigned an incomplete grade. The student can meet with her advisor and explain the circumstances that make it necessary for her to withdraw from a class. A petition must be secured from the registrar and signed by the advisor as well as the course instructor. There will be a fee for such a petition. If a student is too far along in the class and has completed most of the assignments but cannot continue in the course, she may petition the instructor to assign a grade of "incomplete." There is usually no fee for requesting an incomplete from the instructor. However, the student should meet with her advisor, explain why she cannot complete the remaining work in the class on time, and indicate when the remaining work will be completed. Normally, a student must make up the remaining assignments in the course within the next few terms. In some colleges, the student has two years in which to eliminate an incomplete grade. After that, she must petition the college to continue the incomplete or else the grade will be changed to an F.

PETITIONS AND FEES

Latino students must realize that changes to a student's class schedule after the drop and add period, or petitions to withdraw from a course, involve a fee. Most petitions for action that affect a student's records require a fee. There are, however, some ways to avoid a fee. An example is the case of a Latino student who completes a course and earns a B+ grade even though she does not hand in all the assignments. The student may speak with the professor, agree to submit the missing work for the course, and petition to have the grade changed. If the instructor agrees, then a change of grade petition is needed for which a fee is involved. At some colleges, the instructor can request that the fee to change the grade be waived. Again, this depends on the college and on the willingness of the instructor to request the fee waiver. As mentioned earlier, petitions that involve changing a student's records almost always require a fee.

A FAILING GRADE

To show how Latino students can deal with a college or university to understand their rights and make certain they are able to get due process, the example of a student getting a failing grade is informative. There are several things that a Latina student can do to deal with a failing grade in a class. On most campuses, there is a protocol for action that a student needs to know. Each campus procedure for dealing with a student's petition, especially one that involves the assignment of a failing grade, may vary considerably, even if the institution is part of a large multi-campus system. It is common for separate campuses within the same system to have different ways to deal with student petitions. However, some general guidelines include the following: meet with the instructor and determine the nature of the problem that has caused the poor academic performance; seek out tutorial assistance from an on-campus learning resources center or from off-campus academic improvement resources; appeal to the head of the department or to the academic dean of the division; appeal to the advising or counseling center on the campus; contact a student ombudsman[5] or a student government representative for academic matters; contact the academic ombudsman or the dean of students; or contact an off-campus source of support. Each step will be discussed separately.

Before any action is taken, the student should prepare a clear, written statement that details the nature of her petition. In this case, the student should state her background and level of academic preparation, document any skills that are lacking (by securing a copy of her high school transcript), explain extenuating circumstances that may contribute to the failing grade, and make the request to be allowed to withdraw from the class without prejudice. The written petition is essential as a request for action, and it can be used in the event of appeal or at subsequent meetings where the case will be discussed. Once this is done, the student can consider pursuing different alternatives.

The first step a student should take when receiving a failing grade is to immediately make an appointment with the course instructor. At that meeting, the student should inquire of the instructor why a failing grade was given. If it was a failure to comprehend the material and express it to the instructor in a particular way, this should be noted. If it was a lack of skills, such as inadequate preparation in mathematics, the student and the instructor should determine whether it will be possible to earn a passing grade in the class. If the instructor believes the student can acquire the necessary skills to pass the course, the student should find out where to find assistance on campus to develop the learning skills and background that will enable her to earn a passing grade. She should determine if there is a student learning center on campus that offers group or individual assistance to develop the type of skill she requires. Also, she should learn from the instructor or a responsible campus officer if there are free tutorial services for students in this subject. If such free tutorial services are not available, the student should solicit from the instructor the names of paid tutors who might be available to assist her. If the student is on financial assistance, she will need to visit the office of financial aid and ask for her financial aid award to be modified so that she can pay for tutorial services.

The instructor should be candid about the student's chances of passing the course and should inform the student that without the adequate background or preparation she will fail the class. If this is the case, the student should have the instructor provide her with a letter to that effect and ask the instructor if it is possible to withdraw from the class without prejudice.

If the instructor approves, then the student should take the instructor's letter to the teaching department office, notify the chairperson, and seek approval to drop the class or withdraw. The student should also discuss this with her advisor. If the petition is approved, then the student should proceed to the registrar to file a petition to drop or withdraw from the class without prejudice.

But what if the instructor refuses to allow the student to withdraw and is unwilling to offer assistance or provide recommendations about where to get help to pass the course? In this case, it is essential for the student to determine whether the instructor is biased in any way. If a bias or prejudice exists on the part of the instructor toward the student, then a different course of action is required. This will be discussed later. Assuming the instructor is not disposed to offer any assistance to the student and that no biases or prejudices are involved, then the student must first go to the chair of the department and plead her case, indicating that she met with the course instructor and was informed that she would fail the class because of inadequate preparation or learning skills. In such matters, a department chair can act as a mediator and consult with the instructor to arrive at a mutually desirable outcome. A department head may (1) intervene and support a student's request to drop a class, or (2) provide information about on-campus or off-campus support services that will help her gain the background and skills needed to pass the course. If the campus does not have such support services and no tutorial services are available, then the chair must make a decision to support the instructor or approve the student's request to withdraw from the course. If the chair of the department decides in favor of the student, then she should take this written approval to the registrar to drop the course. If the chair refuses to assist the student, then she must consider other alternatives.

Many university campuses have learning resource centers that provide academic support services for students who want to improve their grades. However, there is no guarantee that a particular campus will have such services available for students, especially for those who find themselves in some form of academic difficulty. Another resource for students who may require academic assistance is the campus alumni association. Some alumni associations, especially at the larger public universities, maintain programs that link emeritus faculty and student guidance, counseling, and tutorial services. The services provided by an alumni association represent another possible avenue for academic support that should be made known to the student.

If the department chair cannot be of assistance, then the student can appeal the matter to the academic dean of the particular division or college in which the department is located. The dean can investigate the request by the student and refer the matter back to the department chair and the faculty member; consider intervening on behalf of the student, if circumstances warrant it; or deny the student's petition. If the dean instructs the department chair and the faculty member to work with the student to resolve the matter, due process is served. The dean can (but only on very rare occasions) recommend a decision in favor of a student, in this case allowing the student to drop the class. This may happen when the dean is presented with special circumstances that represent an extreme hardship for the student, a procedural error that worked against the student, or extenuating circumstances that may have resulted in non-academic factors being involved in the awarding of a failing grade. As a matter of practice, a dean usually looks carefully into matters that involve a student petition to withdraw from a course because of extenuating circumstances. In this case, if the student did not have the adequate background and learning skills, was from a low-income group, and was the first in his or her family to attend college, a dean or other college or university official would be justified in seeking ways to prevent the student from failing a course. There is, of course, a third avenue of action available to the academic dean: denying the student's petition. If this occurs, then the student has other paths to consider.

At most campuses, the student government has a group charged with the responsibility for reviewing student petitions, even those that involve academic matters. Usually these groups are located within the broad area of judicial responsibility. Many such student groups have fact-finding responsibility only. Others can recommend further steps and action. At one state-supported university in the Midwest, the student group responsible for reviewing student petitions that involve academic matters has the authority to transmit its recommendations directly to an academic vice president or dean. At some colleges and universities, the student government employs the services of a student ombudsman, usually appointed by the student body president or the elected student senate or assembly. The student ombudsman is charged with the responsibility of reviewing petitions for action in matters that involve differences between students and the institution. The student ombudsman is usually an upper-division student or graduate student. Depending on the campus, the student ombudsman may work with a faculty counterpart on academic matters such as misconduct in a class, charges of cheating, or grade assignment. For the purposes of this case, the student will present her petition to the student ombudsman. That officer will review the matter by checking the facts in the student's petition and interviewing the instructor and the department chair—if necessary—and any other persons who may be essential to rendering a decision on the petition. If the student's petition is reviewed carefully and the ombudsman finds in her favor, a recommendation may be made to the instructor and the department chair that the petitioner be allowed to withdraw from the course. If the student ombudsman denies the petition, then the student must pursue other options.

At some colleges and universities, the president appoints an ombudsman from the faculty, even if a similar officer exists within the student government machinery. This officer usually is concerned with matters of student and faculty conduct and with issues that involve disputes between and among faculty and students. A faculty ombudsman may exercise considerable influence on the campus. In two university settings reviewed by this writer, one faculty ombudsman was a former academic dean and the other was a former academic vice president. Such officers are potentially well versed in campus procedures and due process, and they enjoy the respect of the faculty and the administration in matters involving academic disputes. A positive response to the student's petition by the faculty ombudsman usually carries the blessing of the campus president.

To take this issue to an extreme, it is important to discuss what possible options a student might consider if the internal approaches to her petition are negative. In this situation, the student may turn to a clergyman from her congregation who knows her well and is willing to serve as an intermediary and vouch for her good character. A church official is usually well regarded on a campus and will get the attention of its key officers, even in matters involving the assignment of a failing grade, especially if extenuating circumstances are involved. A second, and perhaps more serious, action is soliciting the assistance of an attorney. Although this might appear to be an extreme measure, some students, when they have not been able to receive what they consider a "fair" hearing on their petition, find it necessary to approach a community-based organization that provides free legal advice and services. If the student feels that the internal courses of action at the college or university have not served her adequately, or that campus officers dismissed her petition without a careful examination and review of the situation, then external legal pressure may be a final resort. In such cases, colleges and universities try to avoid unnecessary legal entanglements, especially where they must explain their procedures of student rights and due process in a public setting. Moreover, the possible exposure of a faculty member who might have acted improperly in assigning a failing grade can never be fully defensible.

As more and more low-income, first-generation students—especially from ethnic/racial backgrounds—attend colleges and universities, their encounters with the institutions' culture and policies will result in a different learning experience from that which takes place in the classroom. Institutions of higher education are a new environment for minority students. Parents, especially those who are immigrants and have never been to college, often do not understand campus requirements and how the academic machinery functions. Many students, even those from middle-class backgrounds, are not fully informed about written policies and guidelines on a campus that state a student's rights and procedures for due process. As more students become aware of such guidelines and test them, there is a cumulative value for students and institutions of higher education. This is still an area of considerable variation in dealing with matters such as cheating, implied student misconduct, and the assignment of grades by faculty. The more such matters are reviewed and added to our reservoir of knowledge, the better we will be able to craft guidelines and procedural steps to deal effectively with students' rights and due process on our campuses.

NOTES

1. The concept of *in loco parentis* has been used by many colleges and universities as a method for them to serve as a surrogate parent for students, especially those under the age of 21.

2. For the purposes of this chapter, the titles *dean of students* and other officers in a division of student services, such as *vice chancellors* or *vice presidents*, are used interchangeably to avoid repetition.

3. The term *Latino* is used to connote persons with family origins from Mexico, Puerto Rico, Cuba, Central and South America, and other Spanish-speaking parts of the world.

4. The terms *Raza* and *Latino* are used interchangeably to avoid repetition and include reference to men and women.

5. The term *ombudsman* is of Swedish derivation. It denotes an official appointed by a governing body to investigate individuals' complaints against a public authority.

SUGGESTED READINGS

Astin, A. "Student Involvement: A Development Theory for Higher Education." *Journal of College Student Personnel* (July 1984): 297–308.

Attinasi, L. "Getting In: Mexican Americans' Perceptions of University Attendance and the Implications for Freshman Year Persistence." *Journal of Higher Education* 60, no. 3 (1989): 247–277.

Cabrera, A. F., and A. Nora. "College Students' Perceptions of Prejudice and Discrimination and Their Feelings of Alienation." *Review of Education, Pedagogy, and Cultural Studies* 16 (1994): 387–409.

Ekeler, W. J., ed. *The Black Student's Guide to College Success*. Westport, CT: Greenwood Press, 1994.

Fleming, J. *Blacks in College*. San Francisco: Jossey-Bass, 1984.

Jalomo, R. "Latino Students in Transition: An Analysis of the First-Year Experience in Community College." Unpublished doctoral dissertation, Arizona State University, Tempe, 1995.

Kraemer, B. A. "The Academic and Social Integration of Hispanic Students into College." *Review of Higher Education* 20 (1997): 163–179.

Kuh, G., and E. Whitt. *The Invisible Tapestry: Culture in American Colleges and Universities*. ASHE-ERICD Higher Education Report.

Lowe, M. "Chicano Students' Perceptions of Their Community College Experience with Implications for Persistence: A Naturalistic Inquiry." Unpublished doctoral dissertation, Arizona State University, Tempe, 1989.

Nora, A., and A. F. Cabrera. "The Role of Perceptions of Prejudice and Discrimination in the Adjustment of Minority Students to College." *Journal of Higher Education* 67, no. 2 (1996): 119–148.

Olivas, M. *The Dilemma of Access: Minorities in Two-Year Colleges.* Washington, DC: Howard University Press, 1979.

Rendon, L. I., and R. O. Hope. *Educating a New Majority.* San Francisco: Jossey-Bass, 1996.

Tierney, W. *Building Communities of Difference: Higher Education in the 21st Century.* Westport, CT: Bergin & Garvey, 1993.

Tinto, V. *Leaving College: Rethinking the Causes and Cures of Student Attrition.* Chicago: University of Chicago Press, 1993.

Extracurricular Activities (Or, Life Beyond Classes and Studying)

VICKI A. LEAL
Doctoral fellow, Arizona State University

The overall number of Latinos enrolled in community colleges and four-year colleges or universities has increased over the past several years. However, even though Latinos boast the fastest growing population segment in the nation, our numbers are not yet adequately reflected in the total enrollments of individuals pursuing college and university degrees. Therefore, it is absolutely critical that each and every Latino student considering college after high school have every tool at his or her disposal to ensure that he or she stays in school and ultimately graduates.

Making the decision to attend college is a very important one. The time commitment is lengthy, and the money required to finance a college career can add up. Many researchers have studied the obstacles that students face as they pursue postsecondary education, including the largest obstacle of all, accessing adequate levels of financial assistance. Because college is one of the most expensive investments individuals will make in their lifetime, it is absolutely critical to make sure, once you've committed yourself to the college experience, that you stay in college and eventually graduate. For Latinos this is especially critical, as our overall contributions to society at large depend to a great extent on the levels of education we're able to successfully complete.

Over the years, educational researchers have identified a number of strategies that students can employ to ensure that they stay enrolled in and graduate from college. The three main ones involve:

1. creating support systems inside and outside of the college classroom; such a support system might include *familia, amigos,* and other individuals you come

to know through your involvement in college, whether academic (classes) or extracurricular (an activity that is in addition to your involvement directly in the classroom).

2. enrolling in a full load of undergraduate coursework (most institutions consider any amount over nine semester hours a full load, although twelve semester hours is the average); furthermore, financial aid requirements may dictate that you take a course load that exceeds the minimum full-time load of nine hours.

3. involving yourself in extracurricular activities (either academic, athletic, or social/cultural); these categories will be further expanded upon throughout this section.

The purpose of Steps 4 to 7 is to assist you in understanding how these retention strategies can enhance your chances of staying in school and successfully completing your college or university degree. Specifically, Step 8 will help you understand how you can involve yourself in the various extracurricular activities that exist on college and university campuses. While reading this Step you will come to understand how, through involvement in extracurricular activities, you can create additional support systems and keep busy while pursuing your goal of getting a college or university diploma. The first section of this Step defines and explains extracurricular activities and can assist you in finding out about the different types of activities that exist on campus. The rest of this Step describes the various types of extracurricular activities, including academic, athletic, and social/cultural ones. The discussion concludes with an overview of where and when to find information regarding extracurricular activities you may be interested in pursuing once you get to the college or university of your choice.

WHAT ARE EXTRACURRICULAR ACTIVITIES?

Extracurricular activities are those activities that students engage in *that are not part of the required curriculum* of the college or university. In other words, any activity a student engages in outside of the academic course schedule is considered extracurricular. Such activities can be informal or formal.

Informal extracurricular activities are those that are casually engaged in by the student. Informal activities happen only occasionally and are not planned. Examples include a game of pick-up basketball at the student recreational gymnasium, a casual game of sand volleyball outside a student dormitory, and participation in a salsa band. Informal activities aren't always athletic in nature, nor are they exclusively devoted to the arts (music, theater, or art). Rather, informal extracurricular activities are ones that a student chooses to participate in that are neither part of the required college curriculum, nor organized by college personnel, nor frequently and consistently engaged in by students.

In contrast, formal extracurricular activities are conducted in a consistent and clearly defined pattern. They take place consistently and on a pre-established, pre-planned schedule. Examples include membership in an academic organization such as a volunteer tutor society, an intramural athletic league (such as flag football, co-ed volleyball, and basketball), or a traditional or nontraditional campus fraternity or sorority. Many formal extracurricular activities focus specifically on the Latino culture. These might include nontraditional fraternities and sororities that devote their mission, goals, and organization to the Latino culture. Formal extracurricular activities usually encompass a wide variety of activities, events, and organizations. Generally, such extracurricular activities can be classified into three types: (1) academic, (2) athletic, and (3) social/cultural. Formal, academic ones are those activities, events, and organizations that fall under the academic umbrella—they are linked to colleges, departments, and majors within a college or university. Formal, athletic ones are those activities, events, and organizations that fall under the athletic umbrella—they are linked to sports and athletics in some way. Finally, formal, social/cultural extracurricular activities are those activities, events, and organizations that fall under the very broad umbrella encompassing events both social and cultural in nature. Thus, formal extracurricular activities are ones a student chooses to participate in that are not part of the required college curriculum. However, they are college approved, usually conducted in a consistent and clearly defined pattern, and take place on a pre-established, pre-planned schedule.

FORMAL, ACADEMIC EXTRACURRICULAR ACTIVITIES

Formal, academic extracurricular activities are linked to colleges, departments, and majors within a college or university. Here, *colleges* are defined as the separate entities or specialized schools on a given four-year university campus that provide students with choices of academic majors and minors. *Departments* are the smaller units or divisions that fall under the different colleges within a university, and *majors* are the designated fields of study in which a student specializes. For example, a student may attend a state university and be part of the College of Fine Arts, Department of Music, and major in string instruments.

Activities are specific actions that occur with varying frequency throughout the course of an academic semester or year. They are usually engaged in by members of a formal, academic organization. Examples of activities include tamales sales, fundraising drives, group volunteer projects, and other philanthropic (that is, charitable) activities. In contrast to activities, *events* are pre-planned, large-scale celebrations that generally occur annually (each year) and consistently as an extension of programming on behalf of a university's colleges, departments, and majors/minors. Examples of events include an annual foreign language day, an annual research day for undergraduate scholars, or an annual conference on multiculturalism.

Organizations are declared groups of students, or clubs, that affiliate themselves with specific colleges, departments, or majors/minors. Such organizations are usually established to provide students an opportunity to become involved with other individuals in similar programs and possessing similar interests. Many organizations under the umbrella of formal, academic extracurricular activities are national in charter; have formal mission statements, bylaws, and expressly stated goals; and in some instances require members to maintain a certain grade point average. An organization that requires its members to have exemplary grade point averages (3.5 or above) is usually referred to as honorary. Most colleges use the four-point system (i.e., A = 4, B = 3, C = 2 and D = 1). Most colleges within universities provide students with the opportunity to become members of these honorary academic organizations. Examples of such organizations include Sigma Tau Sigma (members include volunteer, academic tutors), Phi Beta Kappa (members may or may not be required to maintain a certain grade point average), and MACS (a Macintosh computer–centered organization for individuals possessing a high degree of interest in the world of technology).

Chartered and Nonchartered Organizations

Organizations falling under the category of formal, academic extracurricular activities are either chartered or nonchartered. Chartered organizations are officially recognized by the college or university where they are located. Once an organization has been chartered by the institution, it becomes officially recognized by the institution's student activities office (similar offices may have different names on different campuses). Official recognition and chartering usually mean that an organization can (1) qualify to receive funding through the university's student fees, (2) establish a mailbox within the student activities area of the Student Union (a centrally located building on campus that offers space for many student services and activities), and (3) utilize Student Union space for the organization's meetings (nonchartered organizations may pay a hefty fee to do so). An example of a chartered organization is the Spanish club. By contrast, nonchartered, formal academic extracurricular organizations are not chartered by the college or university. As such, they do not qualify for the benefits that chartered organizations enjoy. An example of a nonchartered organization is MEChA (Movimiento Estudiantil Chicano/a de Aztlan). Some reasons for organizations choosing not to charter are addressed later in this section.

Funding

Funding for formal, academic extracurricular activities usually is received by the organization as a result of going through the chartering process. Organizations officially chartered by the university become eligible for funding collected from student fees (that is, fees all students must pay at the time of registering to take courses). The amount of funding an organization receives is usually determined through a process referred to as the student fee allocation process. This is a lengthy but democratic process that involves only students. In addition to student fees, organizations may collect dues from their members as well as conduct fundraising efforts. Nonchartered organizations do not qualify for student fee monies. These organizations must depend solely on membership dues and/or fundraising. Thus, it may be financially beneficial for organizations to be chartered by the college or university in order to become eligible for student fee dollars.

Expectations and Time Commitment

Organizational expectations of formal, academic extracurricular activities vary. Depending on the student's depth of involvement in an organization, his or her time commitment and responsibilities of membership will vary. The time devoted to an organization can range from very minimal to extremely extensive. The mission, purpose, and goals of an organization; the frequency of meetings; and the student's role within the organization are the primary elements that determine the amount of time he or she spends as a member of that organization. (First-year students should spend a majority of their time on academic studies and minimal time on extracurricular activities.) If the organization is service oriented (in other words, it provides volunteer or other types of services, such as the volunteer tutor society mentioned earlier), the time spent will be considerably greater than if the organization is not service oriented. Organizations that meet weekly take up more time than organizations that meet monthly. Finally, student members who assume a leadership position within an organization usually take on a larger workload than the other members. Again, it is recommended that students wait to take on leadership roles until their second year of college.

Advantages and Disadvantages of Involvement and Membership

The benefits of involvement in extracurricular organizations include, but are not limited to, the following:

- establishing new and lasting networks of friendship,
- creating a busy schedule so that "dead time" is kept to a minimum,
- creating opportunities to release stress and tension,
- establishing a sense of ownership of or belonging to a specific group,
- creating a connection to the university or college, and
- establishing experiences outside the classroom that can enhance a resumé.

There are distinct disadvantages for individuals choosing involvement in formal, academic extracurricular activities:

- becoming overwhelmed with too many commitments,
- lacking adequate time management skills, and
- assuming too much responsibility prior to establishing a strong academic record (grade point average).

There are alternatives to formal, academic extracurricular activities. Students also have the option of participating in athletics (organized, club, and intramural) and social/cultural activities.

ATHLETIC EXTRACURRICULAR ACTIVITIES

Athletic extracurricular activities provide the student with three options: organized athletics, club sports, and intramurals. Each option possesses distinct features that may be attractive to students looking for extracurricular involvement and desiring to pursue athletics.

Organized, athletic extracurricular activities are the varsity sports featured on most college and university campuses, regardless of size, and sanctioned by the National Collegiate Athletic Association (NCAA). Club sports resemble organized, NCAA-sanctioned athletics, as they too are intercollegiate in nature (club sports teams engage in competition with other colleges and universities). Club sports are featured on most college and university campuses, although the option of participation in these sports may not be available at all colleges. However, club sports are not sanctioned by the NCAA and usually do not receive the level of funding that formal, NCAA-sanctioned varsity athletics enjoy.

In contrast to organized and club sports, most campuses feature intramural athletics. These are informal, athletic leagues of play for any number of different sports. Intramurals are not sanctioned by the NCAA, nor do they have club sport status. Rather, intramurals are recreational leagues of varying skill level open to any and all registered students in attendance at a college or university. Intramurals are usually administered through the campus's student recreation complex and, for a slight participation fee, enable students to engage in interleague play with and against other college or university students.

Supporting Organized, Athletic Extracurricular Activities

Many colleges and universities offer opportunities for participation in varsity athletics. Although the majority of students do not participate in organized, varsity athletics, there are plenty of spectator opportunities. Indeed, attending the home games, matches, and meets of the various men's and women's varsity sports teams can provide another opportunity for students to become involved in extracurricular activities.

Many colleges and universities organize "theme" celebrations, such as homecoming, around varsity athletics such as football. Additionally, during the winter months most colleges provide opportunities for students to attend men's and women's basketball, men's wrestling, and (at larger or different types of colleges, depending on location) hockey and water polo. Whereas football season and homecoming occur during the fall semester, the spring semester brings track and field events, as well as baseball. Other sports—such as cross country, tennis, and gymnastics—also provide spectator opportunities for students looking to become more involved in their college and university while also supporting their home teams.

At some colleges and universities, students are able to attend sporting events for free or at a reduced cost. This is an inexpensive source of entertainment. The benefits of supporting varsity athletics include establishing additional friendships and getting to know new or different groups of students.

Club Sports and Intramural Athletics

Both club sports and intramural athletics fall under athletic extracurricular activities. Students interested in maintaining involvement in sports but unable to compete at the varsity level have the opportunity to participate in both club sports and intramural athletics.

Club sports generally include soccer, rugby, and men's volleyball, although the options may vary from campus to campus. Club sports exist for both men and women and tend to not be as time consuming as organized, NCAA-sanctioned athletics. Club sports do not have the level of organization that organized athletics have. Time spent on practicing may be greater than it is for intramurals but much less than for organized athletics, depending on the school, the sport, and the philosophy and attitude of people involved. Students interested in pursuing club sport opportunities should consult either the university's student activities area or the student recreation complex.

Students also have the opportunity for participation in intramural athletics. Because this endeavor is relatively inexpensive and open to the masses of students enrolled in colleges and universities, it is by far the most popular and heavily utilized of all the athletic extracurricular activities.

Intramural athletics include, but are not limited to, flag football, basketball, softball, volleyball, racquet ball, and tennis. Intramural leagues include men's, women's, and co-ed teams playing at the beginner, intermediate, and advanced levels in either recreational or competitive leagues. The cost for participation in intramural athletics is minimal, adding to its popularity. You can form a team, provided you have enough players, and have fun selecting a team name that represents your group character, like Los Picosos, "the hot ones." Usually the time commitment for participation in intramural athletics is small. In fact, many academic advisors and counselors recommend participation in intramurals in order to fulfill students' health and exercise needs in addition to meeting new people and making new friends. Intramurals also provide a great opportunity to release stress and maintain a healthy balance between school studies and "down time."

Finally, there are alternatives to athletic extracurricular activities and academic extracurricular activities. Students also have the option of participating in social/cultural extracurricular activities.

SOCIAL/CULTURAL EXTRACURRICULAR ACTIVITIES

Social/cultural activities, events, and organizations are very broadly defined, as most of what college students participate in outside of class falls under this heading. Social activities are those activities, events, and organizations that exist on most college campuses and can be related to many interests, majors/minors, or clubs and organizations. Examples include involvement in traditional or nontraditional sororities for women and fraternities for men, participation in a campus glee club (a singing group), or involvement with a campus's radio station (note: not all campuses have radio stations). Cultural activities are usually related to specific cultural groups, offices, or centers on a campus. Activities, events, or organizations that have in their mission and make-up a focus on a specific culture, such as Latino/Hispanic, African American, Asian American, Native American, or Women's Culture, serve as examples of cultural extracurricular activities. These might also include groups like MEChA (Movimiento Estudiantil Chicano/a de Aztlan), LULAC (League of United Latin American Citizens), and UMAS (United Mexican-American Students). Social/cultural extracurricular activities share some characteristics with both academic and athletic extracurricular activities, but they also differ in a few ways.

Like the other activities, social/cultural activities may require that students maintain a certain grade point average in order to participate and/or hold office within such organizations. Specifically, both traditional and nontraditional sororities and fraternities may require their members to maintain a minimum grade point average of 2.0. Like the other extracurricular activities, social/cultural organizations may or may not be chartered by the college or university where they are located. As stated previously, an organization's funding may be dependent on campus chartering; organizations not officially chartered by the institution may not receive monies through the student fee allocation process. Choosing not to charter with the institution may be intentional. Many student organizations affiliated with and possessing cultural status, such as MEChA, may decide that not being chartered with the institution provides them with more freedom to act politically and with regard to the mission and goals of their organization.

Finally, expectations and time commitment with regard to social/cultural activities are dependent on the mission, purpose, and goals of an organization; the frequency of organizational meetings; and the student's role within the organization. These primary elements determine the amount of time a student spends as a member of an organization.

The biggest difference between (1) some of the academic and athletic extracurricular activities and (2) the social/cultural activities is the deep commitment and passion that many students have regarding their involvement with social/cultural events, activities, and organizations. This is not to suggest that the academic and athletic extracurricular activities don't inspire such commitment and passion. However, the point being made is that in many cases students' involvement in social/cultural extracurricular activities is the primary force—outside of their studies—that drives, enhances, and complements their college or university experience. (For example, read Polly Baca's vignette of "How I Did It" in Part III.) This is especially true if the student chooses to participate in one of the traditional or nontraditional sororities or fraternities. In fact, the student's participation in other academic and athletic extracurricular activities may occur as a result of participating in social/cultural extracurricular activities. For example, an intramural basketball team may consist entirely of members of an all-Latina sorority. As with the other extracurricular activities, there are both advantages and disadvantages regarding participation in social/cultural activities.

FINDING INFORMATION

As mentioned throughout this step, involvement in extracurricular activities can both enhance a student's opportunities for academic success and retention as well as provide the student with additional support systems throughout his or her time spent in college or at a university. These potential benefits make it very important to find out more about involvement in extracurricular activities.

When can I find out about the different types of extracurricular activities on my campus? There are several options. These include requesting information from the school, attending informational sessions during orientation, and attending campus fairs.

You can write to your college or university and request that a packet of information be sent to you that discusses extracurricular activities in detail. If you have access to a computer and the Internet, look up the college or university Web page. If you do not own a personal computer, you may visit your local library and access the Internet on a computer there; it is free of charge and open for use to the general public. The admissions office is a good place to start. You may also want to contact the student activities office at your college or university.

When you attend you college or university orientation (usually during the summer prior to the first fall that you begin classes), there should be informational sessions about extracurricular activities. If you take note of certain ones that interest you during orientation, you will be prepared to look them up in the fall.

When you arrive on campus, especially at the beginning of each fall semester, most colleges and universities feature fairs to introduce activities, events, and organizations that exist on campus. At most campus fairs, organizations have separate booths staffed by members and featuring literature that explains their goals and activities. It is an especially good idea for you to attend campus fairs because you can find a lot of information regarding extracurricular activities from many organizations at one place and time.

Where can I go and who do I contact to get more information on academic, athletic, and social/cultural extracurricular activities? You should first decide which type of extracurricular activity you are interested in pursuing and then contact the appropriate department, office, or organization. Please consult your college or university phone directory, or campus directory, for additional information and phone numbers. The following table shows you how to get started.

Type of Activity	Department/Office/Organization
Academic	Contact the office of student activities in the Student Union, or the specific academic department of the organization.
Athletic	Contact the office of student activities in the Student Union, or the intercollegiate athletics department, or the student recreation complex.
Social/Cultural	Contact the office of student activities in the Student Union, or any number of organizations, including the different cultural centers that may exist on campus. For sororities and fraternities, the student activities office should be able to provide assistance and information.

Where can I go and who do I contact to get more information on activities, events, programs, and places that deal specifically with Latino issues? If you have a special interest in Latino-focused programming and places on campus, you should consult the campus directory and determine if you are looking for an academically focused program or a social/cultural program. Next, if you are attempting to locate, for example, a Hispanic Studies department, you should begin your search by consulting the various academic departments within the College of Arts and Sciences. If you are attempting to find out if a Latino cultural center exists on the campus, the most helpful contact would be the student activities office. More and more campuses are formally establishing such centers with Latino staff. These centers are separate and different from Chicano or Puerto Rican Studies.

Such types of activities, events, programs, and places provide the Latino student with unique opportunities for cultural enrichment, familiarity, support, and a sense of family or a "home away from home." For other students, Latino-focused activities, events, programs, and places promote intellectual growth, understanding, and involvement with students different from themselves. Diverse campus centers, programming, and departments enable all students to enhance the culture and climate of their college and university campuses.

Finally, if you seek additional information regarding any of the topics discussed here and if you have access to a computer and the Internet, you can consult the Web page or home page of almost any college or university. Most of the information given here should be available and easily accessible on the Internet. If you don't have a computer at home, go to your local library. It has computers that you can use at no cost. All you need is a library card, which is easy to obtain and free of charge.

PART III

"How I Did It"

LEONARD A. VALVERDE

Leonard A. Valverde has been a vice president for academic affairs, a graduate dean, a college dean, and a professor at the university level. He also has held other leadership roles in higher education as well as in the public schools, grades K to 12. He is a second-generation Mexican American, born in East Los Angeles, and the first in his family to go to college. Without a college education, he would not have been able to study for a doctorate and ultimately would not have been able to become an academic professional.

My elementary school experience was typical of the times (1950s) and representative of the kind of education most Mexican Americans in California and the Southwest were getting—or, to be more accurate, not getting. That is to say, we were told in various ways by many people (teachers, business people, elected officials) that we were not smart and that if we finished high school, we would be nothing more than factory workers. The words *college* and *professional* were not known to my fellow students and me. Thus, we did not know that such places like colleges or universities and jobs like lawyers and chief executive officers existed. To this day I do not know how I learned to read, but I do know that I was not taught how to read or spell well in school. Thus, up to and in my junior high school years I had poor language skills and very low self-esteem. About the only two things I felt good about were math and speaking publicly to groups. Doing math and speaking in public came naturally to me; I was at ease doing both.

Then at an open house night during my seventh grade year, my parents, particularly my father, asked a simple question that was to turn my educational experience around and ultimately would enable me to go to college. The junior high school had an honor society for boys and girls. For the boys the honor society was called Knights and Squires. You could join during the middle part of your eighth grade year. The honor society members wore red sweaters and the sweaters had a Knights emblem on the front left side. On this open house night my parents and I were walking on the second floor of the main building, going to one of my classrooms to meet one of my teachers. My parents asked me who these boys were. I explained to them who they were. My father then asked me if I was going to be a Knight. I replied that I did not feel I could be one. He asked simply, "Why not?" How could I say to my father that after all my years in school, I had come to believe I was a dummy! Instead I said nothing. However, I valued highly my father's view of me and his belief in me. So what I decided after that night was to try, to study hard to get good grades, so I might become a Knight—not so much for me, but for my father and mother. To my surprise, after long hours of studying, over many months, I did earn good grades during my eighth grade year and did become a member of the honor society.

As I think back about this, I am somewhat amazed. For the first seven years of my schooling (from age 5), I came to believe I was a dummy. But after I decided I would work hard to prove my parents' belief in my ability, after I had set a goal for myself, I was successful! I was able to overcome bad teaching from my first seven years and do well. I was too young to understand then that I was not stupid, that most of the teachers had come to accept the stereotype, "Mexicans don't want to or can't learn. So don't expect anything from them." I did not know that at the time I was ignoring the perception that my teachers had caused me to disbelieve in myself. I proved that Mexicans could not only learn but excel, if we decided to do so.

In high school, because of my junior high school grades and taking a typing class, I was placed in a college track. Even though I worked hard and did get good grades in college preparatory courses while in high school, I did not believe I would go to college. The high school counselors did not talk to me or many of my classmates about going to college. They did not tell me what I had to do to apply for college. College recruiters did not come to my high school. And when it came time to test the seniors for after-high-school employment, I was not scheduled for the ACT or SAT test. Instead I was tested for hand dexterity in the high school cafeteria. When I graduated from high school, I decided to join the Navy. When my mother, who did not finish high school, learned of what I was going to do, she encouraged me to attend the local junior college. Again, my mother, as my father earlier, believed in me. Because the local junior college was very inexpensive and had open admission (i.e., no SAT score required), I was able to live at home, drive to college, and work part-time, so I enrolled.

My years at the junior college were great. For the first time, I was excited about learning and competing. I taught myself how to succeed in college. First, I learned that it did not matter how intelligent you were as measured on an IQ test or a national examination, what your grade point average in high school was, or what high school you attended. Instead, I learned that in order to be successful in college you had to believe in yourself, first above all. Second, you had to put in many hours in your studies (i.e., take notes, read the textbooks more than once, review your class notes, go over your textbook notes). Third, I had to sacrifice Friday nights and weekends to work on my studies. I learned to organize my time and make my studies a high priority. I spent many hours in the library during the day, between classes, at night, on weekends, and during holidays. Fourth, I was stimulated by and enjoyed taking interesting courses such as cultural anthropology, astronomy, philosophy, and world literature.

I earned an Associate of Arts degree from the junior college and transferred to a nearby four-year university. During my university study I learned that believing in yourself ("I can do it, and I can do it well") and being organized paid off in other ways. Because I had taught myself to take copious notes in class, other students wanted to copy my notes. I let them do this for a price. Also, my confidence had grown to a point that I was no longer satisfied to take required classes. Now I wanted to take courses with the most difficult professors, those instructors whom most students wanted to avoid. I enrolled in these faculty members' classes and in so doing was recognized by one of them. This faculty member had served in World War II with the famous tank commander General George Patton. The professor called me into his office one day to say two things. One, I had gotten the highest score ever on one of his tests. Later he made this fact known to the class members. (My class notes now were in real demand.) Two, he encouraged me to think about going for a master's degree in history after I earned my baccalaureate degree.

This high praise and recommendation by a well-known "hard" professor told me not only that I could complete an undergraduate program of study, but that I could do it better than most students. I did get my B.A. degree and decided to become a public school teacher. I wanted to return to schools in East Los Angeles so I could encourage other Mexican American students to go to college. I taught mathematics and, without formal training in English as a second language, also taught math to non-English speaking students.

After about three years of teaching, I did start a master's program and earned all A's while in the program. I had learned to organize my time, be focused, and be disciplined (i.e., stay organized and stick to my schedule of study). But most important, I believed in myself. Before completing my Master's program of study, I was identified because of my outstanding work and selected to participate in an interdisciplinary doctoral studies program with a Ford Foundation fellowship. The competition for the fellowship was national. By applying what I had come to learn on my own during my undergraduate and graduate programs, I was recognized by my professors in the doctoral program as a bright fellow and recommended for an assistant professor's position in Texas. I interviewed and was selected. What I learned during my doctoral studies was to set goals and to identify some purposes. For example, (a goal) in which courses did I want to earn a grade of A, and (a purpose) what in particular did I want to learn from either a course or a professor? I set these goals at the beginning of the semester. I found that courses in business, religion, English, and sociology were fascinating and stimulating. I learned more about (1) how people think about problems and solve such problems, than about (2) subject matter or class content.

Epilogue: Even though I was not encouraged by my schoolteachers at all grade levels to think about attending college, through self-determination and persistence I discovered I could be very successful in college. By starting in an open enrollment community college and without financial assistance, I ended up with a terminal degree. All this college study permitted me to be a professor and academic administrator. My work has taken me around the world to observe, experience, and learn firsthand what I could never have imagined. I am extremely pleased to say that my son and daughter have just completed their college education, and as a result they should have a much better life and more income than I or my wife, who is also a college-educated person.

EDUARDO J. PADRÓN

Eduardo Padrón is district president of Miami-Dade Community College. He was recognized by President Clinton as "one of America's outstanding educators." He has served on the Board of Trustees of the College Board; as chair of the Hispanic Association of Colleges and Universities; on the Board of Directors of the American Council on Education; on the Editorial Board of *The Hispanic Outlook in Higher Education*; and on the Executive Advisory Board of the *Harvard Journal of Hispanic Policy*.

I came to the United States from Cuba when I was 14 years of age. My parents were prohibited from leaving Cuba at the time, so my younger brother and I came into the care of friends of my family living in Miami.

To say that everything was overwhelming would be an understatement. I could not speak English, and American culture was indeed a shock. Most important, my new school, Miami Senior High, conducted all its classes in English, presenting me with an enormous challenge each day. My confidence was shaken, and only the help of teachers and counselors who cared for my development kept me on track. In my most difficult moments I remembered my mother's words: "The three most important things are education, education, and education." Although she never finished the third grade in Cuba, she had the wisdom to know what she had missed.

From Miami Senior High I enrolled at Miami-Dade Community College. There, my doubts about achieving a worthwhile career only intensified. I worked at several part-time jobs to support myself and pay college bills, all the while trying to get my feet on the ground academically. I can point to two experiences that helped me turn the corner and believe in myself.

The first was meeting Professor Joseph Leon. He literally went out of his way for me, providing transportation to and from college. We reviewed assignments and talked about life. His care made all the difference in the world. Second, as my English improved, I ventured into an extracurricular club activity. I became an officer of the club and began to discover that I had leadership ability. Instead of being a shy teenager struggling with the English language, now I was standing at a microphone expressing my views and expanding my horizons. It had a profound effect on me. My doubts were disappearing and I began to believe in myself and my abilities.

This transformation was all about small victories. I realized then, as I do now, that a mountain cannot be climbed with one giant step. I began to set realistic goals and to take the small and practical steps that would bring me closer to my goals. I began to make important connections with my peers, and together we organized informal study groups. All of us benefited from the simple pooling of our questions and intelligence, not to mention that it transformed a sometimes tedious chore into an enjoyable social experience.

Financing my education remained problematic. I continued to work at several jobs, but need-based scholarships simply were not available anywhere near the level they are today. I continued to take inspiration from my parents' encouragement and focused intently on qualifying for merit-based scholarship funds. My efforts proved successful. I completed my A.A. degree at Miami-Dade and then transferred to Florida Atlantic University, where I graduated summa cum laude (i.e., with highest academic honors) and was named valedictorian of my graduating class. I continued my studies at the University of Florida, where I received my master's and Ph.D. degrees in economics.

I cite these accomplishments because I once doubted that any of this was possible. I wondered how in the world I would overcome the fact that many obstacles placed limits on my dreams.

MARI-LUCI JARAMILLO

Mari-Luci Jaramillo has served in a wide variety of leadership positions. In 1955 she started her career as an elementary school teacher and quickly became the language arts supervisor for an entire county school system. At the University of New Mexico, from 1964 to 1987, she was a department chair and associate dean, assistant to the president and vice president for student affairs. From 1987 to 1993 she was an assistant vice president for the Educational Testing Service. She served as U.S. ambassador to the Republic of Honduras from 1977 to 1980, and from 1993 to 1995 she was deputy assistant secretary of defense for Latin America. Also, she has been a board member of the Thomas Rivera Policy Center, the Children's Television Workshop, and the Hispanic Scholarship Fund.

Although we were a very poor Hispanic family in Las Vegas, New Mexico, I went through my high school years in the 1950s without any traumas. I was known as a good student both by my friends and teachers because I was quiet and well mannered. In other words, I didn't make any waves.

I was so naïve that up to graduation night I did not know if I was going to go to college. And, mind you, I had attended a laboratory school at New Mexico Highlands University! At the time we had no counselors, no scholarships, no support for such ventures. But today, even with all these conditions, there are still many Latino students who are not prepared to take advantage of these opportunities due to lack of knowledge about such programs. Many students have not taken Advanced Placement (AP) courses (AP courses are offered in only a select few high schools) when they could have; some have not taken enough science and math courses even when they are talented in these fields. Preparation for success in college really begins much earlier than high school. But it is never too late to study hard and become a good student. All one has to do is try hard and dedicate quality time to the effort.

I attended Las Vegas High School, and although I cleaned homes for money to help my family, I excelled as a student. I loved studying, mostly to please my teachers and my autocratic, demanding dad. Some of my friends talked about going to college, but I knew I could not afford it and it was out of the question. But the night I graduated, my whole world turned around. It was a pivotal point in my life. I was the recipient of the five awards given that night! My father was so impressed that he promised to give me $100 to partially help me enroll for one semester. It was not much, but what a jump-start it was for me. So who influenced me to go to college? A dad who had a fourth-grade education is certainly to be counted among the many.

During your college years there are usually many, many people who influence you and keep egging you on toward success. Sometimes their help is so subtle that you are not aware of it until years later. I was blessed in having good teachers in my early schooling, so I was pretty well prepared for college. But there were always the poverty issues that I had to contend with. We were extremely poor and its effects were always there. But the angels come from somewhere. One was my wonderful high school English teacher, Ms. Nell Doherty, who kept up with me as a college student at New Mexico Highlands University. When she found out I would have to drop out during my last semester because I had no money for tuition, she volunteered to lend me $300 to finish. She took a risk and it paid off. Within six months I had graduated, gone to work, and repaid the loan in full!

There was also Mr. Blas Lopez, the only U.S.-born Spanish-speaking person I ever had as a professor who cheered me on as being a brilliant woman. Though I did not believe him, his remarks certainly boosted my ego. Because there were no counselors, one seldom heard anything from the professors about personal matters. But this professor took my student life seriously and even advised me not to marry too young. He urged me to first get my degree and then marry. But when one is young, sometimes good advice goes unheeded. Because I did not listen, I had to work much harder later on.

My extended family and friends supported me with encouragement and praise for my good grades. They were also poor, so I never received financial help from them, but to this day I believe their moral support helped more than anything else did.

However, I owe most everything to my wonderful mother. She always created an environment so I could study, even after I was married and had children. I could not have done it without her caring ways. My father, on the other hand, was my model of an active learner. He was self-educated and always reading. My parents were not formally educated, but in their own very different ways they became a winning combination to spur me on.

Upon arrival at New Mexico Highlands University, I quickly selected education as my major. Not knowing what I wanted to do for a living, I knew I wanted a job that would get me out of poverty. Teaching satisfied my criteria of getting a well-paying job as soon as I graduated. The idea of becoming a teacher became my goal, for which I studied day and night for several years. Luckily for me and the children, I loved what the career entailed and I later became a passionate teacher. Perhaps my vision in selecting education as a major was unduly influenced because at the time no one tried to encourage economically poor students to study for other careers. There were lots of closed doors for Latinos and other people of color in those days. However, I am delighted I chose to become a teacher. That profession has been a springboard for the many things I have done with my life.

Recalling my years in college so very long ago has been both rewarding and fun. I now realize that although I worked hard during those crucial years, they were some of the best ones of my life. Those experiences gave me a strong foundation to help me later on in my various careers. Any new road I took was always based on something I had learned in college, either directly or indirectly. Internalizing your college experiences is like having a private tutor with you at your beck and call—almost like a guardian angel sitting on your shoulder ready to be called to work.

Confidence is a very necessary ingredient for success in college, but I have a mixed report on my confidence level. I was extremely confident when it came to my studies because I had always been a good student rewarded with good grades and lots of pats on the back. I thought college would be the same, but it was much harder and I had to study twice as hard to keep my top rank when I was competing in a much larger arena.

Another component of my confidence was my intense, passionate pride in my Mexican American heritage, in spite of the fact that Mexicans were not especially well liked in the area where I grew up. I was so very proud of the beautiful Spanish language, and even though we were punished for speaking it in school, I knew mine was better than average in my group and I used it whenever I possibly could. My father, a Mexican from Durango, Mexico, had instilled in his children the belief that Mexico is a great country with a beautiful culture, outstanding art and music, and a proud history.

But on the other hand, my confidence was nil when it came to my looks. I was the tallest and skinniest Mexican American girl in school, with ugly teeth that had needed correcting long ago, but by now it was too late. My lower bite was longer than my upper, so I constantly used my hand to cover my mouth and not display my unattractive smile. Even though I had a well-developed and mischievous sense of humor and was always making people laugh, I was teased unmercifully and constantly about my looks. To add insult to injury, I was very timid and withdrawn and would seldom volunteer an opinion unless asked. My clothes were all hand-me-downs that seldom did me justice—to say nothing of my shoes, which never fit because my feet grew way ahead of me. My mother often made many of my skirts from flour sacks with funny prints. My blouses had drawstrings so I could puff the sleeves and make it look like I had a little flesh on my arms. There were also pieces of material wadded up to make me appear as though I was blossoming!

Although I was well liked and had many friends, I did not have the material things others had. I did not have access to a car so I had to walk everywhere, carrying large stacks of books, whether it was a hot or cold day. I did not have the money needed for either books or supplies, so I had to find ways around that problem. Nor did I have the funds for all the extras that are so necessary in a college setting. Thus, lack of money was a barrier to my future success, or so it seemed at the time. Another apparently limiting factor was that I was not the slightest bit athletic, which all the popular girls seemed to be (or was it that they looked cute in their shorts and I looked like a stick?). I definitely was not into sports, although I could talk up the scores with the best of them. Participating in sports seemed to make students popular and placed them at the center of cliques. I soon became aware that to be a leader I would have to shine in the areas in which I was talented and try to ignore those areas in which I could do little to improve because they were beyond my control. I could not let these matters erode my confidence.

I had strong study habits that I acquired in high school, so later I simply upgraded them. A master juggler is what I became during my college days. No, I did not throw balls up in the air, but I did learn to juggle my time to the minute in order to accomplish all I wanted to. I had several outside jobs; my studies, which always included a full load of credits so I could graduate as early as possible; and my family. My blessed mother and grandmother were there to help with the family component. What a godsend extended families were when I was a young person! But the jobs and my studies were my responsibility alone, so I had to find a way to manage my time wisely. That is usually very hard for a young person to do, and I had to work at it seriously.

Another skill I was able to master was note taking, whether for lecture notes or assigned reading. I would rewrite my notes completely and very carefully as soon as I could. I would then use them while tutoring other students, which helped me learn the material all the better. That is a good way to get depth in your knowledge base.

In looking back at how I financed my education, it almost seems impossible that the skinny girl with no money would even think it could be done. I was working in my father's shoe shop and cleaning homes when I started college. Also, I worked in a parachute factory for several months. I didn't know how to sew all that well, so I constantly prayed that the parachutes I sewed would never be used. I had to balance those activities that earned me a little money with my new responsibilities as a student. And as if that weren't enough of a heavy load, I married at the end of my freshman year and became a mother of three youngsters in short order, so money was extremely tight. I could not have survived financially if I had not learned how to manage every minute of my waking hours. But God was with me and I did!

Another way I helped reduce my schooling expenses was to not buy books. That is not as simple as it sounds. I became a master at finding out ahead of time what text was to be required for a given class and quickly checked it out of libraries or asked professors to place a copy on the reserved shelves. I would find out when books were to be returned and was always able to get them when needed. It didn't hurt that I became close friends with the librarians. (Now I have told you all the trade secrets, but you will still have to develop some of your own and pass them on to others.)

My system to read the textbooks was very rewarding. When a friend would buy a book, I would promise to read it carefully, outline it, and on the margins write questions the professors might ask on a future test. These notes became great study aids, and I even tutored my friends using them. Friends thought I could psych out the professors, but I really couldn't. Can you imagine how much I learned while doing this? And it did not cost me a penny.

I had managed to turn poverty around and use the skills I learned fending it away. My mother had used the bartering system by offering her work for a piece of meat or something else the family needed. I was a keen observer and followed her example. It worked like magic; still does. Discover what special talent you have and exchange it for what you need. The only price involved is hard work.

I have learned lots in these many years since I graduated from college. I know that supportive parents and friends are very important, but there are some nitty-gritty things that you alone are responsible for. I have decided to list some suggestions that may be crucial to your success.

First and foremost, believe in yourself. You must tell yourself that you can do whatever you propose to do. In addition, do it to the very best of your abilities. *Si se puede* when you give it your all. Be true to yourself.

Be realistic and give yourself the proper amount of time to pursue your studies and graduate in a timely fashion. But work hard and take advantage of every opportunity that arises to shorten the time it will take to get your diploma. Are there special courses you can take? Are there workshops? Would you be allowed to take an extra class? Look around. Don't short-change yourself from a good solid education, but don't waste precious time that you could use to start working on an advanced degree or to go into your chosen field of work.

Develop every skill needed to succeed in college to the utmost. Not only will they help you in school, but the majority of those skills are needed in the work force also. Who ever heard about being late to work? Not doing your best work and not handed in on time? That is what the work world is about, so start learning early and internalize those skills. But your most important skill is reading. Practice your reading. Do you know how to speed-read? Skim with deep understanding? And so on. You get the picture.

Associate with people a heck of a lot smarter than you. When possible, make those people your best friends. Think of all the informal learning that is going on when you are with them. It is definitely one of the best ways to learn. Just remember that pretty soon you will be as smart as they are.

When there is something you need to know, do not be afraid to ask questions until you understand the situation. This does not have to be limited to asking the professors. Ask anyone who you think might know. Often, all you need is an inkling to get on the right track and go off on your own.

Read and reread your assignments. Never assume you know everything. There is always more to truly understanding a problem. Remember, depth in knowledge is crucial.

Visit your counselor often and before there is a problem. Become friends with him or her. If possible, become acquainted with several counselors. Never be satisfied with just one advisor's opinion. Check around and compare what you are told with what other students are being advised. Advisors can make mistakes too, you know. Seek the best information you can from a variety of sources.

Participate in extracurricular activities, but be careful you do not overdo it. They should not interfere with your studies or other responsibilities. But remember, there is much learning in these activities and you should take advantage of them.

Keep adding new members to your support groups, but never forget all the people who have helped you along the way. Call them for advice or just to chat occasionally. Remember that probably you are in a more favorable position because of their support.

Hindsight is such a help to understanding fully. I was very poor growing up. Living in a small, dark adobe hut with no running water was no fun. Not having access to health services or adequate food started me on the road to some health problems, like losing all my teeth by age 37. Those are serious setbacks, but we must have the drive to move past them. By the time I was in college, my life was a little better but not by much. But by then I was rich in spirit and knew I would graduate.

There are many Latino students today who face some of the same obstacles that stood in my way. But I know that with perseverance and dedication one can get a college degree even when faced with lots of dilemmas. My wish is that no one be satisfied with simply racing through college and not taking advantage of studying really hard and learning as much as one possibly can. Take advantage of study groups; attend extra lectures; go to conferences to begin networking but more important to learn more about your field; make friends with knowledgeable people wherever you are; and above all, motivate others to follow in your footsteps.

May your college days be as fruitful as mine—and do not forget to smell the roses on your way to success.

RONALD T. VERA

Ronald T. Vera graduated from the UCLA Law School and worked for the Mexican American Legal Defense and Education Fund at its San Francisco office. He is in private law practice and providing civic service by serving on boards, for example, the Claremont Hospital Board.

The question of how one person "made it through college" may be difficult to answer inasmuch as one student's travails may be another student's bounty or steppingstone for success in college. For me, the better question is *what mistakes not to make in college.* To put things in perspective, let me also add that I was a first-generation college student, the oldest of five brothers, and neither of my parents graduated from high school, not for lack of desire but lack of money, World War II, and pressing family concerns. Further, the question of doing well in college means more than just doing well academically or matriculating in four years. Rather, as a first-generation college student, the college experience for me conjured the ability to partake in the full enjoyment of the educational milieu socially, culturally, and academically.

For example, the student who delves straight ahead, taking the maximum units, and who graduates in three years but never ventures to explore the university art museum, join a club, or encounter a student outside of one's major may not view college in the same way as the student who realizes his or her initial major is a mistake, meets students from other cultures and places, or opts to take a semester off to travel or study abroad. Granted, not every student can partake in these adventures. For many students, the realities of college are such that they have to juggle family demands, work at a part-time job or complete course requirements after transferring from a two-year college in order to receive the next promotion. It becomes a task-oriented education bereft of social or cultural aspects. Although this student may be successful, what I speak of here is somewhat different. To be blunt, I happened to make it into college because of an initial failure. Let me explain.

There is one day that comes to mind vividly about my college experience. It was my first year in college, at one of California's state colleges, and I was enrolled as a freshman civil engineering major taking a full academic load with courses in calculus, organic chemistry, and strength of materials. My parents had steered me into a local state college because it was inexpensive and close to home. I knew nothing about majors and my parents less so. Even though they valued education, neither one had much experience to pass on to me. My father had urged me to consider civil engineering because it was tangible, something you could do with your hands, unlike sociology or the liberal arts.

On the day I speak of, I had just returned to my calculus professor's office to get my grade for the first semester and was shocked to learn that I received an F on my semester exam. Not only did the F put me on probation for the next semester, but the professor announced my grade in front of two unsuspecting friends who had accompanied me to get my grade, and this dashed any hopes of playing baseball for the year. Not knowing the severity of my situation in calculus, I had invited my friends along as I told them that Professor Chang had announced midway through the semester that there would be only one exam, the final, and the grade in the class would be determined solely by the final exam.

I smugly told my friends, on my way to get the grade, that I was confident in my abilities. Why should I be forced to attend the thrice weekly classes when I could study on my own and simply take the final exam? I didn't tell them that I had missed the last three weeks of class and was somewhat anxious about the exam, but still I had crammed for several days leading up to the exam. Although an A was out of the question and it was a very hard exam, I felt that I might sneak a B or at least a C and be done with the course. Thus, with my two friends I walked into Professor Chang's office and asked him what my grade was on the exam. At first he looked puzzled, as if trying to recall my face, and then he got up and said loudly, "Ah yes, Mr. Vera, the student who decided to skip my classes, you received a 20, Mr. Vera, a 20 out of 200 on the exam, Mr. Vera. That is an F, and never in my twenty years of teaching has anyone received such a low score." I was too stunned at these remarks to hear him mumble something about the insolence of missing his class and grading me harshly because of my absences. My friends were of little consolation, and they quickly told everyone of my arrogance and apparent stupidity.

During the rest of the week I was disconsolate, feeling that I had been undisciplined, ignorant of what college requires, and perhaps even mistaken about my interests in college and my life's goals. There were few friends I could confide in about my self-doubts. That day spawned a period of self-reflection on what I needed to do to make it in college. The immediate impact was the realization that even though college provided a greater degree of independence than ever before, it also required more self-discipline and a greater degree of awareness of my personal goals and aspirations.

That week I realized the effort one must make to succeed academically in college. I also realized that I did not really enjoy working late at night on calculus equations or attending seminars on the strength of metal materials. If I was going to work hard at something, I decided that I would do it in a subject or courses that I enjoyed. What took hold that week was the realization that *college is not just an academic exercise but a pathway to life's aspirations and interests.*

The next semester I changed my major to urban planning and went head-long into my classes. I focused completely on academics, studying twice as hard and enjoying the newness of cities, social planning, and the gridlock of freeways. Although I did not have the resources that other students had, I used part-time jobs as an extension of my academic experience, either working on campus or in positions that were related to my courses. Over-coming a fear of being labeled ignorant, I purposefully sought out teachers for advice and shared with them my goals and hopes. Many years later as I taught at a university, I realized that teachers welcomed this interchange. Had I known then, I would have pursued this interchange more and sought professors more from the very start of my college career.

In addition to the academic aspects, I encountered students who were taking a semester abroad or were part of various clubs. This led me to another realization. Every student brought a uniqueness, and I sought out different students as friends. I also benefited from a friend's advice that all colleges are cultural museums, so I attended as many college "art or music" events as I could. For me there was an adjustment period, attempting to balance these new experiences with the demands of college; but once I attained this balance and kept it in focus with the help of a few professors, college became a wonderful academic experience.

For me it did not stop there. The final chapter was a decision to drop out of college for a year. Because I did not have the financial resources for a semester abroad, I applied for and was accepted in a domestic-type Peace Corps program that gave me the benefit of working in the inner city in Michigan and working with an urban planning program for a year. The year gave me the opportunity to travel and whet my appetite for pursuing a graduate degree and choosing to stay in the Midwest and graduate from an excellent university there. Refocused, recharged, and with some added maturity, I did very well upon my return and was eventually accepted into law school, where I had plans to combine urban planning and a legal career.

In all these endeavors, I learned several valuable lessons from the first day when I flunked calculus. First, college is hard work, and although it provides great freedom, it also requires a great degree of self-discipline and awareness of choices we make. Second, the hard work should be in an area that is of interest to you, otherwise it loses value and becomes less enjoyable. I took the time to explore what really interests me and realized that I enjoyed social interaction with people, which I did not get from civil engineering. Third, the more interaction you have with the school, the more you derive the benefits of the college and its resources, staff, and facilities. Thus, I chose purposefully to seek part-time jobs that were a part of my campus experience. This greatly benefited me.

Eventually, self-reflection made me realize that time away from college was also good. My year away was even more helpful as I came back to finish my last semesters with an even greater self-discipline and maturity. In looking back, I had the assistance of many individuals who took the time to help and guide me, but it was the painful self-realization of one's goals and aspirations—the ability to see what you enjoy and to take the time to partake of the college experience—that helped me make it through my undergraduate years.

CONSUELO NIETO

Consuelo Nieto is a professor in the College of Education, California State University, Long Beach. Prior to this she was a teacher of history and English in the Los Angeles Unified School District. She is also a member of the following groups: California State Council of Education; Board of Directors of the California Faculty Association; National Education Association's Women's Rights Task Force; National Education Association's Leadership Cadre; and National Education Association's Minority Affairs Committee.

My parents came from a small village in Central Mexico. It is located in an isolated area of San Luis Potosí. The town had no school for the children to attend. My parents never had the opportunity for any formal education. My father told me how he used to cry as a child because he could not go to school. When he and my mother came to this country, he vowed that his children would have every opportunity for an education; he saw no sacrifice too great to achieve this end.

When I began high school I entered a large four-year Catholic girls high school in Los Angeles. On the day of registration there were two lines available; one was for the college program, the other for general education. I got in the general education line as I certainly was not qualified to prepare for college. A former classmate from my elementary school was in the other line; she asked me to join her, saying that I shouldn't sign up for general education courses because they were too easy and would be a repeat of what we had already taken. I joined her line mainly because I knew her and it was reassuring to be with a friend in such a big and lonely place. And so my work for college preparation began.

At the beginning of my second year in high school, I was surprised to learn that my homeroom section had been changed. During my freshman year I had been in section 9S1 for high achievers; now I had been placed in 10S12 for students at the other end of the spectrum. I had done well in my freshman year, so I could not understand the change. I walked into my new homeroom on the first day of the semester and was bewildered. I didn't like what I saw and at the same time felt guilty because of my negative feelings. All the girls in the class were Mexican; we had been segregated from the other students. When we went to our classes, we were in all the low-achieving classes. The teachers felt they were addressing our needs because they believed we were not capable of doing well in school. The classes were very easy and boring, and I didn't feel challenged by any of the classroom activities. I was embarrassed by the work required of me compared to the assignments I saw other girls doing from other sections.

I thus doubted my ability to enter college and succeed. But my mother, since my days in elementary school, kept telling me of her hopes that I would become a schoolteacher. My mother and father both worked very hard to help pay my way to college. My parents took a lot of criticism from members of our extended family. My parents were sending me, a girl, to college. My family was poor; I should not have been given such a luxury, and I should be going to work to help support my family. So with all the sacrifices my parents had made, I couldn't let them down. I had to go to college and I had to succeed.

Once at Immaculate Heart College, I wasn't sure what it meant to be a student. I had many questions, and my parents couldn't answer them. I needed advice, but I was afraid to seek it. Finally, in desperation I went to the student advisement office to seek help. The woman who was there said, "Hurry up, I haven't got all day, what do you want?" Flustered, I muttered an apology and scurried out of the office. Where was I to go for help? Fortunately, during the first semester of my freshman year I had an English professor who was a very warm and caring woman. In class she suggested that we students stop by her office to review our work. I took her up on her suggestion and went to visit her. She was wonderful. Not only did she help me with English, but she gave me programmatic advice as well. As time went on, my visits to her office became a regular part of my schedule. It was so nice to have someone whom I could talk with, someone who could help me with my academic and personal life as well. There was only one problem. She thought I was more intelligent and capable than I really was. I didn't want her to find out the truth. So I worked very hard to live up to her expectations of me. She in turn encouraged me, supported me, and showed me how to move step by step to my goals—a Bachelor's degree, then a teaching credential. She was there for me when I needed her. There were times when I wanted to give up and walk away. For example, I figured I could get a job in a department store because I didn't need all the frustrations that went with college. But she wouldn't let me give up, so I picked myself up and tried again. I did not realize it at the time, but what she had become was my mentor—a mentor without whose help I don't believe I could have achieved success.

As a freshman I had a physical science class that posed a big problem for me. I didn't know how I could learn all the material for my exams, so I got together with a group of students and we formed a study group. It was a great success. As time went on, study groups became an important means of mastering content for many courses.

I soon discovered that the library was a place I could use as my own private study hall. Hidden away in a cubicle, I could study with no distractions and with all the needed resources at hand. If I were at home, there would always be additional chores to do or errands to run. Furthermore, my non-college friends would come by to visit or to talk me into going on some excursion with them. They could not, would not, understand that I had to study, that I had to do my assignments. So the library became a place of refuge.

The college had various resources to help students. There were learning labs, assistance centers, and language labs, to name just a few. I collected brochures on all the learning resources and then followed up by visiting them to see which ones would help me. I found some that were very useful and they were all free. These resources were put to good use to help me achieve my goals.

Although both my parents worked to help subsidize my education, I had to work part-time as a retail clerk to help pay the bills. I chose to go to a state university because that was the only institution I could afford. I combed the financial aid office looking for sources of funding. With the monies I obtained I was able to stay in school.

Because I was focused on succeeding as a student, I had no time for extracurricular activities. If I were back in college now, I think I would be more involved. There are activities that can enhance, not hinder, one's education. Furthermore, some activities, especially community service, would broaden one's perspective on how and why one should serve people in the community.

As you begin your academic journey, reflect on the goals you wish to achieve. Explore the many choices that are yours to make. First, you and your family must discuss your options. Which college should you attend? This will depend on your academic status and your financial situation. These conversations should begin when you are in high school. Applications should be made to more than one campus so that you have more than one choice. Plans should be made carefully to determine how you will pay for your education, year by year. The family should understand what a difference college will make in your life. Accommodations must be made so that you have the necessary time to study and do your assignments. Once accepted into the school, you and your family should take a tour to understand the "lay of the land" and the resources that the campus has to offer. You should seek appropriate help when you plan your program and the courses you are to take. As you begin attending classes, keep a log of how you spend your time. You may find that some non-school activities have to be reduced or eliminated completely. Always remember to keep your eyes on your goal. This way you will succeed. *Si Se Puede.*

LARRY VILLARREAL

Upon graduating from college, Mr. Villarreal joined the U.S. Air Force and was commissioned as a second lieutenant after completing Officer Training School in San Antonio, Texas. Service in the Air Force provided many exciting and challenging opportunities. Assignments included the Pentagon in the nation's capital; Korea; and several places in the Midwest. Mr. Villarreal had the opportunity to lead and manage people, including the opportunity to command a squadron. He considered it an honor and privilege to serve his country. After twenty years of service, he retired from the Air Force as a colonel.

How I made it through college is a question I still ask myself as I look back at the self-doubts and uncertainty about my abilities and future I had at the time. As I was going through college, there were many times when I asked myself if it was worth the sacrifices and "good times" I was losing out on. I was definitely one of a very few Latinos from my high school (Theodore Roosevelt High School in East Los Angeles) to attend college. The majority of the senior class graduates went to get jobs and make money, while I was still studying and attending classes. There were many times when I asked myself if college was worth the time and effort.

The most important reason I went to college and hung in there was because my parents encouraged me and emphasized the importance of education. They would say that if I were to get ahead and have a better life, I needed a college education. No one in our family had previously gone to college. Both my parents worked, my dad as a spray painter and my mom in a meat-packing plant. Both wanted me to get an education to improve my life. They had the foresight to know that education was the key to getting a better job and to achieving success. It was because of their support and the support of some of my friends, who also planned to go to college, that I studied hard in high school and developed the study habits that would later help me get through college. Also, it was in high school while I was a senior that I got a part-time job after school and on weekends to help meet school expenses and provide some gas money, as I now had my driver's license.

Upon graduating from high school I attended a community college (East Los Angeles College) because of the low tuition and, I guess, because in the back of my mind I was not confident I could complete a four-year college program. I was not sure I had the ability, commitment, and willingness to make the sacrifices to graduate. I planned to continue to work part-time to help finance my college education. A pleasant surprise that helped me out tremendously upon graduating from high school was that I was a winner of the Armando Castro Scholarship, which assisted with my tuition and book costs at East Los Angeles College.

Because I had doubts about my long-term commitment to graduating, I decided right from the first to do my very best during the first semester. I wanted to get off to a good start in college. I wanted to prove to myself that I could do well in terms of the studies. Also, I wanted to thank my parents for all their support by earning good grades right from the beginning. If I did not succeed, at least I knew I had given college my best shot and would have the peace of mind knowing I had done my best. Thinking about it now, I am glad that I had this attitude rather than not even trying college or, worse, not doing my best to study and graduate. I took one semester at a time and did my very best each semester. While focusing on the short term and taking a semester at a time, I was able to get over the intimidating thought of making a four-year commitment. Four years can seem like a lifetime when you are a young high school graduate. As it turned out, it actually took me five years to graduate from college.

My goal and focus were to do my very best, learning all I could and getting good grades one semester at a time. Between my studies and part-time job, I had to set priorities and manage my time. I had limited time for a social life or extracurricular activities. The little free time I had I chose to spend with family and close friends, as well as going to church on a regular basis.

Upon graduating from East Los Angeles College and getting my Associate's degree, I attended California State University, Los Angeles, to get my Bachelor's degree. When I graduated from East Los Angeles College, again I was awarded a scholarship from a local Latino group, which helped cover the cost of my tuition and books. It was the award of these scholarships that helped me and my parents get me through college. While I was attending the university, I continued my approach of focusing on my studies one semester at a time and doing my best.

In summary, there is not any one thing that got me through college. A combination of things made it all happen: the never-ending support of my family and friends, the financial support afforded by scholarships, and a commitment and faith on my part to do my best each semester. I cannot help but thank God for giving me the strength and commitment to continue with my education when there were moments when I thought the sacrifices on my time and life were too great. It was family, friends, and faith that got me through college.

A footnote: Because I learned that education is a process that never ends, I went on to earn a Master's of Business Administration (MBA) at the University of Missouri.

Thank you for taking the time to read my story. I hope that in some small way it strengthens your confidence and commitment to make it through college.

POLLY B. BACA

Ms. Baca was born on a small farm in Weld County and grew up in Greeley and Thornton, Colorado. After attending Colorado State University, she did graduate work at the American University in Washington, D.C. She began her career as an editorial assistant for a labor union newspaper in Washington, D.C. A member of the Colorado legislature for twelve years, she was first elected to the state's House of Representatives in 1974 and the Colorado Senate in 1978. Nationally known for her leadership skills and motivational presentations, Ms. Baca has appeared on numerous television and radio programs. Additionally, she has been recognized by many groups; for example, she was one of the original fourteen members to be inducted into the National Hispanic Hall of Fame.

It's a myth! You can't have it all—not until you graduate from college, that is. You cannot get good grades, work to help pay for your college education, participate in extracurricular activities, and also party every night. Something has to give. Make sure it is not your college degree.

So what's the answer? Why are you going to college anyhow? If it's to make friends, you can do that without ever setting foot in a college classroom. If it's to find a spouse, join a dating service—it's a lot less expensive. However, if you're going to college to better your chances of getting a job that you will like and that will also provide a decent salary and good future, *then make the decision now that getting that degree is the most important thing you have to do now, and act accordingly.* That was the most important decision I made when I was in college.

My parents didn't have the money to send me to college, but they gave me the encouragement to go and the confidence that I could make it. I had a tuition scholarship, but I had to work to provide for my board and room. That meant I didn't have a lot of extra time. I had to have a certain grade point average to keep my scholarship, and I still had to work. I made the decision early that getting my degree was more important than anything else I was doing at that time in my life. But it wasn't easy to keep focused on my decision. I enjoyed belonging to organizations, but this activity sometimes interfered with my studies.

My freshman year at Colorado State University, I worked in the dorms and got interested in politics. I got very involved in student body politics and the Young Democrats, although I was majoring in physics. Fairly soon my extracurricular activities started interfering with my homework. Near the end of the year, the faculty advisor to the Young Democrats asked me if I belonged to any organizations related to my major. I didn't. *That's when I realized that if I wanted to succeed, I should major in something I liked to do outside of the classroom*—which was the second most important decision I made in college. Before the end of the year, I changed my major from physics to political science. Then I limited my extracurricular activities to (1) those that related to my major, and (2) those that gave me spiritual nourishment.

God gives us each unique gifts and talents. We can usually tell what those gifts and talents are because they make certain subjects easier and more fun to do than others. Although I was majoring in physics at first, I found that courses related to political science were much more interesting and enjoyable for me. Also, I found out that it is much easier to excel if you like the subjects you are taking and find them interesting. Throughout my career, I have found that you can make money in anything you like to do. If you like the job you have, it doesn't seem like work and you spend more of your own time doing it well.

The same thing goes for college. If you like your major, you will want to get involved in extracurricular activities and join organizations related to it. Involvement will help you in developing the networks you will need to succeed in your chosen field after college. As a political science major, I got involved in the Young Democrats and the International Relations Club. That's what led me to getting involved in the John F. Kennedy campaign for president in 1960 and my first job in Washington, D.C., when I graduated from college in 1962.

But you have to watch how much time you spend on extracurricular activities. It will not help if you are not spending enough time on your studies to get the grades you need to graduate. *Your first priority, above everything else, should be to go to class and do your homework.* It's that simple. Nothing else is more important while you are in college. Also, I found out that it helped when I got to know my professor and made sure he or she knew me, too. When I had some problems understanding a particular assignment or text, I asked my professor for clarification. That is how I made sure she or he knew who I was. This little trick helped me out later in life, too. My first boss told me that as a young woman I could ask any question I wanted—and it would always make the person I was asking feel good about helping me. As a state legislator, I found out that there is no such thing as a dumb question unless you don't ask it. People are always flattered when you ask for their help or opinion, especially if you are a student.

Another critical component in getting through school and life is *attitude*. If you think you cannot do it, then you probably can't. You have to believe that you can do it—because you can. You don't have to be a genius to get through college; you just have to be willing and disciplined enough to attend class and do your coursework. If you are majoring in something you find interesting and like, you'll have a better attitude about learning. And if you have a good attitude about learning, you'll find your classwork and homework much more interesting. If you can discipline yourself and keep focused on getting that college degree, you *can* do it!

Remember, study what you like to do. Develop those gifts and talents God gave you first. Excel in whatever it is you like to do without worrying about money. If you like to do it, you can always make money. I changed majors from physics to political science, although at the time I couldn't imagine how I was going to make money with a degree in political science. In retrospect, as a physics major I probably would not have been the first woman on the moon. However, as a political science major I was the first woman to be elected to the State Senate from Adams County and the first minority woman to ever be elected to the Colorado State Senate.

You can work part-time and get grades good enough to graduate; many of us are living proof of that. My freshman year I worked in the dorms. My sophomore through senior years I worked in the Student Center at various jobs, including cashier in the cafeteria and receptionist in the office. I got involved in extracurricular activities that related to my major. But then I chose to limit my social activities to only those that did not interfere with my studies.

We have to make choices throughout out lives, so you might as well start learning how to make good choices now. *It's the quality of the choices you make in the present that will determine the quality of your life later on.*

So go for that college degree. *You can do it!*

MARIA "CUCA" ROBLEDO MONTECEL

Currently, Dr. Robledo Montecel is the executive director of the Intercultural Development Research Association, a nonprofit educational consultant and advocacy group located in San Antonio, Texas. As the executive director, she works with federal officials in Washington, D.C.; with universities and school districts throughout the United States; and with state departments of education.

I always knew I would go to college. I did not know how. I did not know where. But I did know why. College was a way of giving back—giving back what I was so generously given.

I was given, most important, an insight that has stayed with me for life: that schooling, regardless of how much, does not make an educated person. An educated person, I was taught, is one who treats others with dignity and respect. Being an educated person would take more than schooling. Being an educated person would mean following the example of my parents, who, despite having little formal schooling in Mexico, were and continue to be the most educated people I know.

I was given another fundamental lesson: that learning and achieving are worth the effort. When the school year was beginning and with the need to pick crops in California, my parents would stay and work while we children were enrolled in school or we would be sent back to Texas to stay with relatives in order to start school. When monies were insufficient for school, my mother worked in the cafeteria of my elementary school. Beginning with the summer after eighth grade, I began working every summer to help the family and to help with school. In high school, I worked in the school office during the regular terms.

At the beginning of my senior year in high school, my class visited several colleges in San Antonio, Texas. San Antonio was 150 miles and a world away from Laredo, the small town on the U.S.-Mexico border in which I had grown up and spent most of my life. We visited several colleges. I made my choice by the end of that day, even before getting information about the financial aid packages that each college could offer. I selected Our Lady of the Lake College because it is a Catholic institution and, thus, would ease my mother's fears about her daughter being away from home. The fact that it was small, friendly, and had at least some students with brown faces like mine who spoke Spanish like I did eased my own fears. Before moving to San Antonio to begin my first semester in the fall, I completed twelve hours of coursework that summer at Laredo Junior College. Taking courses at home during the summer, as well as the following summer, made for a good transition. It was also much cheaper than taking them as part of a regular undergraduate course load. And I needed to minimize my college cost! The costs of attending college were taken care of through a combination of a small scholarship, federally guaranteed student loans (the National Defense Student Loan program), need-based state grants (Texas Equalization Grant), and twenty hours a week of work-study in the chemistry department on campus.

Initially my major was psychology, but I changed my major after someone told me that "I couldn't do anything" with a psychology degree. At the time I had no plans for graduate school, and it was clear to me that I needed to "do" something—work, that is. I graduated Cum Laude (with honors) with a Bachelor of Science degree in social work.

After three years of working in education, I realized that I missed the challenge of school. Thirteen years after completing my bachelor's degree and ten years after completing my master's degree in educational evaluation, my mother and I braved single-digit temperatures in December to attend my doctoral degree graduation ceremonies at the University of Wisconsin, Milwaukee. After the ceremony we celebrated with dinner at a Serbian restaurant, joined by those who had helped me along the way.

Along the way I had found people who, like my parents, were truly educated—people who treated others, myself included, with dignity and respect. Of those people, I asked for their help. I asked help of the freshman-year English teacher who gave me a mid-term grade of C during my first semester in college (I was always a good student and had never gotten a C). I asked help of the chemistry department chair when I needed work-study to help finance college. I asked help of friends and other students when I felt lonely or needed help studying. I asked help of fellow Laredoans when I needed rides to go home and be *apapachada* ("cuddled," "taken care of"). When I decided to go to graduate school, I asked help of mentors who helped me find a graduate school, a financial aid package, and a job while I studied. I tried also to give back—by tutoring both friends and strangers who requested help, by completing tasks entrusted to me, by completing a job well done, by treating others with dignity and respect.

So, I got help and I helped others. Learning and schooling are worth the effort, and being educated is more than being schooled. Over the years, I have met people—too many people—who believe that educational achievement among Latinos is merely an individual feat of those few who manage to divest themselves of the baggage that is their family, their culture, and their language. These people are wrong. The broad and strong shoulders of our families, of our communities, of our culture, and of our language are helping many of us to meet the challenge of educational institutions that too often remain closed to Latino students.

LORETTA SANCHEZ

Loretta Sanchez was elected in 1996 and re-elected in 1998 by citizens of Orange County in Southern California to serve in the U.S. House of Representatives.

As one of seven children of immigrant parents from Mexico, I always knew I would attend college. Ever since I was a little girl, my father and mother would tell me that I had to study hard so that I could graduate from college. My parents' mission to send all of their children to college stemmed from the fact that each of their fathers had died when they were young children and therefore they had to suspend their education to work to support their families.

My parents made sure we did well in school and took the right courses to prepare for college. My father required me to take math every year through calculus and all the sciences (biology, chemistry, and physics). In addition, because I was a shy girl, my father made me take speech class and participate in debate and speech tournaments.

It was not a big surprise to me that many of the Ivy League schools wanted me to matriculate at their schools. My parents had done everything right to ensure that I would qualify for acceptance to any university. However, because my parents had never been to college, they had no idea about the differences in colleges and how that would affect my future choices. They thought all colleges were the same. In fact, I remember my father suggesting I go to the University of Southern California (USC) because he knew it had a good football team.

I sought help from my high school counselor, who suggested I go to the local community college. Here I was a 4.0 student with 1350 SAT scores, and he suggested I go to a local two-year college because being from a Latino family, I should not go too far from my family. I told him he was crazy!

I decided to attend Chapman University, a private university in Orange County in Southern California. It had a good pre-medical program, was close to home, and offered me a manageable way to pay for college. At the time, my older brother was at USC, taking classes and working, and my mother was cleaning houses on Saturday and Sunday to help pay his tuition bills. My parents couldn't borrow any more money to help me, and I also had a younger brother entering college the following year.

I paid for my four years at Chapman through a patchwork of financial aid. I received a California Grant A (state scholarship), a Pell grant (federal scholarship), a scholarship from United Farm Workers Local 324 (a union), and a student loan. In addition, I worked during my entire time at Chapman, sometimes three jobs at a time. I was a sales clerk, an aerobics instructor, a photographer's assistant, and a financial analyst.

Most important, I carried the Pralle Scholarship at Chapman. This was a privately donated scholarship by the Pralle family. Aside from good academics, the other requirement of the scholarship was to have lunch once a year with Bob Pralle. Every year, as the date of this lunch would approach, Bob would cancel it. It wasn't until ten years later when I was asked to sit on a nonprofit board that I met Bob Pralle, who also was one of the board members. The day I told him he had helped me so much to finance my college education, he doubled his commitment of scholarship monies to Chapman. Today, Bob and Helga Pralle are still some of the greatest supporters in my education.

One of the greatest friends I had at Chapman was Alan Mishne, the financial aid director. He helped me to finance my education, including my Master's in Business Administration (MBA) in finance from the American University in Washington, D.C. He guided me toward the Anaheim Rotary Club, which, through an International Rotary Scholarship, paid for the second year of my Master's program in Rome, Italy. Alan was a true friend, the type who would take me to dinner because he knew I had no money to eat well.

During the first two years at college I studied pre-med (math and science), but in the last semester of my second year I took my first economics class and knew I wanted to graduate in business. Two great professors, Scott Harris and James Doti, helped me to craft a plan to graduate with a degree in economics. I spent the last two years of college taking twenty-two units a semester in order to graduate with my entering class. When my name was called at graduation, the whole pre-med section yelled excitedly. They had not seen me for two years and were thrilled I was able to graduate as planned.

Both Drs. Doti and Harris helped me to get into a doctoral program in economics, but it was my marketing professor who convinced me to be a generalist and go east to work on my MBA. It was Dr. Doti, now the president of Chapman, who later supported me and helped me with the business community in Orange County to win my seat in Congress.

Going to college is never easy, but for many it will be the step that enables you to have choices in life. I can decide to be a businesswoman, a congresswoman, or whatever I dream about. An education gives me the knowledge and courage that I can succeed at anything. *Latinos can succeed at anything!*

To do well and get through college, one should be as well prepared as possible in entering college—the way my parents prepared me and each of my six siblings, all of whom have graduated from college. Take the hard courses, read well, don't be afraid of math. Ask people for help in researching college. Think about what you want to do with your life, and find a college that has a solid reputation in that field.

Do not be afraid to apply, even if you think you cannot afford the college. Worry about how you will finance your education after you have been accepted to the college of your choice. Seek help from financial aid counselors and community leaders. They can help you finance your education.

Do not get discouraged. In your life, there will be many ups and downs, and plenty of chances to try again. Work hard and be smart, in high school, in college, and in life. There is nothing as satisfying as working hard and seeing the payoff. Partner with people. It not only makes life easier, but it is fun!

FÉLIX GUTIÉRREZ

Mr. Gutiérrez has been a professor of journalism at California State University at Northridge, an associate dean at the University of Southern California, and is currently the senior vice president and executive director of the Freedom Forum, Pacific Coast Center, located in San Francisco, California.

My story of getting to and through college is a little different from most Latinos' in the early 1960s. My parents, as well as most of my aunts and uncles, had gone to college and were working as educators in California and Arizona to help other young persons of Mexican descent advance their education. Going to college was something my sisters, my cousins, and I heard about while growing up and most of us knew we would do. It wasn't a question of "if" but "how" we would get through college.

When we were living in East Los Angeles and attending predominately Mexican American schools, I had plenty of family encouragement and support from my parents. After my father died of cancer in 1955, and when I was 12 years old, my mother moved me and my two sisters to a predominately Anglo community (Pasadena, California) where the schools had a better reputation for preparing graduates for college.

I made it through a college preparatory track there with mixed success, doing well in social studies and not so well in math and science. I did well enough that I received scholarships from two East LA organizations, one being the Armando Castro Scholarship. Although most of my friends went on to a local community college, I decided to go to a new and nearby Los Angeles State College (now called California State University, Los Angeles). I enrolled at LA State because I could get in and it was close to home, cost only $47.50 a semester, and required no math to graduate. Like most Cal State LA students, I was a commuter: living at home, working part-time, and attending college classes. My mother was able to provide a home in which to sleep and eat. I took on part-time and summer jobs as a factory worker, janitor, fast-food delivery person, and gas station attendant. These jobs generated the money for school fees and books.

I was both intimidated and excited by the prospect of going to college. The first day I rode five miles to school with a couple of high school friends, then quickly parted company as we headed in different directions for classes among strangers on a strange campus. The first lunch break I ate alone, looking at people talking, laughing, and walking. All of them seemed to know each other. But I didn't know anyone and none of them knew me.

I figured I would find a way to make it through the classes as long as I didn't take any that were too hard. But I didn't know how I would ever make friends on a campus that was so big, so impersonal, and where everyone lived away from the school. The high school friends were a good first anchor, but I figured college was also a place to make new contacts.

Opportunity struck unexpectedly during registration week for my second semester. I had worked on the high school paper and enjoyed it, but I didn't figure I had a shot at making the college paper in my first year. Most of the staffers were community college transfers and the editor was a mother with teenage sons nearly my age. But when I returned home after registering for classes, I noticed in the college newspaper a small item headlined "Staffers Wanted" that indicated those who were interested in writing for the paper should contact the faculty advisor. Even though I was at home (five miles away from the campus), I headed back, sought out the advisor at the registration tables, and asked if he would accept a freshman not majoring in journalism. He looked me over, apparently figured I couldn't do much damage, and said yes. I added the class and went home on cloud nine.

For me, journalism was the great equalizer. The newspaper newsroom gave me a place to hang out on campus, even if I was the youngest by far, and the reporting assignments gave me a chance to cover stories all around the school and make new friends in the process. The newsroom experience even helped in my coursework as I learned to quickly absorb information, perform under deadline, and write with confidence.

For young Mexican Americans in the early 1960s, going to college was as much a process of assimilation as it was a process of education. We knew who we were and where we came from, but racial slights and slurs from some classmates were very common. Some of my classmates claimed they were Spanish, not Mexican, which usually worked until someone asked what part of Spain they were from. Others were proudly assertive but found little support for that visibility even on a campus located in East Los Angeles, the largest Spanish-speaking city in the world after Mexico City.

For me it was two trips to the interior of Mexico during and after my sophomore year that helped turn the identity tide. It was there for the first time that I saw Mexicans of all shapes and sizes doing all kinds of work. It was the first time I had not felt like I was part of a permanent minority. Also, it was there that I bought Mexican records that I would play as I did my homework at home at night. Still, it was a Mexican American identity. I felt like my cultural identity was divided into two different, distinct cultures; not a unified identity drawing strength from two cultures that others saw as divided, but that had been integrated in the lives of my parents, aunts, and uncles.

The five years I was a student at Cal State LA (four years as an undergraduate and one year completing a teaching credential) were probably the most important in my life. From the start as a cub reporter on the campus newspaper I moved up in two years to become editor and from there to student body president. I branched out into religious and service organizations, community volunteer work, and even a social fraternity in my senior year.

Most of all, I was able to build a sense of self-confidence and ambition that I didn't have before. Based on those campus successes, I was able to be successful through most of the three-plus decades since I left Cal State LA in 1966 for graduate degrees at Northwestern University and, later, Stanford University.

For me, college turned out to be a great experience. But it might not have been, if I hadn't looked beyond the classroom and taken that drive back to campus to see if I could work on the school paper.

PART IV

College and University Directory

SYLVIA PEREGRINO AND MIRANDA LOPEZ
Doctoral Fellows at Arizona State University

Latinos traditionally have been underrepresented in higher education. As such, there may not be any college graduates as role models in your family. Therefore, you may begin with less information about college admission and attendance than some of your peers. In addition, when you attend college recruitment events, the recruiters may not seek you out. However, this does not mean you are not college material. It just means you may have to seek out information on colleges on your own and be persistent in order to find out about colleges in which you are interested.

Where to go to college is a very important decision for you and your family to make together. You will want to consider many things, such as: Do I want to attend a four-year university or a two-year community college? How much will it cost? Can I get a scholarship or other financial aid? What programs of study or degrees are offered that I might be interested in? Do I want to attend a large school or a medium- or small-size school? Will I attend on a full-time basis or attend part-time while working? Keep in mind that community colleges have "open door" enrollment; that is, students with a high school diploma or GED (general equivalency diploma) are automatically admitted. Universities, on the other hand, may be highly selective or moderately competitive, with admission usually based on a combination of standardized test (SAT or ACT) scores, high school grades (GPA), and letters of references. (Please see Steps 1, 2 and 3.)

Other factors will also have to be considered. For example, do you want to attend a school that large numbers of other Latinos attend? Will you want to enroll where your friends will be attending? Do you want to leave the state or stay close to home? Do your grades and test scores seem competitive for those schools that are highly selective?

These and many other questions will cross your mind in making your ultimate decision of where to go to college. First, you will want to prioritize these questions and decide which are most important to you. Then, you should discuss these questions and others you may have identified with your family, friends, and high school guidance counselor. They are sources of information, support, and encouragement that you should be able to rely on. After discussing your questions, you must weigh and consider the answers and make some decisions. The most important thing is that you make definite plans to attend college. In today's highly competitive world, good jobs and top salaries go to those with a college education. Even if you are the first in your family to attend college, do not be discouraged. There are many other students just like you who are facing the challenges of a new experience. In fact, many colleges have special programs such as peer mentoring, freshman experience, Latino cultural center, student success programs, orientation, special clubs, and others just to help you make the transition from high school to college and to give you a sense of belonging. You should inquire about any program targeted at Latinos and get involved in some of these activities in order to ease your sense of isolation and to find sources of support and encouragement.

It is always a good idea to visit the school(s) you are interested in attending, if at all possible. Sometimes schools have weekend visit programs during which you can stay in the dorms and meet other students. Be sure to talk to presently enrolled students and ask them about their experiences. If you cannot visit the colleges of your choice personally, check each school's Web page. Most schools today have their own Web pages full of great, up-to-date information. We provide the Web addresses of the colleges listed here for your easy use. If you do not have a computer, very often you can use one at your local public library or possibly at your guidance counselor's office. The more information you get, the better informed you will be when you make your final decision. For the schools listed in the following pages, the phone number given is for the admissions office unless otherwise noted.

Once you've done some initial information gathering on the colleges of your choice, you should apply to at least three or more schools. It is always good to have a choice. The admissions office is where you can call to obtain an application and find out about deadlines. (Applications may also be available electronically on the Web or downloadable, if you prefer a hard copy.) Applications usually have a processing fee. *In financial hardship cases you can ask for a fee waiver*. Also, you should call the financial aid office to get the appropriate aid forms and to find out about any scholarships or loans that may be available. It is a good idea to apply for financial aid about four to six months prior to your first semester, even if you believe you'll be awarded a scholarship, loan, or other means to pay. You may be eligible for a federal Pell grant, which you do not need to repay. The Free Application for Federal Student Aid (FAFSA) only needs to be completed once, but you may include several schools to which the report may be sent. See Step 3 for more information about financial aid.

CRITERIA USED TO DETERMINE TOP UNIVERSITIES AND COMMUNITY COLLEGES

This part presents key lists to help in your decision making about where to attend college. Three of the lists give short descriptions of 50 universities and 20 community colleges from across the country, as well as 5 universities in Puerto Rico, that have been selected on the basis of the number of degrees they awarded to Latino students in 1996–1997. They are ranked in declining order, beginning with the highest number of degrees awarded. This information comes from the May 2000 issue of *The Hispanic Outlook* magazine and is based on the most current data from the U.S. Department of Education. The Degrees Awarded criterion was selected because it represents a realistic outcome measure of schools that have been successful in graduating Latinos and will likely continue to do so. Within each description is other information regarding tuition cost, cost of books and supplies, ethnic breakdown, and most popular majors and programs. Although our goal was to obtain the most current data, it should be noted that these figures change from year to year. You should check the most current issue of *The Hispanic Outlook* magazine as well as access data from individual college Web pages for the latest information.

Two other lists identify the top 10 universities and 10 community colleges nationally with the highest percentage of Latino enrollment in 1997 and 1998. These lists are presented in table form for easy reading, from highest to lowest percentage. The lists were obtained from the Integrated Postsecondary Education Data System (IPEDS) Peer Analysis system designed for educational researchers.

Information about the colleges was obtained from the schools' Web sites and also from the U.S. Department of Education's Web site (*www.nces.gov/ IPEDS/COOL*), specifically the Integrated Postsecondary Education Data System's Colleges On-Line (COOL) program.

You will notice that most of the colleges and universities that are graduating the largest numbers of Latinos are concentrated in four states: California, Texas, Florida, and New York. That is no accident. These states also have the largest Latino populations, with Mexican Americans/Chicanos concentrated in Texas and California, Cubans in Florida, and Puerto Ricans and Dominicans in New York. In the twenty-first century, as the demographics of the country continue to show rapid growth and population shifts, it is likely that other states besides these will emerge as leaders in educating Latinos. For now, we salute those institutions that have made concerted efforts to recruit, retain, and graduate large numbers of Latinos. We hope you will find your unique place among the many colleges presented here. *Adelante!*

TOP 50 UNIVERSITIES IN THE UNITED STATES FOR LATINOS (graduation numbers)

1
Florida International University
University Park
11200 SW 8th St.
Miami, FL 33199
(305) 348–2363
www.fiu.edu

Tuition, Full-time (Fall '99):
In State: $2,322 per year
Out of State: $9,311 per year
Books and Supplies: $1,080

Undergraduate Enrollment: (Fall '98):
24,807

Race/Ethnicity (Fall '98):
Black   14.9%
American Indian   0.1%
Asian   3.5%
Hispanic   54.2%
White   20.3%

Most Popular Majors or Programs (Fall '98):
Business, Health Professions & Related Sciences, Education

Bachelor's Degrees Awarded to Latinos (1997–98):
2,004

2
University of Texas—Pan American
1201 W. University Dr.
Edinburg, TX 78539
(956) 381–2206
www.panam.edu

Tuition, Full-time (Fall '99):
In State: $2,101 per year
Out of State: $8,157 per year
Books and Supplies: $565

Undergraduate Enrollment (Fall '98):
10,737

Race/Ethnicity (Fall '98):
Black   0.5%
American Indian   0.1%
Asian   0.8%
Hispanic   86.4%
White   7.9%

Most Popular Majors or Programs (Fall '98):
Multi/Interdisciplinary Studies, Business, Health Professions & Related Sciences

Bachelor's Degrees Awarded to Latinos (1997–98):
1,114

3
University of Texas at El Paso
500 W. University Ave.
El Paso, TX 79968
(915) 747–5576
www.utep.edu

Tuition, Full-time (Fall '99):
In State: $2,244 per year
Out of State: $7,428 per year
Books and Supplies: $546

Undergraduate Enrollment (Fall '98):
12,545

Race/Ethnicity (Fall '98):
Black   2.5%
American Indian   0.3%
Asian   1.3%
Hispanic   70.8%
White   14.7%

Most Popular Majors or Programs (Fall '98):
Business, Multi/Interdisciplinary Studies, Health Professions & Related Sciences

Bachelor's Degrees Awarded to Latinos (1997–98):
1,069

4
University of Texas at Austin
Main Bldg., Room 7
Austin, TX 78712
(512) 475–7399
www.utexas.edu

Tuition, Full-time (Fall '99):
In State: $3,128 per year
Out of State: $9,608 per year
Books and Supplies: $694

Undergraduate Enrollment (Fall '98):
37,203

Race/Ethnicity (Fall '98):
Black 3.5%
American Indian 0.5%
Asian 13.7%
Hispanic 13.9%
White 65.0%

Most Popular Majors or Programs (Fall '98):
Social Sciences & History, Business, Communications

Bachelor's Degrees Awarded to Latinos (1997–98):
1,060

5
University of Texas at San Antonio
6900 N. Loop 1604 West
San Antonio, TX 78249
(210) 458–4530
www.utsa.edu

Tuition, Full-time (Fall '99):
In State: $2,974 per year
Out of State: $9,454 per year
Books and Supplies: $494

Undergraduate Enrollment (Fall '98):
15,536

Race/Ethnicity (Fall '98):
Black 4.7%
American Indian 0.4%
Asian 3.6%
Hispanic 44.4%
White 45.6%

Most Popular Majors or Programs (Fall '98):
Business, Multi/Interdisciplinary Studies, Biological & Life Sciences

Bachelor's Degrees Awarded to Latinos (1997–98):
889

6
San Diego State University
5500 Campanile Dr.
San Diego, CA 92182–7455
(619) 594–5384
www.sdsu.edu

Tuition, Full-time (Fall '99):
In State: $1,776 per year
Out of State: $9,156 per year
Books and Supplies: $810

Undergraduate Enrollment (Fall '98):
25,773

Race/Ethnicity (Fall '98):
Black 5.2%
American Indian 1.0%
Asian 14.9%
Hispanic 21.7%
White 43.9%

Most Popular Majors or Programs (Fall '98):
Business, Social Sciences & History, Psychology

Bachelor's Degrees Awarded to Latinos (1997–98):
867

7
California State University–Los Angeles
5151 State University Dr.
Los Angeles, CA 90032
(323) 343–3901
www.calstatela.edu

Tuition, Full-time (Fall '99):
In State: $1,722 per year
Out of State: $9,106 per year
Books and Supplies: $810

Undergraduate Enrollment (Fall '98): 13,935

Race/Ethnicity (Fall '98):
Black 8.5%
American Indian 0.5%
Asian 22.5%
Hispanic 47.1%
White 10.5%

Most Popular Majors or Programs (Fall '98):
Business, Education, Social Sciences & History

Bachelor's Degrees Awarded to Latinos (1997–98):
858

8
University of California–Los Angeles
405 Hilgard Ave.
Los Angeles, CA 90095–1361
(213) 825-3101
www.ucla.edu

Tuition, Full-time (Fall '99):
In State: $3,683 per year
Out of State: $13,857 per year
Books and Supplies: $902

Undergraduate Enrollment (Fall '98): 24,102

Race/Ethnicity (Fall '98):
Black 5.4%
American Indian 0.7%
Asian 37.3%
Hispanic 15.5%
White 32.8%

Most Popular Majors or Programs (Fall '98):
Social Sciences & History, Biological & Life Sciences, Psychology

Bachelor's Degrees Awarded to Latinos (1997–98):
808

9
California State University–Fullerton
800 N. State College Blvd.
Fullerton, CA 92834–9480
(714) 278-2370
www.fullerton.edu

Tuition, Full-time (Fall '99):
In State: $1,780 per year
Out of State: $9,160 per year
Books and Supplies: $810

Undergraduate Enrollment (Fall '98): 21,279

Race/Ethnicity (Fall '98):
Black 3.1%
American Indian 0.7%
Asian 24.1%
Hispanic 22.9%
White 36.0%

Most Popular Majors or Programs (Fall '98):
Business, Communications, Social Sciences & History

Bachelor's Degrees Awarded to Latinos (1997–98):
735

10
California State University–Northridge
18111 Nordhoff St.
Northridge, CA 91330
(818) 677-3700
www.csun.edu

Tuition, Full-time (Fall '99):
In State: $1,814 per year
Out of State: $9,194 per year
Books and Supplies: $810

Undergraduate Enrollment (Fall '98): 20,955

Race/Ethnicity (Fall '98):
Black 8.7%
American Indian 0.7%
Asian 15.2%
Hispanic 23.7%
White 32.6%

Most Popular Majors or Programs (Fall '98):
Business, Social Sciences & History, Psychology

Bachelor's Degrees Awarded to Latinos (1997–98):
714

11
University of New Mexico (Main Campus)
University Dr.
Albuquerque, NM 87131
(505) 277–2446 or
1–800–CALL–UNM
www.unm.edu

Tuition, Full-time (Fall '99):
In State: $2,430 per year
Out of State: $9,172 per year
Books and Supplies: $680

Undergraduate Enrollment (Fall '98):
16,295

Race/Ethnicity (Fall '98):
Black 2.7%
American Indian 5.7%
Asian 3.4%
Hispanic 30.2%
White 54.2%

Most Popular Majors or Programs (Fall '98):
Education, Health Professions & Related Sciences, Business

Bachelor's Degrees Awarded to Latinos (1997–98):
711

12
University of Arizona
University Dr.
Tucson, AZ
(520) 621–3237
www.arizona.edu

Tuition, Full-time (Fall '99):
In State: $2,264 per year
Out of State: $9,416 per year
Books and Supplies: $700

Undergraduate Enrollment (Fall '98):
26,155

Race/Ethnicity (Fall '98):
Black 2.7%
American Indian 2.4%
Asian 5.3%
Hispanic 14.5%
White 69.2%

Most Popular Majors or Programs (Fall '98):
Business, Social Sciences & History, Biological & Life Sciences

Bachelor's Degrees Awarded to Latinos (1997–98):
706

13
University of California at Berkeley
110 Sproul Hall
Berkeley, CA 94720
(510) 642–3175
www.berkeley.edu

Tuition, Full-time (Fall '99):
In State: $4,046 per year
Out of State: $14,220 per year
Books and Supplies: $854

Undergraduate Enrollment (Fall '98):
22,261

Race/Ethnicity (Fall '98):
Black 5.2%
American Indian 0.9%
Asian 39.3%
Hispanic 11.3%
White 30.2%

Most Popular Majors or Programs (Fall '98):
Social Sciences & History, Biological & Life Sciences, Engineering

Bachelor's Degrees Awarded to Latinos (1997–98):
674

14
Texas A&M University
College Station, TX 77843
(409) 845–1060
www.tamu.edu

Tuition, Full-time (Fall '99):
In State: $2,640 per year
Out of State: $7,824 per year
Books and Supplies: $772

Undergraduate Enrollment (Fall '98):
35,889

Race/Ethnicity (Fall '98):
Black   3.0%
American Indian   0.4%
Asian   3.4%
Hispanic   10.2%
White   80.2%

Most Popular Majors or Programs (Fall '98):
Business, Engineering, Multi/Interdisciplinary Studies

Bachelor's Degrees Awarded to Latinos (1997–98):
667

15
California State University–Fresno
5241 N. Maple Ave.
Fresno, CA 93740
(559) 278–2191
www.csufresno.edu

Tuition, Full-time (Fall '99):
In State: $1,670 per year
Out of State: $9,050 per year
Books and Supplies: $720

Undergraduate Enrollment (Fall '98):
14,518

Race/Ethnicity (Fall '98):
Black   5.7%
American Indian   1.2%
Asian   11.4%
Hispanic   27.8%
White   37.9%

Most Popular Majors or Programs (Fall '98):
Liberal/General Studies & Humanities, Business, Health Professions & Related Sciences

Bachelor's Degrees Awarded to Latinos (1997–98):
654

16
University of Florida
201 Criser Hall
Gainesville, FL 32611
(352) 392–1365
www.ufl.edu

Tuition, Full-time (Fall '99):
In State: $2,141 per year
Out of State: $9,130 per year
Books and Supplies: $700

Undergraduate Enrollment (Fall '98):
31,447

Race/Ethnicity (Fall '98):
Black   6.8%
American Indian   0.3%
Asian   6.2%
Hispanic   10.1%
White   75.0%

Most Popular Majors or Programs (Fall '98):
Business, Engineering, Social Sciences & History

Bachelor's Degrees Awarded to Latinos (1997–98):
627

17
New Mexico State University (Main Campus)
Box 30001, Dept. 3A
Las Cruces, NM 88003
(505) 646–3121
www.nmsu.edu

Tuition, Full-time (Fall '99):
In State: $2,502 per year
Out of State: $7,790 per year
Books and Supplies: $634

Undergraduate Enrollment (Fall '98):
12,621

Race/Ethnicity (Fall '98):
Black   2.6%
American Indian   2.9%
Asian   1.7%

Hispanic 40.6%

White 50.6%

Most Popular Majors or Programs (Fall '98):

Business, Education, Engineering

Bachelor's Degrees Awarded to Latinos (1997–98):

614

18
California State University–Long Beach
1250 Bellflower Blvd.
Long Beach, CA 90840
(562) 985–1887
www.csulb.edu

Tuition, Full-time (Fall '99):
In State: $1,688 per year
Out of State: $9,068 per year
Books and Supplies: $810

Undergraduate Enrollment (Fall '98):
22,868

Race/Ethnicity (Fall '98):
Black 7.9%
American Indian 0.9%
Asian 24.1%
Hispanic 21.4%
White 32.2%

Most Popular Majors or Programs (Fall '98):
Business, Social Sciences & History, Psychology

Bachelor's Degrees Awarded to Latinos (1997–98):
608

19
Arizona State University (Main Campus)
Tempe, AZ 85287
(480) 965–7788
www.asu.edu

Tuition, Full-time (Fall '99):
In State: $2,261 per year
Out of State: $9,413 per year
Books and Supplies: $700

Undergraduate Enrollment (Fall '98):
33,268

Race/Ethnicity (Fall '98):
Black 3.0%
American Indian 2.3%
Asian 4.8%
Hispanic 10.9%
White 72.8%

Most Popular Majors or Programs (Fall '98):
Business, Social Sciences & History, Communications

Bachelor's Degrees Awarded to Latinos (1997–98):
562

20
Southwest Texas State University
601 University Dr.
San Marcos, TX 78666
(512) 245–2364
www.swt.edu

Tuition, Full-time (Fall '99):
In State: $3,056 per year
Out of State: $9,536 per year
Books and Supplies: $750

Undergraduate Enrollment (Fall '98):
18,486

Race/Ethnicity (Fall '98):
Black 4.7%
American Indian 0.6%
Asian 1.8%
Hispanic 18.8%
White 73.4%

Most Popular Majors or Programs (Fall '98):
Business, Multi/Interdisciplinary Studies; Parks, Recreation, Leisure & Fitness

Bachelor's Degrees Awarded to Latinos (1997–98):
541

21
University of California–Santa Barbara
Admissions Office

Santa Barbara, CA 93106
(805) 893–2881
www.ucsb.edu

Tuition, Full-time (Fall '99):
In State: $3,844 per year
Out of State: $14,018 per year
Books and Supplies: $889

Undergraduate Enrollment (Fall '98): 17,059

Race/Ethnicity (Fall '98):
Black   2.6%
American Indian   1.0%
Asian   15.1%
Hispanic   13.6 %
White   58.2 %

Most Popular Majors or Programs (Fall '98):
Social Sciences & History, Business, Biological & Life Sciences

Bachelor's Degrees Awarded to Latinos (1997–98):
526

22
University of Houston (University Park)
4800 Calhoun
Houston, TX 77004–2162
(713) 743–1010
www.uh.edu

Tuition, Full-time (Fall '99):
In State: $2,638 per year
Out of State: $8,686 per year
Books and Supplies: $824

Undergraduate Enrollment (Fall '98): 24,268

Race/Ethnicity (Fall '98):
Black   14.1%
American Indian   0.6%
Asian   19.3%
Hispanic   18.3%
White   42.8%

Most Popular Majors or Programs (Fall '98):

Business, Psychology, Social Sciences & History

Bachelor's Degrees Awarded to Latinos (1997–98):
519

23
University of Southern California
University Park
Los Angeles, CA 90089
(213) 740–1111
www.usc.edu

Tuition, Full-time (Fall '99):
In State: $22,636 per year
Out of State: $22,636 per year
Books and Supplies: $650

Undergraduate Enrollment (Fall '98): 15,553

Race/Ethnicity (Fall '98):
Black   6.0%
American Indian   0.7%
Asian   23.2%
Hispanic   14.5%
White   46.0%

Most Popular Majors or Programs (Fall '98):
Business, Social Sciences & History, Engineering

Bachelor's Degrees Awarded to Latinos (1997–98):
507

24
University of Central Florida
4000 Central Florida Blvd.
Orlando, FL 32816
(407) 823–3000
www.ucf.edu

Tuition, Full-time (Fall '99):
In State: $2,297 per year
Out of State: $9,285 per year
Books and Supplies: $772

Undergraduate Enrollment (Fall '98): 25,151

Race/Ethnicity (Fall '98):
Black   7.3%
American Indian   0.5%

Asian 4.8%
Hispanic 10.4%
White 74.6%

Most Popular Majors or Programs (Fall '98):
Business, Health Professions & Related Sciences, Education

Bachelor's Degrees Awarded to Latinos (1997–98):
499

25
California State Polytechnic University–Pomona
3801 W. Temple Ave.
Pomona, CA 91768
(909) 869–2000
www.csupomona.edu

Tuition, Full-time (Fall '99):
In State: $1,777 per year
Out of State: $9,157 per year
Books and Supplies: $810

Undergraduate Enrollment (Fall '98):
15,351

Race/Ethnicity (Fall '98):
Black 3.6%
American Indian 0.6%
Asian 34.4%
Hispanic 22.5%
White 25.8%

Most Popular Majors or Programs (Fall '98):
Business, Engineering, Liberal/General Studies & Humanities

Bachelor's Degrees Awarded to Latinos (1997–98):
494

26
San Jose State University
1 Washington Square
San Jose, CA 95192–0001
(408) 283–7500
www.sjsu.edu

Tuition, Full-time (Fall '99):
In State: $1,780 per year
Out of State: $9,237 per year
Books and Supplies: $810

Undergraduate Enrollment (Fall '98):
20,681

Race/Ethnicity (Fall '98):
Black 4.6%
American Indian 0.7%
Asian 37.5%
Hispanic 14.7%
White 27.4%

Most Popular Majors or Programs (Fall '98):
Business, Engineering, Health Professions & Related Sciences

Bachelor's Degrees Awarded to Latinos (1997–98):
490

27
CUNY Lehman College
250 Bedford Park Blvd. West
Bronx, NY 10468–1589
(718) 960–8706
www.lehman.cuny.edu

Tuition, Full-time (Fall '99):
In State: $3,320 per year
Out of State: $6,920 per year
Books and Supplies: $600

Undergraduate Enrollment (Fall '98):
7,302

Race/Ethnicity (Fall '98):
Black 37.4%
American Indian 0.1%
Asian 3.8%
Hispanic 44.5%
White 13.0%

Most Popular Majors or Programs (Fall '98):
Social Sciences & History, Health Professions & Related Sciences, Psychology

Bachelor's Degrees Awarded to Latinos (1997–98):
478

28
University of Miami
University Station
PO Box 248025
Coral Gables, FL 33124
(305) 284–4323
www.miami.edu
admission@miami.edu

Tuition, Full-time (Fall '99):
In State: $21,354 per year
Out of State: $21,354 per year
Books and Supplies: $720

Undergraduate Enrollment (Fall '98):
8,391

Race/Ethnicity (Fall '98):
Black   11.0%
American Indian   0.3%
Asian   4.8%
Hispanic   29.5%
White   44.4%

Most Popular Majors or Programs (Fall '98):
Business, Health Professions & Related Sciences, Visual & Performing Arts

Bachelor's Degrees Awarded to Latinos (1997–98):
462

29
Texas A&M University–Kingsville
955 University Blvd.
Kingsville, TX 78363
(361) 593–2315
www.tamuk.edu

Tuition, Full-time (Fall '99):
In State: $2,482 per year
Out of State: $8,962 per year
Books and Supplies: $562

Undergraduate Enrollment (Fall '98):
4,779

Race/Ethnicity (Fall '98):
Black   5.3%
American Indian   0.3%
Asian   0.6%

Hispanic   66.0%
White   25.9%

Most Popular Majors or Programs (Fall '98):
Engineering, Multi/Interdisciplinary Studies, Business

Bachelor's Degrees Awarded to Latinos (1997–98):
450

30
California State University–Dominguez Hills
100 East Victoria Ave.
Carson, CA 90747
(310) 243–3601
www.csudh.edu

Tuition, Full-time (Fall '99):
In State: $1,735 per year
Out of State: $9,115 per year
Books and Supplies: $810

Undergraduate Enrollment (Fall '98):
7,834

Race/Ethnicity (Fall '98):
Black   28.8%
American Indian   0.8%
Asian   10.3%
Hispanic   28.9%
White   20.1%

Most Popular Majors or Programs (Fall '98):
Health Professions, Business, Liberal/ General Studies & Humanities

Bachelor's Degrees Awarded to Latinos (1997–98):
438

31
University of Illinois at Chicago
601 South Morgan St.
Chicago, IL 60680
(312) 996–4350
www.uic.edu

Tuition, Full-time (Fall '99):
In State: $4,684 per year
Out of State: $10,924 per year
Books and Supplies: $630

Undergraduate Enrollment (Fall '98): 16,384

Race/Ethnicity (Fall '98):
Black   10.3%
American Indian   0.3%
Asian   22.2%
Hispanic   16.9%
White   45.2%

Most Popular Majors or Programs (Fall '98):
Business, Health Professions, Engineering

Bachelor's Degrees Awarded to Latinos (1997–98):
437

32
San Francisco State University
1600 Holloway Ave.
San Francisco, CA 94132
(415) 338–2411
www.csusf.edu

Tuition, Full-time (Fall '99):
In State: $1,862 per year
Out of State: $9,242 per year
Books and Supplies: $810

Undergraduate Enrollment (Fall '98): 21,044

Race/Ethnicity (Fall '98):
Black   6.7%
American Indian   0.8%
Asian   33.6%
Hispanic   12.6%
White   26.8%

Most Popular Majors or Programs (Fall '98):
Business, Social Sciences & History, Psychology

Bachelor's Degrees Awarded to Latinos (1997–98):
430

33
Rutgers, The State University of New Jersey
83 Somerset St.
New Brunswick, NJ 08901
(732) 932–3770
www.rutgers.edu

Tuition, Full-time (Fall '99):
In State: $5,852 per year
Out of State: $10,782 per year
Books and Supplies: $700

Undergraduate Enrollment (Fall '98): 27,086

Race/Ethnicity (Fall '98):
Black   8.1%
American Indian   0.3%
Asian   17.5%
Hispanic   7.8%
White   56.4%

Most Popular Majors or Programs (Fall '98):
Social Sciences & History, Psychology, Biological & Life Sciences

Bachelor's Degrees Awarded to Latinos (1997–98):
418

34
University of California–Davis
1 Shields Ave.
Davis, CA 95616
(530) 752–2971
www.ucdavis.edu

Tuition, Full-time (Fall '99):
In State: $4,034 per year
Out of State: $14,208 per year
Books and Supplies: $844

Undergraduate Enrollment (Fall '98): 19,403

Race/Ethnicity (Fall '98):
Black   3.0%
American Indian   1.1%
Asian   34.7%

Hispanic 10.2%
White 42.1%

Most Popular Majors or Programs (Fall '98):
Biological Sciences, Social Sciences & History, Psychology

Bachelor's Degrees Awarded to Latinos (1997–98):
409

35
University of South Florida
4202 E. Fowler Ave.
Tampa, FL 33620
(813) 974–3350
www.usf.edu

Tuition, Full-time (Fall '99):
In State: $2,256 per year
Out of State: $9,245 per year
Books and Supplies: $700

Undergraduate Enrollment (Fall '98)
25,565

Race/Ethnicity (Fall '98):
Black 10.4%
American Indian 0.4%
Asian 5.3%
Hispanic 9.5%
White 71.8%

Most Popular Majors or Programs (Fall '98):
Education, Social Sciences & History, Psychology

Bachelor's Degrees Awarded to Latinos (1997–98):
400

36
California Polytechnic State University–San Luis Obispo
One Grand Ave.
San Luis Obispo, CA 93407
(805) 756–2311
www.calpoly.edu

Tuition, Full-time (Fall '99):
In State: $2,126 per year
Out of State: $9,506 per year
Books and Supplies: $810

Undergraduate Enrollment (Fall '98):
15,347

Race/Ethnicity (Fall '98):
Black 1.4%
American Indian 1.6%
Asian 11.5%
Hispanic 12.5%
White 61.9%

Most Popular Majors or Programs (Fall '98):
Engineering, Business, Agriculture

Bachelor's Degrees Awarded to Latinos (1997–98):
395

37
California State University–San Bernadino
5500 University Pkwy.
San Bernadino, CA 92407
(909) 880–5000
www.csusb.edu

Tuition, Full-time (Fall '99):
In State: $1,747 per year
Out of State: $9,127 per year
Books and Supplies: $810

Undergraduate Enrollment (Fall '98):
9,636

Race/Ethnicity (Fall '98):
Black 9.4%
American Indian 1.3%
Asian 8.6%
Hispanic 26.4%
White 41.4%

Most Popular Majors or Programs (Fall '98):
Business, Liberal/General Studies & Humanities, Social Sciences & History

Bachelor's Degrees Awarded to Latinos (1997–98):
386

38
California State University–Sacramento
6000 J St.
Sacramento, CA 95819
(916) 278–6723
www.csus.edu

Tuition, Full-time (Fall '99):
In State: $1,747 per year
Out of State: $9,127 per year
Books and Supplies: $810

Undergraduate Enrollment (Fall '98):
9,636

Race/Ethnicity (Fall '98):
Black   9.4%
American Indian   1.3%
Asian   8.6%
Hispanic   26.4%
White   41.4%

Most Popular Majors or Programs (Fall '98):
Business, Liberal/General Studies & Humanities, Social Sciences & History

Bachelor's Degrees Awarded to Latinos (1997–98):
386

39
University of California–Irvine
Campus Dr.
Irvine, CA 92697
(949) 824–6703
www.uci.edu

Tuition, Full-time (Fall '99):
In State: $3,871 per year
Out of State: $14,044 per year
Books and Supplies: $948

Undergraduate Enrollment (Fall '98):
14,336

Race/Ethnicity (Fall '98):
Black   2.0%
American Indian   0.5%
Asian   55.3%
Hispanic   11.0%
White   20.9%

Most Popular Majors or Programs (Fall '98):
Biological Sciences, Social Sciences & History, Psychology

Bachelor's Degrees Awarded to Latinos (1997–98):
381

40
Barry University
11300 NE Second Ave.
Miami Shores, FL 33161
(305) 889–3000
1–800–756–6000
www.barry.edu

Tuition, Full-time (Fall '99):
In State: $15,530 per year
Out of State: same
Books and Supplies: $700

Undergraduate Enrollment (Fall '98):
5,086

Race/Ethnicity (Fall '98):
Black   13.4%
American Indian   0.1%
Asian   1.4%
Hispanic   31.8%
White   36.6%

Most Popular Majors or Programs (Fall '98):
Liberal/General Studies & Humanities, Health Professions, Education

Bachelor's Degrees Awarded to Latinos (1997–98):
371

41
Florida State University
321 Wescott Bldg.
Tallahassee, FL 32306
(850) 644–2525
www.fsu.edu

Tuition, Full-time (Fall '99):
In State: $2,196 per year

Out of State: $9,148 per year
Books and Supplies: $702

Undergraduate Enrollment (Fall '98):
24,699

Race/Ethnicity (Fall '98):
Black   12.5%
American Indian   0.4%
Asian   2.6%
Hispanic   7.2%
White   76.1%

Most Popular Majors or Programs (Fall '98):
Business, Social Sciences & History, Education

Bachelor's Degrees Awarded to Latinos (1997–98):
361

42

University of California–San Diego
9500 Gilman Dr.
La Jolla, CA 92093–0021
(858) 534–4831
www.ucsd.edu

Tuition, Full-time (Fall '99):
In State: $3,842 per year
Out of State: $14,022 per year
Books and Supplies: $886

Undergraduate Enrollment (Fall '98):
15,837

Race/Ethnicity (Fall '98):
Black   1.7%
American Indian   0.8%
Asian   36.4%
Hispanic   9.8%
White   39.8%

Most Popular Majors or Programs (Fall '98):
Biological & Life Sciences, Social Sciences & History, Psychology

Bachelor's Degrees Awarded to Latinos (1997–98):
353

43

CUNY–Hunter College
695 Park Ave.
New York, NY 10021
(212) 772–4490
www.hunter.cuny.edu

Tuition, Full-time (Fall '99):
In State: $3,347 per year
Out of State: $6,947 per year
Books and Supplies: $600

Undergraduate Enrollment (Fall '98):
15,251

Race/Ethnicity (Fall '98):
Black   19.7%
American Indian   0.2%
Asian   14.4%
Hispanic   22.1%
White   39.0%

Most Popular Majors or Programs (Fall '98):
Social Sciences & History, Psychology, Health Professions

Bachelor's Degrees Awarded to Latinos (1997–98):
343

44

CUNY–City College
160 Covenant Ave.
New York, NY 10031
(212) 650–6977
www.ccny.cuny.edu

Tuition, Full-time (Fall '99):
In State: $3,309 per year
Out of State: $6,909 per year
Books and Supplies: $600

Undergraduate Enrollment (Fall '98):
8,934

Race/Ethnicity (Fall '98):
Black   36.8%
American Indian   0.2%
Asian   11.7%
Hispanic   32.1%
White   9.3%

Most Popular Majors or Programs (Fall '98):

Engineering, Education, Social Sciences & History

Bachelor's Degrees Awarded to Latinos (1997–98):

338

45
CUNY–Baruch College

17 Lexington Ave.
New York, NY 10001
(212) 802–2000
www.baruch.cuny.edu

Tuition, Full-time (Fall '99):
In State: $3,330 per year
Out of State: $6,930 per year
Books and Supplies: $600

Undergraduate Enrollment (Fall '98): 12,386

Race/Ethnicity (Fall '98):
Black   21.9%
American Indian   0.2%
Asian   22.7%
Hispanic   19.7%
White   27.9%

Most Popular Majors or Programs (Fall '98):

Business, Marketing Operations/Marketing & Distribution, Computer Information Systems

Bachelor's Degrees Awarded to Latinos (1997–98):

324

46
Texas A&M International University

5201 University Blvd.
Laredo, TX 78041
(956) 326–2200
www.tamiu.edu

Tuition, Full-time (Fall '99):
In State: $1,985 per year

Out of State: $7,169 per year
Books and Supplies: $629

Undergraduate Enrollment (Fall '98): 2,114

Race/Ethnicity (Fall '98):
Black   0.2%
American Indian   0.1%
Asian   0.3%
Hispanic   92.7%
White   4.5%

Most Popular Majors or Programs (Fall '98):

Business, Education, Multi/Interdisciplinary Studies

Bachelor's Degrees Awarded to Latinos (1997–98):

319

47
Florida Atlantic University–Boca Raton

777 Glades Rd.
Boca Raton, FL 33431
(561) 297–3040
www.fau.edu

Tuition, Full-time (Fall '99):
In State: $2,253 per year
Out of State: $9,241 per year
Books and Supplies: $610

Undergraduate Enrollment (Fall '98): 16,017

Race/Ethnicity (Fall '98):
Black   13.3%
American Indian   0.6%
Asian   3.7%
Hispanic   11.5%
White   66.1%

Most Popular Majors or Programs (Fall '98):

Business, Social Sciences & History, Education

Bachelor's Degrees Awarded to Latinos (1997–98):

318

48
Texas Tech University
P.O. Box 42013
Lubbock, TX 79409
(806) 742–1482
www.texastech.edu

Tuition, Full-time (Fall '99):
In State: $3,107 per year
Out of State: $9,587 per year
Books and Supplies: $770

Undergraduate Enrollment (Fall '98):
20,024

Race/Ethnicity (Fall '98):
Black   3.1%
American Indian   0.4%
Asian   2.0%
Hispanic   10.4%
White   83.4%

Most Popular Majors or Programs (Fall '98):
Business, Home Economics, Engineering

Bachelor's Degrees Awarded to Latinos (1997–98):
311

49
CUNY–John Jay College of Criminal Justice
889 10th Ave.
New York, NY 10019
(212) 237–8000
www.jjay.cuny.edu

Tuition, Full-time (Fall '99):
In State: $3,309 per year
Out of State: $6,909 per year
Books and Supplies: $600

Undergraduate Enrollment (Fall '98):
9,690

Race/Ethnicity (Fall '98):
Black   31.7%
American Indian   0.2%
Asian   4.6%
Hispanic   37.8%
White   25.1%

Most Popular Majors or Programs (Fall '98):
Protective Services, Public Administration & Services, Psychology

Bachelor's Degrees Awarded to Latinos (1997–98):
305

50
University of California–Riverside
900 Riverside Ave.
Riverside, CA 92521
(909) 787–3411
www.ucr.edu

Tuition, Full-time (Fall '99):
In State: $3,751 per year
Out of State: $13,925
Books and Supplies: $1000

Undergraduate Enrollment (Fall '98):
9,130

Race/Ethnicity (Fall '98):
Black   5.1%
American Indian   0.6%
Asian   40.4%
Hispanic   20.5%
White   25.4%

Most Popular Majors or Programs (Fall '98):
Biological Sciences, Business, Social Sciences & History

Bachelor's Degrees Awarded to Latinos (1997–98):
302

TOP 10 UNIVERSITIES IN THE UNITED STATES WITH THE GREATEST PERCENTAGE OF LATINO UNDERGRADUATES

University	1997 (%)	1998 (%)
1. Texas A&M International University	93	93
2. University of Texas–Pan American	87	86
3. University of Texas at Brownsville	80	N/A
4. University of Texas at El Paso	65	71
5. Texas A&M University–Kingsville	62	66
6. New Mexico Highlands University	60	66
7. Florida International University	49	54
8. Sul Ross State University	46	53
9. California State University–Los Angeles	41	47
10. CUNY Lehman College	41	45

Source: Integrated Postsecondary Education Data System (IPEDS) Peer Analysis System, Survey Year 1997. Institutional characteristics: General Information and Response Status Information, Fall Enrollments by Race/Ethnicity, Sex, Attendance and Level of Student.

TOP 20 COMMUNITY COLLEGES IN THE UNITED STATES FOR LATINOS (graduation numbers)

1
Miami-Dade Community College
300 NE 2nd Ave.
Miami, FL 33132
(305) 237–3221
www.mdcc.edu

Tuition, Full-time (Fall '99):
In State: $1,787 per year
Out of State: $6,242 per year
Books and Supplies: $760

Undergraduate Enrollment: (Fall '98):
48,222

Race/Ethnicity (Fall '98):
Black   20.0%
American Indian   0.1%
Asian   1.6%
Hispanic   63.5%
White   12.5%

Most Popular Majors or Programs (Fall '98):
Liberal/General Studies & Humanities, Health Professions & Related Sciences, Business

Associate's Degrees Awarded to Latinos (1996–97):
2,993

2
El Paso Community College
P.O. Box 20500
El Paso, TX 79998
(915) 831–2150
www.epcc.edu

Tuition, Full-time (Fall '99):
In State: $1,437 per year
Out of State: $2,070 per year
Books and Supplies: $900

Undergraduate Enrollment (Fall '98):
20,744

Race/Ethnicity (Fall '98):
Black   3.1%
American Indian   0.6%
Asian   0.8%
Hispanic   81.7%
White   11.4%

Most Popular Majors or Programs (Fall '98):
Health Professions & Related Sciences, Business, Vocational Home Economics

Associate's Degrees Awarded to Latinos (1996–97):
506

3
CUNY–La Guardia Community College
31–10 Thomson Ave.
Long Island City, NY 11101
(718) 482–7206
www.lagcc.cuny.edu

Tuition, Full-time (Fall '99):
In State: $2,622 per year
Out of State: $3,198 per year
Books and Supplies: $600

Undergraduate Enrollment (Fall '98):
11,058

Race/Ethnicity (Fall '98):
Black   20.5%
American Indian   0.1%
Asian   11.9%
Hispanic   37.8%
White   17.9%

Most Popular Majors or Programs (Fall '98):
Business, Health Professions & Related Sciences, Social Sciences & History

Associate's Degrees Awarded to Latinos (1996–97):
493

4

East Los Angeles College
1301 Avenida Cesar Chavez
Monterey Park, CA 91754
(323) 265–8605
www.elac.cc.ca.us

Tuition, Full-time (Fall '99):
In State: $308 per year
Out of State: $3,584 per year
Books and Supplies: $810

Undergraduate Enrollment (Fall '98):
14,876

Race/Ethnicity (Fall '98):
Black   1.8%
American Indian   0.3%
Asian   15.5%
Hispanic   77.1%
White   2.9%

Most Popular Majors or Programs (Fall '98):
Business, Liberal/General Studies & Humanities, Health Professions & Related Sciences

Associate's Degrees Awarded to Latinos (1996–97):
467

5

CUNY–Borough of Manhattan Community College
199 Chambers St.
New York, NY 10007
(212) 346–8102
www.bmcc.cuny.edu

Tuition, Full-time (Fall '99):
In State: $2,590 per year
Out of State: $3,166 per year
Books and Supplies: $600

Undergraduate Enrollment (Fall '98):
16,022

Race/Ethnicity (Fall '98):
Black   40.9%
American Indian   0.2%
Asian   9.7%

Hispanic   31.4%
White   9.2%

Most Popular Majors or Programs (Fall '98):
Business, Liberal/General Studies & Humanities, Health Professions & Related Sciences

Associate's Degrees Awarded to Latinos (1996–97):
452

6

Southwestern College
900 Otay Lakes Rd.
Chula Vista, CA 91910–7299
(619) 482–6550
www.swc.cc.ca.us

Tuition, Full-time (Fall '99):
In State: $296 per year
Out of State: $3,296 per year
Books and Supplies: $810

Undergraduate Enrollment (Fall '98):
15,452

Race/Ethnicity (Fall '98):
Black   6.1%
American Indian   0.6%
Asian   17.4%
Hispanic   55.7%
White   16.5%

Most Popular Majors or Programs (Fall '98):
Liberal/General Studies & Humanities, Business, Health Professions & Related Sciences

Associate's Degrees Awarded to Latinos (1996–97):
434

7

Laredo Community College
1 West End Washington St.
Laredo, TX 78040
(956) 722–5108
www.laredo.cc.tx.us

Tuition, Full-time (Fall '99):
In State: $1,606 per year
Out of State: $2,246 per year
Books and Supplies: $550

Undergraduate Enrollment (Fall '98):
7,463

Race/Ethnicity (Fall '98):
Black   0.2%
American Indian   0.1%
Asian   0.4%
Hispanic   95.5%
White   2.5%

Most Popular Majors or Programs (Fall '98):
Liberal/General Studies & Humanities, Business, Health Professions & Related Sciences

Associate's Degrees Awarded to Latinos (1996–97):
399

8
CUNY–Bronx Community College
W. 181 St. & University Ave.
Bronx, NY 10453
(718) 289–5888
www.bcc.cuny.edu

Tuition, Full-time (Fall '99):
In State: $2,610 per year
Out of State: $3,186 per year
Books and Supplies: $600

Undergraduate Enrollment (Fall '98):
7,298

Race/Ethnicity (Fall '98):
Black   37.9%
American Indian   0.2%
Asian   2.0%
Hispanic   52.9%
White   4.6%

Most Popular Majors or Programs (Fall '98):
Public Administration, Business, Health Professions & Related Sciences

Associate's Degrees Awarded to Latinos (1996–97):
383

9
Cerritos College
11110 Alondra Blvd.
Norwalk, CA 90650–6298
(562) 860–2451
www.cerritos.edu

Tuition, Full-time (Fall '99):
In State: $324 per year
Out of State: $3,750 per year
Books and Supplies: $810

Undergraduate Enrollment (Fall '98):
19,173

Race/Ethnicity (Fall '98):
Black   7.8%
American Indian   1.2%
Asian   13.5%
Hispanic   43.6%
White   14.7%

Most Popular Majors or Programs (Fall '98):
Liberal/General Studies & Humanities, Business, Health Professions & Related Sciences

Associate's Degrees Awarded to Latinos (1996–97):
368

10
Rancho Santiago Community College District (Santa Ana College)
2323 N. Broadway
Santa Ana, CA 92706
(714) 564–6000
www.rancho.cc.ca.us

Tuition, Full-time (Fall '99):
In State: $308
Out of State: $3,500
Books and Supplies: $810

Undergraduate Enrollment (Fall '98):
17,734

Race/Ethnicity (Fall '98):
Black   2.8%
American Indian   0.9%
Asian   25.0%
Hispanic   41.8%
White   23.8%

Most Popular Majors or Programs (Fall '98):
Liberal/General Studies & Humanities, Business, Protective Services

Associate's Degrees Awarded to Latinos (1996–97):
360

11
Texas Southmost College
80 Fort Brown
Brownsville, TX 78520
(956) 544–8200
www.sa.utb.edu

Tuition, Full-time (Fall '99):
In State: $1,788 per year
Out of State: $6,756 per year
Books and Supplies: N/A

Undergraduate Enrollment (Fall '98):
N/A

Race/Ethnicity (Fall '98):
N/A

Most Popular Majors or Programs (Fall '98):
N/A

Associate's Degrees Awarded to Latinos (1996–97):
344

12
Eugenio María de Hostos Community College of the City University of New York
500 Grand Concourse
Bronx, NY 10451

(718) 518–4444
www.hostos.cuny.edu

Tuition, Full-time (Fall '99):
In State: $2,552 per year
Out of State: $3,128 per year
Books and Supplies: $600

Undergraduate Enrollment (Fall '98):
3,619

Race/Ethnicity (Fall '98):
Black   17.2%
American Indian   0.1%
Asian   1.6%
Hispanic   78.4%
White   2.3%

Most Popular Majors or Programs (Fall '98):
Liberal/General Studies & Humanities, Health Professions, Home Economics

Associate's Degrees Awarded to Latinos (1996–97):
307

13
Valencia Community College
Downtown Center
190 South Orange Ave.
Orlando, FL 32801
(407) 299–5000
http://valencia.cc.fl.us

Tuition, Full-time (Fall '99):
In State: $1,419 per year
Out of State: $5,149 per year
Books and Supplies: $600

Undergraduate Enrollment (Fall '98):
24,655

Race/Ethnicity (Fall '98):
Black   12.5%
American Indian   0.6%
Asian   5.7%
Hispanic   16.9%
White   61.8%

Most Popular Majors or Programs (Fall '98):

Liberal/General Studies & Humanities, Health Professions, Business

Associate's Degrees Awarded to Latinos (1996–97):
302

14
Del Mar College
101 Baldwin
Corpus Christi, TX 78404
(361) 698–1255
1–800–652–3357
www.delmar.edu

Tuition, Full-time (Fall '99):
In State: $814 per year
Out of State: $1,620 per year
Books and Supplies: $800

Undergraduate Enrollment (Fall '98):
9,958

Race/Ethnicity (Fall '98):
Black 1.8%
American Indian 0.1%
Asian 1.4%
Hispanic 52.9%
White 42.2%

Most Popular Majors or Programs (Fall '98):
Health Professions, Business, Liberal/General Studies & Humanities

Associate's Degrees Awarded to Latinos (1996–97):
292

15
Fresno City College
1101 East University Ave.
Fresno, CA 93741
(559) 442–4600
www.fcc.cc.ca.us

Tuition, Full-time (Fall '99):
In State: $358 per year
Out of State: $3,746 per year
Books and Supplies: $648

Undergraduate Enrollment (Fall '98):
16,532

Race/Ethnicity (Fall '98):
Black 7.9%
American Indian 0.0%
Asian 11.5%
Hispanic 33.0%
White 35.3%

Most Popular Majors or Programs (Fall '98):
Liberal/General Studies & Humanities, Health Professions, Business

Associate's Degrees Awarded to Latinos (1996–97):
291

16
Mt. San Antonio College
1100 N. Grand Ave.
Walnut, CA 91789
(909) 594–5611
www.mtsac.edu

Tuition, Full-time (Fall '99):
In State: $330 per year
Out of State: $3,830 per year
Books and Supplies: $864

Undergraduate Enrollment (Fall '98):
22,715

Race/Ethnicity (Fall '98):
Black 6.4%
American Indian 0.7%
Asian 24.9%
Hispanic 38.0%
White 26.9%

Most Popular Majors or Programs (Fall '98):
Liberal/General Studies & Humanities, Health Professions, Protective Services

Associate's Degrees Awarded to Latinos (1996–97):
290

17
Imperial Valley College

380 E. Aten Rd.
P.O. Box 158
Imperial, CA
(760) 352–8320
www.imperial.cc.ca.us

Tuition, Full-time (Fall '99):
In State: $364 per year
Out of State: $2,052 per year
Books and Supplies: N/A

Undergraduate Enrollment (Fall '98):
4,860

Race/Ethnicity (Fall '98):
Black   1.4%
American Indian   0.4%
Asian   1.2%
Hispanic   82.6%
White   12.5%

Most Popular Majors or Programs (Fall '98):
Education, Business, Liberal/General Studies & Humanities

Associate's Degrees Awarded to Latinos (1996–97):
279

18
Los Angeles Trade and Technical College
400 West Washington Blvd.
Los Angeles, CA 90015–4181
(213) 744–9058
www.lattc.cc.ca.us

Tuition, Full-time (Fall '99):
In State: $308 per year
Out of State: $3,584 per year
Books and Supplies: $810

Undergraduate Enrollment (Fall '98):
6,971

Race/Ethnicity (Fall '98):
Black   33.0%
American Indian   0.4%
Asian   9.9%
Hispanic   50.3%
White   3.7%

Most Popular Majors or Programs (Fall '98):
Liberal/General Studies & Humanities, Business, Health Professions

Associate's Degrees Awarded to Latinos (1996–97):
264

19
Chaffey Community College
5885 Haven Ave.
Rancho Cucamonga, CA 91737
(909) 987–1737
http://www.chaffey.cc.ca.us/

Tuition, Full-time (Fall '99):
In State: $333 per year
Out of State: $4,030 per year
Books and Supplies: $810

Undergraduate Enrollment (Fall '98):
13,468

Race/Ethnicity (Fall '98):
Black   11.5%
American Indian   0.8%
Asian   9.1%
Hispanic   33.9%
White   39.5%

Most Popular Majors or Programs (Fall '98):
Education, Liberal/General Studies & Humanities, Health Professions

Associate's Degrees Awarded to Latinos (1996–97):
247

20
Pima Community College
2202 W. Anklam Rd.
Tucson, AZ 85709
(520) 206–6132
www.pima.edu

Tuition, Full-time (Fall '99):
In State: $826 per year
Out of State: $4,210 per year
Books and Supplies: $700

Undergraduate Enrollment (Fall '98):
28,316

Race/Ethnicity (Fall '98):
Black   3.5%
American Indian   3.3%
Asian   2.8%
Hispanic   27.0%
White   58.0%

Most Popular Majors or Programs (Fall '98):
Liberal/General Studies & Humanities, Health Professions, Business

Associate's Degrees Awarded to Latinos (1996–97):
241

TOP 10 COMMUNITY COLLEGES IN THE UNITED STATES WITH THE GREATEST PERCENTAGE OF LATINO STUDENTS

College	1997 (%)	1998 (%)
1. Laredo Community College	94	96
2. South Texas Community College	94	95
3. Texas Southmost College	90	N/A
4. Texas State Technical College—Harlingen	87	87
5. El Paso Community College	82	82
6. Imperial Valley College	81	83
7. CUNY Hostos Community College	79	78
8. Southwest Texas Junior College	77	75
9. East Los Angeles College	74	77
10. Northern New Mexico College	73	72

Source: Integrated Postsecondary Education Data System (IPEDS) Peer Analysis System, Survey Year 1997. Institutional characteristics: General Information and Response Status Information, Fall Enrollments by Race/Ethnicity, Sex, Attendance and Level of Student.

TOP 5 UNIVERSITIES IN PUERTO RICO, RANKED BY BACHELOR'S DEGREES AWARDED TO LATINOS

1
Universidad de Puerto Rico
Recinto de Río Piedras
PO Box 23303
San Juan, PR 00931–3303
(787) 764–0000
http://upracd.upr.clu.edu:9090/

Tuition, Full-time (Fall '99):
In Puerto Rico: $1,245 per year
Out of State: pay tuition equal to their state of origin
Books and Supplies: $1000

Undergraduate Enrollment (Fall '98): 17,779

Race/Ethnicity (Fall '98):
Hispanic   100%

Most Popular Majors or Programs (Fall '98):
Business, Education, Biological & Life Sciences

Bachelor's Degrees Awarded to Latinos (1997–98):
1,949

2
InterAmerican University of Puerto Rico Metro
Carreterra #1
ESQ Calle Fransico Sein
Rio Piedras, PR 00919
(787) 765–1270
http://metro.inter.edu/

Tuition, Full-time (Fall '99):
In Puerto Rico: $3,186 per year
Out of State: same
Books and Supplies: $640

Undergraduate Enrollment (Fall '98): 14,000

Race/Ethnicity (Fall '98):
N/A

Most Popular Majors or Programs (Fall '98):
Business, Education, Biological & Life Sciences

Bachelor's Degrees Awarded to Latinos (1997–98):
870

3
Universidad del Turbao
PO Box 3030, University Station
Gurabo, PR 00778
(787) 746–3009
www.suagm.edu/UT/main/default.htm

Tuition, Full-time (Fall '99):
In Puerto Rico: $3,084 per year
Out of State: same
Books and Supplies: N/A

Undergraduate Enrollment (Fall '98): 6,649

Race/Ethnicity (Fall '98):
Hispanic   100%

Most Popular Majors or Programs (Fall '98):
Business, Education, Social Studies & History

Bachelor's Degrees Awarded to Latinos (1997–98):
610

4
InterAmerican University of Puerto Rico–San German
PO Box 5100
San German, PR 00683
(787) 892–3090
www.sg.inter.edu

Tuition, Full-time (Fall '99):
In Puerto Rico: $3,666 per year
Out of State: same
Books and Supplies: $640

Undergraduate Enrollment (Fall '98):
N/A

Race/Ethnicity (Fall '98): N/A

Most Popular Majors or Programs (Fall '98):
Business, Biological & Life Sciences, Education

Bachelor's Degrees Awarded to Latinos (1997–98):
609

5
University of Sacred Heart
Calle Rosales Esq San Antonio

PDA 26 ½
Santurce, PR 00907
www.sagrado.edu

Tuition, Full-time (Fall '99):
In Puerto Rico: $4,280 per year
Out of State: same
Books and Supplies: $1,000

Undergraduate Enrollment (Fall '98):
4,747

Race/Ethnicity (Fall '98):
Hispanic   100%

Most Popular Majors or Programs (Fall '98):
Communications, Business, Marketing

Bachelor's Degrees Awarded to Latinos (1997–98):
533

Index

About the Editor and Contributors

SILAS ABREGO is an associate vice president for student affairs at California State University at Fullerton. He earned his doctorate in education from the University of Southern California.

BALTAZAR ARISPE Y ACEVEDO JR. was the founding president of the Community College Without Walls in Houston. He earned his doctorate in community college leadership from the University of Texas at Austin. He went to Western Michigan University for his master's degree and worked at Grand Valley State University and Michigan State University.

GUADALUPE ANAYA is a professor in the College of Education at Indiana State University. She earned her doctorate from the University of California at Los Angeles and has been a counselor and assistant director in higher education.

A. REYNALDO CONTRERAS is a professor at San Francisco State University. He earned his doctorate in education from Stanford University.

CARLOTA CARDENAS DE DWYER is a high school teacher in San Antonio, Texas. She earned her doctorate in English from the State University of New York at Stony Brook and has also been a professor of English at the University of Texas at Austin.

ROBERTO HARO is a professor of ethnic studies at San Francisco State University and the director of research for the Cesar E. Chavez Institute for Public Policy. He has been a faculty member at University of California at Berkeley, the University of Southern California, and the University of Maryland. He has published five books and written eighty articles/chapters.

VICKI A. LEAL is a doctoral fellow at Arizona State University. She has been the director of the Cesar Chavez Cultural Student Center at the University of Northern Colorado.

MIRANDA LOPEZ is a doctoral fellow at Arizona State University. Prior to her formal studies, she was an administrator at Laredo Community College in Texas.

RONALD S. MARTINEZ is the director of student financial aid at the University of New Mexico. Previously he was with the College Board office in San Jose, California.

SYLVIA PEREGRINO is a doctoral fellow at Arizona State University. Previously she worked in Washington, D.C., with an advocacy organization. She earned her Master's degree from the New College in New York. She is originally from El Paso, Texas.

LEONARD A. VALVERDE is the executive director of the Hispanic Border Leadership Institute, a consortium of six universities and two community colleges located in Arizona, California, New Mexico, and Texas. He is also a professor of educational leadership and policy studies at Arizona State University. He has been a public school teacher and administrator in Southern California and a vice president of academic affairs in Texas as well as a college dean in Arizona.